s altar

DATE DUE			
OCT. 1 0 1984 MLF			
OCT 3 1 1984 LF			
NOV 0 8 1986			
OCT			

God's
Altar

God's Altar

THE WORLD
AND THE FLESH
IN PURITAN POETRY

ROBERT DALY

University of
California Press
BERKELEY
LOS ANGELES
LONDON

University of California Press
Berkeley and Los Angeles, California

University of California Press, Ltd.
London, England

Copyright © 1978 by
The Regents of the University of California

ISBN 0–520–03480–5
Library of Congress Catalog Card Number: 77–76182
Printed in the United States of America

1 2 3 4 5 6 7 8 9

for Sharon

Contents

Acknowledgments
ix

Introduction:
Puritanism and Poetry
1

I. The World's Body
6

II. *Ars Poetica*
40

III. Anne Bradstreet and the Practice of
Weaned Affections
82

IV. Gnostics and Naturalists
128

V. Edward Taylor:
Christ's Creation and the
Dissatisfactions of Metaphor
162

Appendix:
In Critic's Hands:
A Bibliographical Essay
201

Notes
225

Index
249

Acknowledgments

THIS BOOK has been something of a community project, and I owe many debts, as pleasant to remember as they have been to incur. I am grateful to the Trustees of Lever House for a Leverhulme Fellowship that made possible a year's research in England, and to several librarians, especially D. W. Downes of the Plume Library in Maldon, Janice Wallace of the Rare Books Room at the Cambridge University Library, Robert Latham of the Pepys Library at Magdalene College, Cambridge, and the librarians of the Emmanuel College Library and the British Museum, for the good counsel and good cheer that helped to make the year worthwhile.

Professors Michael Colacurcio, Norman Grabo, Sanford Budick, Harrison T. Meserole, and Michael Kammen assisted generously in the long work of writing and revision. Though each suggested valuable revisions and left the manuscript far better than he found it, none should be held responsible for errors that remain. Evelyn Primus, Rita Swick, and Hilda Ludwig typed and retyped. Among the many others who aided and abetted in more ways than I can recount or repay are Ralph and Margaret Daly, Ralph Durbin, and William Holvey of Doylestown, Ohio; Gerald Levin, Charles Duffy, and John Phillipson of the University of Akron; David Novarr of Cornell University; Gabriel Pearson of the University of Essex; Dorothy Klopf of Princeton University; Karl Keller of San Diego State University; William McClung and Susan Welling of the University of California Press; and my wife and good friend, Sharon.

Parts of Chapter 2 appear in "Puritan Poetics: The World, the Flesh, and God" in the Fall, 1977, issue of *Early American Literature*. I am grateful to its editor, Everett Emerson, for permission to reprint them.

November 1977   R. D.

INTRODUCTION
Puritanism and Poetry

God's Altar needs not our polishings.
JOHN COTTON

I stretched thy joints to make thee even feet,
Yet still thou run'st more hobbling than is meet;
In better dress to trim thee was my mind,
But nought save homespun cloth i' th' house I find.
In this array 'mongst vulgars may'st thou roam.
In critic's hands beware thou dost not come,
And take thy way where yet thou art not known.
ANNE BRADSTREET

APOLOGIES for American poetry began in 1640. *The Whole Booke of Psalmes Faithfully Translated into English Metre* was, after all, a book of poetry, and John Cotton apparently felt the need for a carefully wrought preface. He assured the reader that the translators' intention was religious, not literary. He justified the standardized aspects of psalm-singing by citing numerous biblical precedents and based his defense of standardized psalms on a careful distinction between psalm and prayer: standardized prayer was papist ritual since any good minister could "pray in the spirit," that is, conceive and extemporize his own prayers; but, said Cotton, "every good minister hath not a gift of spiritual poetry to compose extemporary psalms as he hath of prayer." The good minister was permitted, therefore, to depend upon those skilled in meter and rhyme to provide him with standardized psalms. This vaguely literary justification, however, was as far as Cotton was willing to go in the direction of aesthetic concerns. He quickly added: "Neither let any think, that for the meter's sake we have

I

taken liberty or poetical license to depart from the true and proper sense of David's words in the Hebrew verses, no; but it hath been one part of our religious care and faithful endeavor, to keep close to the original text." In one sense this is no more than a prime tenet of good translation: the authors had not sacrificed meaning to prosody. But having justified their efforts in part on literary grounds, Cotton repeatedly asserted that the central consideration was not literary. Because the translators "have attended Conscience rather than Elegance, fidelity rather than poetry," those who read the book for the regularity of its numbers or the elegance of its style will have misinterpreted its intention and will be disappointed. Cotton answered such readers: "If therefore the verses are not always so smooth and elegant as some may desire or expect; let them consider that God's Altar needs not our polishings: Ex 20."[1]

Turning to Exodus 20, we find the central biblical admonitions concerning the religious uses of the things of this world. The Israelites are forbidden to make and worship graven images and are given directions for building a proper altar for worship. That altar may be built of earth, or of stone so long as the stone is not hewn or worked with tools. Such artificing would pollute the altar. Cotton cited the text, then, to justify the translators' refusal to polish, or put into smooth meter and elegant diction, this new aid to worship, fashioned by men from the materials of this world.

We can better understand Cotton's apparently antiliterary statements if we consider their context. The *Bay Psalm Book* was intended to replace the Sternhold and Hopkins versification of the psalms that had been added to the Prayer Book in 1562 and that remained quite popular in Anglican churches throughout the seventeenth century. The principal Puritan objections to Sternhold and Hopkins were that it departed from the original Hebrew and often sacrificed a literal rendering for poetic effect.[2] The Puritans were not alone in their objections. Dryden cited as evidence of the unreliability of popular taste that "the people . . . stick to Hopkins and Sternhold's Psalms and forsake those of David. . . ."[3] In *The Second Part of Absalom and Achitophel*, Dryden leveled a satiric blast at some poetic incompetents by characterizing them as "Poor slaves in metre, dull and addlepated, / Who rhime below ev'n David's Psalms translated."[4] Even Rochester, whose objection could hardly have been on religious grounds, opined that if King David could hear what Sternhold and Hopkins had done to his psalms, the experience would drive him mad.[5] One function of Cotton's preface was to justify the *Bay Psalm Book* by contrasting it, not with all literary efforts, but with the careless translation of Sternhold and Hopkins. And as the reactions of Dryden and Rochester indicate, one could deplore the efforts of Sternhold and Hopkins without contemning literature itself or revealing an unliterary sensibility.

Indeed, we have some evidence that, even in their translations of the psalms, the Puritan clergy neither ignored nor scorned literary considerations. Ten years after Cotton's preface, other Puritan ministers undertook to revise the *Bay Psalm Book* itself and to smooth the rough verse that Cotton had felt compelled to justify. President Dunster of Harvard and Richard Lyon revised some of the psalms and added translations from other books of the Bible, mostly from the Song of Solomon, "having a special eye," as they explained in the preface, "both to the gravity of the phrase" and "sweetness of the verse."[6] In recording this event Cotton Mather noted the aesthetic intentions of Dunster and Lyon: "It was thought that a little more of Art was to be employed upon the verses."[7] It is clear, then, that in 1640 the Puritan translators had reacted to the poor translations in the Sternhold and Hopkins version. They had therefore emphasized a literal rendering. And their Puritan successors, satisfied with the translation, had devoted themselves to concerns that were openly aesthetic. Even in the 1640 edition, moreover, the poetry is hardly so uniquely pathetic as subsequent detractors have claimed. All metrical translations of the psalms must not only fit a simple and familiar melody but also bear comparison with the magnificent free verse of the English Bible. Few translators have created verses that do both, and one reader has noted that anyone "who compares the *Bay Psalm Book* with versions similarly adapted by Sandys, Donne, Milton, and Dryden need not single out the colonial versifiers for apology."[8]

Subsequent critics have nevertheless done just that and have constructed a variety of theories to account for the Puritans' failure to write poetry. Usually in works centered on other subjects, these critics have offered major statements on Puritan poetry. Since so many such statements exist and since even modern critics of Puritan poetry have taken little note of their predecessors, we can understand the bases for current descriptions of Puritan poetry only by examining their development.[9] A detailed examination of such criticism reveals that the numerous descriptions of Puritan poetry over the last century are variations on a few core descriptions, descriptions that do not entirely and accurately describe either Puritan poetry or the constellation of ideas and attitudes that informed it.

Taken collectively, the critics have written that the Puritans were hostile to art and consequently produced none whatever. Or, they have maintained that the Puritans produced art consisting merely of religious abstractions, art that ignored or contemned the physical world and the concrete images needed to render it. Even if the Puritans were not opposed to art or to naturalistic imagery, we are told, they objected to the use of sensuous or even sensual imagery to illustrate religious doctrine; they considered the use of sensuous appeals in religious art peculiarly Catholic and

4

avoided it. Finally, those critics who allow the Puritans a rudi-
mentary imagistic art assert that it was never symbolic, that for
the Puritan the gap between the visible world of creation and the
invisible Creator was too great to be bridged by symbol; the
creatures could tell depraved man nothing whatever of the in-
finite and inscrutable God about Whom the Puritans predicated
nothing.

I

The World's Body

The Puritans are still thought by many to have had little figural art and no religious art. Both notions are fictitious.
ALLAN I. LUDWIG

Cast as art within a craft framework, gravestone carving provides many insights into the Puritan culture of New England. First and foremost, the conception of Puritans as iconoclasts must be revised or qualified.
DICKRAN AND ANN TASHJIAN

. . . when he is satisfied with her breasts, he is ravished with her love; so hope hath an expectation of mercy, and is satisfied herewith.
THOMAS HOOKER

to deny
Theyr Great Dominion, is to defie
The sacred Oracle itself, besides
Each dayes Experience in *Winds* and *Tydes*:
Theyr Maker made them *signs* and why I grow
Except to *signify*; then men may *know*
By Observation and Experience
What 'tis they signify, (In my poor sense).
SAMUEL DANFORTH II

LEAVING ASIDE for the moment the difficult question of Puritan theories about the world and the religious uses of images drawn from it, we can evaluate the critical generalizations set forth in previous criticism by referring to what the Puritans actually practiced. We can begin by asking, not whether it would seem that the Puritans should have been hostile to art, for example, but whether they were in fact hostile to it and in fact avoided it in their own

6

culture. To be sure, they were hostile to some forms of art. During the English Civil War, for example, Puritan troops destroyed religious statuary in the cathedrals at Exeter, Canterbury, and Winchester. God had forbidden man to worship graven images, and the Anglicans, no less than the Catholics, had violated that commandment. The Puritans obeyed it; they neither painted pictures of God the Father on the ceilings of their meeting houses, nor knelt before statues of their fellow saints, nor treasured the grinning skulls of martyred virgins. But we cannot conclude from this iconoclasm that they defined themselves only in opposition to Catholics and rejected all religious art.

As Allan I. Ludwig, Dickran and Ann Tashjian, and others have pointed out, the Puritans left us graven images of their own. They "began as early as 1668 to fill their burial grounds with emblems and symbols." Instead of simple stones bearing only names and terminal dates, the Puritans honored their dead with elaborately carved stones bearing images of skeletons, hourglasses, picks, shovels, coffins, scythes, winged death's heads, candles being snuffed out, Death carrying an arrow, the Tree of Life, the Palm of Righteousness, the Crown of Victory, flowers, souls figured as doves, souls being carried toward heaven in the bellies of birds, and living roots and flowers growing from skulls and cinerary urns. In Chapter 2 I shall discuss the differences between this permissible imagery and the idols that Puritans scrupulously avoided. It is enough to note here that such figural and religious art exists and that its very existence contradicts the oft-repeated generalization that since the Puritans had no art, they must have been hostile to it.

The power and durability of such generalizations are evident from the refusal of even excellent critics to trust their own best instincts. Murdock and Johnson both noted that they had found no evidence that the Puritans were hostile to plastic art, but we have had to wait until quite recently for detailed analyses of that art. And even Ludwig was somewhat cautious before the unsupported but commonly accepted notion that the Puritan meeting house was intentionally plain to the point of dreariness. He could only wonder "why the Puritans cut graven images for their tombs but would not allow the same imagery into their meeting houses."[1] Though we cannot be sure what ornaments adorned the meeting houses, Marian Card Donnelly has recently provided evidence that they were not so plain as was formerly imagined: "The many instructions for architectural ornament on the meeting houses and the obvious admiration of contemporaries for the more handsome buildings argue against claims that the meeting houses were built in a belligerently doctrinaire spirit of ostentatious austerity." One such contemporary was Edward Johnson, who, in his own history of New England, commented on which meeting houses were beautiful, which "unbeautified," and clearly preferred the former.[2] Even in the plastic arts, then, the Puritans were willing to record the truth as they saw it and to appreciate the beauty of that record. On gravestones, in meeting houses, and in the works of over two hundred poets, they were not, in Moses Coit Tyler's words, "at war with nearly every form of the beautiful." Their practice clearly does not reflect a belief "that there was an inappeasable feud between religion and art."[3]

Granting that they had produced some art and a good deal of verse, one might still argue, as earlier critics have, that because of their "unconscious Manichaeism," because "God, not the world, inspired their 'noble numbers,'" they created a poetry characterized by "otherworldliness" and consisting only of "religious abstractions," art which tells "us almost nothing of the concrete, existential experience of people, places, or things."[4] But if we advert to the poetry itself, we find that the world's body, the physical world sensorily perceived, inspired many Puritan poems and that

8

such poems, though not divorced from considerations of that other world, are filled with an undisguised appreciation of this one. Anne Bradstreet's "Contemplations" were spiritual exercises, intended to raise her thoughts and affections to God; yet they begin with and never entirely discard the creatures of this world:

> . . . on the glistering Sun I gazed
> Whose beams was shaded by the leavie Tree;
> The more I looked, the more I grew amazed,
> And softly said, "What glory's like to thee?"
> Soul of this world, this universe's eye,
> No wonder some made thee a deity;
> Had I not better known, alas, the same had I.
>
> Thou as a bridegroom from thy chamber rushes,
> And as a strong man joys to run a race;
> The morn doth usher thee with smiles and blushes,
> the Earth reflects her glances in thy face.
> Birds, insects, animals, with vegative,
> Thy heat from death and dullness doth revive,
> And in the darksome womb of fruitful nature dive.[5]

The speaker's relation to the natural world is not Romantic. She would clearly rather not be "a pagan suckled in a creed outworn" nor would she agree with Coleridge and Emerson that her metaphoric association of the sun, bridegroom, and (figurally) Christ was the result of her transforming imagination. For the Puritan such correspondences existed in nature by God's will and were merely seen and uttered, not made, by the poet. But neither is her relation to the natural world "Manichaean" or "Gnostic,"[6] as Tyler and Waggoner have written. The natural world is clearly beautiful and the appreciation of that beauty is neither foolish nor sinful.

Bradstreet's delight in the beauties of the sensible world was hardly unique. In 1634, a book entitled *New Englands Prospect* was entered in the Stationers' Register in London. It is generally

attributed to one William Wood who came to New England in
1629, settled at Lynn, Massachusetts, and was made a freeman
in 1631. To be a freeman at that time, one had to be a member
of the local congregation. We can be almost certain, then, that
Wood was a Puritan. And he was so stricken by the beauty and
abundance of the new world that these, and apparently little else,
inspired his poetry. His poems are explosions of images drawn from
the natural world and appreciated for their intrinsic beauty and
limitless variety. They catalogue and celebrate

> The kingly Lyon, and the strong arm'd Beare
> The large lim'd Mooses, with the tripping Deare,
> Quill darting Porcupines, and Rackoones bee,
> Castelld in the hollow of an aged tree;
>
> . . . .
>
> The Princely Eagle and the soaring Hawke,
> Whom in their unknowne ways there's none can chawke:
>
> . . . .
>
> The swift wing'd Swallow sweeping to and fro,
> As swift as arrow from *Tartarian* Bow.
>
> . . . .
>
> The king of waters, the Sea shouldering Whale,
> The snuffing Grampus, with the oyly Seal,
> The storm presaging Porpus, Herring-Hogge,
> Line shearing Sharke, the Catfish, and Sea Dogge.[7]

Wood's poems were intended, of course, to promote colonization;
but Wood achieved that end by portraying the new world, not as
a place where the Gnostic Christian would find rest from distractions of the sensible world, but as a beautiful world worth seeking
and enjoying.

Much the same attitude pervades the numerous almanac verses
by Puritan poets. Though Samuel Danforth was thought "un-
wholesomely pious" while in college, he must have come to enjoy

both natural beauty and pagan mythology by the time he composed his almanac for 1647.[8] In happy ignorance of our critical expectations, the minister at Roxbury wrote:

> Awake yee westerne Nymphs, arise and sing:
> And with fresh tunes salute your welcome spring.
>
> (p. 417)

And Samuel Bradstreet, eldest son of the poet, told in his verses for the almanac of 1657 the familiar story of the sun god Apollo coming in spring to woo the earth goddess Tellus, also a goddess of fertility and marriage:

> It was, when scarce had rang the morning bells
> That call the dead to rise from silent tombes,
> Whilst yet they were lockt up in darker Cells
> Ne had the light possess'd their shady roomes,
> That slumbering Tellus in a dream did see
> Apollo come to cure her Lethargie.

She wakes, sees the morning twilight herald the god's approach, and uses the welkin as a mirror to dress herself with dew,

> Whilst fleet-fire-foming-steeds from farre appear
> In speedy race the lofty hills to stride:
> They Scout the smoking Plaines, and then draw near
> With burning Carre, that none but he can guide
> Who baulks their course with curb and gars [holds]
>   them bound
> Whilst he steps down to Sublunary-round:
>
> To greet his Tellus then he hies apace,
> Whom sprusely deckt he finds i'th verdant gown
> He whilom sent. Each other doth embrace
> In loving arms, and then they sitten down
> Whilst high-born states, and low Tellurean bands
> Rejoice to see sage Hymen joyn their hands.
>
> Eftsoones Apollo gives a Girlond rare
> With flowers deckt (for Tellus front alone)

11

To her: and sayes in mind of me this weare
And Babyes deft will thence arise anon.
She dons it strait: And buds that erst were green
Now sucklings at her milkey papps they been.
(pp. 427–428)

Though less skilled a prosodist than either Wood or Bradstreet, Benjamin Lynde also combined a love of the sensible world and of the pagan classics in his poem describing Thompson's Island and the landscape surrounding Boston Harbor (pp. 491–494). Lynde often exchanged verses with Samuel Sewall, whose poems on the springs at Plymouth and Sandwich Beach also exemplify this version of the American pastoral (pp. 306–307).

But if the created world was a source of beauty and delight for the Puritan poet, it was also an *a fortiori* argument for the beauty and generosity of its Creator and the delights He had prepared for His people. Though the writers of almanac verse often saw and uttered this connection, the most explicit poem devoted entirely to the aesthetic and religious uses of nature is the Puritan layman Richard Steere's *Earth Felicities, Heavens Allowances* (pp. 252–265). Steere's poem begins with the conventional disclaimer that the poet cannot possibly do justice to his subject:

Upon the Earth there are so many Treasures
Various Abounding objects of Delight,
That to Enumerate, would be a Task
Too ponderous for my Imperfect Skill.
(lines 1–4)

Yet such pleasures may be classified according to the senses they please, and examples of each may be given, at great length:

To please the *Eye* how many various Sights?
The fair and glorious Aspect of the *Heav'ns*,
The Darling brightness of the *Sun Moon Stars*,

12

The naked *Air*, the Curled Silver *Streams*,
The *Birds* Enamel'd with their Divers *Plumes*;
Orchards, whose *Trees*, with *blossoms, leaves and fruit*
Of various Kinds, all pleasing to the Eye.
The ev'n *Meadows*, in their Tap'stry green.
(lines 33–40)

All these delight the eye of this Puritan. He hears

Sweet Musicks pleasant and harmonious Sounds;
The chirping notes of winged *Choresters*,
And Purling Murmurs of the Gliding *brooks*
Modulate Accents of a *well Tun'd voice*.
(lines 50–53)

. . . .

Pleasing discourses, *Histories and Novals*
Am'rous Converse, when Innocent and clean
All give a Charming Sweetness to the Muse.
(lines 57–59)

Having delighted in things that "Gratifie the sence of *Tasting*" and the "*Olfactal*" faculty, the speaker ends his opening catalogue with neither a good Gnostic's condemnation of such sensory delusions nor the descent of a wrathful God; rather, he asserts an undefined harmony between his God and the delights of the natural world:

When we make our selves
Sensible, of the sweetness all affords;
We may perceive a Possibility
By bounteous Heav'ns Allowance, on the Earth,
To find in Temp'ral good felicity.
(lines 82–86)

But Steere's poem is no proleptic *Nature*, and the speaker goes on to list some pains that flesh is heir to and to recommend a certain irreducible toughness as the only way of dealing with them. He spends, however, only a few lines on the obvious difficulties of human experience, before returning to the subject of earthly delights and assuring his hearer

> That lo by Looking up to heav'n above,
> From whence these Lower joys to us descend,
> We may a Heav'nly Paradise possess,
> Of sweet and Comforting delights on Earth.
> (lines 188–191)

God has bridged the gap between heaven and earth. Joys of heaven and joys of earth come from the same Creator and are sufficiently similar that one can be used to describe the other. Indeed Steere reversed the usual metaphoric equation by asserting not that heaven would be a garden of earthly delights but that earthly joys were in source and nature of heaven. The speaker accepts these gifts and ridicules the "Stoicks" to whom he imputes the simpleminded brand of *contemptus mundi* usually imputed to Puritans:

> However Superstitious *Stoicks*, may
> Refuse those blessings which are freely giv'n:
> As if not making use of Earthly good,
> Were to obtain Heav'ns Glory in Exchange
> (lines 199–202)
>
> . . . .
>
> And seeming fearful of their sweets to taste,
> As if within their good were Lodg'd infection:
> And so deny themselves their harmless use;
> (lines 206–208)
>
> . . . .
>
> Whereas without abuse we may, nay aught,
> Freely Enjoy Earths good in its good use.
> Nature Invites, and Reason bids us tast;
> Temp'rance, as well Condemns Stupidity,
> As Glut'ny and Excess it disallows,
> Since both prohibit and deny us Comfort.
> (lines 211–216)

Having asserted that one ought to accept earth's felicities as the gifts of a generous God, the speaker undertakes, in good Puritan fashion, to pose and answer objections. "Tis certain there are many Dangers, hid / In Temporary, *Riches, Honours, Pleasures*" (lines 265–266) he admits, but answers that only where temptations are greatest can the wayfaring Christian practice virtue. No more than Milton could Steere "praise a fugitive and cloistered virtue." It is far more virtuous

> to do well,
> When in the middest of Great Temptations,
> Than to be good for mere necessity;
> (Who in an Eunuch Chastity admires?)
>   (lines 275–278)

To shut oneself away from the temptations of the world, "to bind ourselves by Sequestration, . . . Argues a feeble and distrustful mind" (lines 281, 285).

With considerable dialectic skill, the speaker demolishes or side-steps several more specific arguments for rejecting the world. It is said no man can serve two masters.

> What tho' no man can serve two Masters well,
> The Supream God and the Inferiour Mammon,
> He's [the saint's] not concern'd, as being not the Man;
> This Man subjects to one, Commands the other,
> Owns God his Master, makes the World his Slave.
>   (lines 295–299)

But man is not to scorn that slave. Earthly joys are the creatures and gifts of God. And though

> . . . in Comparison of Heav'nly joys,
> Earth's best of Blessings scarce deserve a name:
> Yet in themselves, and in Respect to us,
> And our necessities, to disesteem 'em
> Would make us guilty of a heinous Crime.
>   (lines 245–249)

15

Only when compared to God and heaven do the joys of the sensible world sink to nothingness. In all other contexts, they are necessary and delightful, certainly not to be scorned by man, who is, like them, a creature. In the temporal world, they merit respect:

> They are in worth and time to be Regarded,
> As they're free gifts to us giv'n by the hand
> Of God himself as Tokens sent from Heav'n
> Not only for our needs, But to delight us,
> Which may appear, because unto our sense,
> They do afford us various Delectations,
> Beyond necessity to Satiate.
>   (lines 250–256)

The sensible world, then, is the creation of God, not of the Gnostic's Ialdabaoth. It delights our senses, and this delight, far from delusion, is evidence that God intends us to enjoy it:

> Nor is this all, God doth not only give,
> But lovingly Commands us to Enjoy,
> Those Gracious Ernests of his future Love.
>   (lines 257–259)

If this command to enjoy the suitor's gifts that God has sent before His coming should appear to contradict another command, say the command to forsake the world, we must have faith that God's word, however complex, is consistent; guided by our reason, we must make distinctions:

> When we're Commanded to forsake the World,
> 'Tis understood its Vices and Abuses;
> For certainly its good is not intended.
>   (lines 393–395)

Since it cannot "justly be supposed" that God "contradicts him self," it would be absurd to take the command to forsake the world as literal and all-inclusive. This univocal predication of God's

rationality lies behind the speaker's assertion that God obviously
does not intend for us "to forsake our Parents, Wives, and Children" who are part of this world and whom He has commanded
us to love (lines 395–398). It would seem, then, that man's reason can tell him something of God, can be of some use in man's
quest for heaven.

For the speaker of this poem, earth and heaven, reason and
faith, man and God, are not separated by the unbridgeable abyss
that we would expect to find in the writings of a Gnostic dualist:

> By the dim Eye of Reason we may view,
> Through this perspective of our Earthly joy,
> As t'were, a glance of Heav'ns Felicity.
> (lines 410–412)

God has created the joys of the sensible world, then, both to delight
the creatures He loves and to lead us to Him. The center of the
poem is this climax, and Steere's blank verse, which had begun
well but slacked into the structure and language of debate during
the long and prosaic middle section, becomes in this final hymn
to the harmony of God's universe the sprawling, image-packed,
uneven, argumentative language of the Puritan enthusiast, who
cannot and should not separate the passionate intensity of his experience from the theological doctrine and commentary that inform and express it. Poetic conventions, sophisticated theological
distinctions, sheer joy in the beauties of a clean new world, and
the longing for God and certainty all composed Steere's view of
the world and of his experience in it. They formed the lens through
which he viewed his life, through which he brought the chaos of
experience into focus, as well as the language in which he uttered
his vision:

> When we the Azure Cannopy Survey,
> Deck'd *with those bright* and Glorious Rouling *Torches*;

17

It mounts our minds in Raptur'd Contemplation,
With Rev'rence, up to the Admired Author.

(lines 422–425)

. . . .

We with our Corp'ral Eye, can gaze unto
The *Spangled* Spheres, and *view those* Lights *of* Heav'n,
Whose dazling, glorious, silver brightness, gives
A pleasant delectation; higher thence
Our Sprightly Souls, by winged Reason mounts,
To view the Impartial Throne, and Contemplate
Those Sence-Surpassing glories that attend it:
So that through Earthly Comforts, our dull Eyes
By Reason's Light, as through a Tellescope
May look to Heav'n, to God himself, and see
Some Glimpses of his Goodness, and his Pow'r,
And in some measure may already Taste,
Of those Reserved Sweets of Heav'nly Pleasures.

(lines 430–442)

It is noteworthy that so far the speaker has said nothing of faith. Sense perception and human reason have taken us this far. They are dim, but they are not delusory. Faith supports them and improves upon them:

But when we add Faiths Light, to Reasons Eye,
We far more plain, and clearly, can discern
God, in the mid'st of his Reserv'd Rewards,
Touching the Longing Palates of our Souls,
With fuller Cups of those Caelestial Joys,
And by a Spiritual conveyance feasts,
Our Ravish'd souls with symptoms of his Love.

(lines 443–449)

For Steere's speaker, then, the world and all in it were made, designed by God and are therefore in themselves good. They dim only when compared with their Creator. Man's senses, though weak, are not completely unreliable, are quite sufficient to see the real beauty of the sensible world. Man's reason, though dim, is sufficient to lead man part of the way to God, Who has ordered all things to aid such a pilgrimage. And finally, what may be said of God's creature may also be said of God, so long as one recognizes that the creature can never comprehend, or encompass, or say everything there is to be said about the Creator.

Indeed, the only way to say anything about God's glory is through the creatures, through metaphor, a literary device implicit in God's creation and sanctioned by its use in Scripture:

> How frequent may we find in Sacred Writ
> Metaphors, Similes, Comparisons,
> Drawn from those Temp'ral Things that are in sight,
> To signify to us Heav'ns unseen Glory,
> As Riches, Honours, Pleasures, Kingdoms, Crowns,
> Speaks to our sense the Highest State of Glory,
> By such known Language Heav'n conveys to us,
> High Apprehensions of Eternal Bliss.
>   (lines 450–457)

A system of metaphors made by God and explicated in the Bible, the world itself had its place in salvation history. God had made the metaphors, but as Steere's example shows, man could see them, meditate on them, utter them in language:

> Faith Exercis'd on these is of such force,
> As to present our minds with future things,
> Faith Soars aloft, and thence (preventing time)
> Descends with Samples of those Joys to come.
>   (lines 458–461)

Steere's vision of the world contained no necessary conflict between duty and enjoyment. Like most Puritan poets, he ended with a moral imperative, a coda that comprised both the argument and the tone of his poem:

If thus the Earths Felicities we use,
Looking through them up to those joys beyond,
And so enjoy them with a heav'nly mind,
We may in them feel heav'nly joys below,
That when our days shall Terminate, we may
From Heav'n on Earth, to Heav'n in Heav'n ascend,
Where our Felicities can know no
　　　　　　　　　End.
　　　　　　(lines 521–527)

Steere's attitude toward the created world was far more positive and far more complex than such descriptions as "Gnostic dualism" and "unconscious Manichaeism" would lead us to believe. Neither was it unusual among the Puritans, as has been shown by references to the poetry of Anne Bradstreet, William Wood, Samuel Danforth, Samuel Bradstreet, Benjamin Lynde, and Samuel Sewall.

Nor was Steere somehow a crypto-Catholic whose belief in such extreme forms of Divine immanence as transubstantiation enabled him to use metaphors forbidden to his more sober colleagues. Like most Puritans, he loathed the Catholic Church and said so. In 1682 he published a broadside entitled *Antichrist Display'd* in which he gave the usual Puritan reading of Revelation: the "Whore of Babylon" was the Roman Catholic Church. Antichrist was its Pope. And as for the doctrine of transubstantiation, presumably so poetically fecund, Steere reserved for that one of his finest snarls: true Christians, he wrote, "would not own a *Breaden God*" (pp. 244–245). From what little we know of him, Steere seems to have been orthodox, even conservative.[9] And he wrote imagistic poems filled with the beauty of the sensible world and wrought with some care.

In describing "a Sea-Storm nigh the Coast," for example, he played line length off against rhyme rather in the manner of Herbert—an orderly way to give the effect of disorder:

The weighty Seas are rowled from the Deeps
In mighty heaps,
And from the Rocks foundations do arise
To Kiss the Skies
Wave after wave in Hills each other Crowds,
As if the Deeps resolv'd to Storm the Clouds.
(p. 265)

Such poetry was inspired by the sensible world, a world clearly presented as "real." It was and is far more than a collection of "religious abstractions." We need to begin to realize how authentically Jonathan Edwards spoke for his ancestors as well as his own generation in his brief essay on "The Beauty of the World": "The beauty of the world consists wholly of sweet mutual consents, either within itself or with the supreme being."[10] The Puritan poet could delight in the beauty of the natural world merely because of its own harmonies, the "sweet mutual consents . . . within itself"; or he could value the sensible world because it figured forth, albeit imperfectly, the mind of its Creator.

Even in the face of such evidence, one might, while abandoning the generalizations that the Puritans were hostile to art and to the sensible world, still maintain the third generalization of previous criticism—that Puritans objected to the use of sensuous imagery to illustrate religious doctrine. Joseph Crouch, for example, argued that the English Puritans were not hostile to all art, but concluded that they did reject the "sensuous and emotional." "It is probable," he concluded, "that one of the reasons of the extraordinary success of the Evangelical Revival of the eighteenth century was because Protestantism had gone too far in rejecting the sensuous and emotional . . . for two centuries."[11] And Kenneth Murdock concluded that any appeal to the senses might "so stir the sensual in man as to blind him to anything spiritual in the poem." Murdock

21

then distinguished between "good" and "bad" imagery. "If a simile or metaphor made truth more intelligible and rationally more convincing it was good; . . . if it distracted the reader's attention from the doctrine, it was clearly bad." [12] Now of course we cannot attach wires to the original readers of Puritan poetry and hearers of Puritan sermons to see if the sensual in them was aroused or if they were distracted from the doctrine by the images with which it was illustrated. We can, however, examine Puritan appeals to both the sensuous and the sensual in man. Such an examination reveals that one who believes that Puritans avoided sensuous and even erotic imagery in expressing religious doctrine or describing spiritual states does so in the face of considerable evidence to the contrary.

Puritan writing is filled with appeals to the senses, with exhortations that the believer use his senses and the creatures perceived through them to raise his apprehensions and affections to God. And the relation between God and earth is seen neither as a contrast nor even a dualism, but as a simple hierarchy in which God creates the world and gives us the senses to perceive it in order that this sensuous experience might lead us to Him. In 1628, Thomas Taylor, an English Puritan divine, published his *Meditations from the Creatures*, an image-filled book about the religious uses of imagery. Asking "Who can discern the darkness of his mind, and not open his windows, and hereby let in some light into his dark house?" Taylor argues that "we have not only a sensual use of the creatures . . . but a spiritual; and profiteth not only our bodies, but our souls by them. Wherefore else did the Lord create them." He cites the example of the psalmist David who "extolleth the Majesty of God 1. By contemplating the works of nature, in the world," and he concludes that "These two are the great works, wherein the Lord's greatness shineth out: the

Creation and Redemption; the one written in the volume of the Creatures, the other in the volume of the Scriptures." Taylor goes on to list the religious use of each kind of creature, beginning with the sun and going on through moon, stars, clouds, air, beasts, birds, and trees to fish and all that lives in the sea. So completely does he trust this use of his senses that his meditation on the wind comes to sound like Wordsworth's lines on the "correspondent breeze": "He findeth a secret voice and sound of the wind, making request in him, with sighs which cannot be expressed. This secret breath and inspiration of the Spirit, giveth him breath . . . and whereas before he was as the ship that lay wind-bound: now having a fair gale of wind, he is as a ship under sail, that goeth swift as an arrow."

The sighing wind and all the other creatures made by God were "fruits of his love, his love tokens" and were to be loved and used accordingly. To those who might argue that "the Heathens had this knowledge, and it is fitter for them," Taylor replied with rhetorical questions that indicate his belief that God's creation was verbal and metaphoric and therefore had to be understood verbally and metaphorically, through figures that linked the visible and natural to the invisible and supernatural. Having argued that "hands and fingers are ascribed to God metaphorically," he now asked: "must we not know God in his works, because the Heathen did? Nay, if they by his works came to know the invisible things of God, may not we much more, who by faith know, that the world was made by the Word of God."[13] The senses and their objects, then, were no distraction. They were the love tokens of a loving God and were, therefore, to be attended rather than denied or ignored.

Among American Puritans, truths of the spirit were often expressed in worldly terms, that is, terms that appealed to man's physical senses and experience. Though Anne Bradstreet meditated on man's journey to the next world, her figures are drawn from this one: "The spring is a lively emblem of the resurrection: after a long winter we see the leafless trees and dry stocks (at the approach of the sun) to resume their former vigor and beauty in a more ample manner than what they lost in the autumn; so it shall be at that great day after a long vacation, when the Sun of righteousness shall appear; those dry bones shall arise in far more glory than that which they lost at their creation, and in this transcends the spring that their leaf shall never fail nor their sap decline" (p. 279). The figure is admittedly limited in that the saint's resurrection is far more perfect and irrevocable than the yearly revivification of plant life. But the temporal and eternal, worldly and divine orders of reality were not so disparate for the Puritan as for the Gnostic. The lower world could be seen to figure the higher, a figuration apparent and comforting to the wayfaring Puritan. "The hireling that labours all the day comforts himself that when night comes he shall both take his rest and receive his reward; the painful Christian that hath wrought hard in God's vineyard and hath born the heat and drought of the day, when he perceives his sun apace to decline and the shadows of his evening to be stretched out, lifts up his head with joy, knowing his refreshing is at hand" (p. 273).

Even in her poem "The Vanity of All Worldly Things," Bradstreet expressed the soul's yearning for heaven in biblical symbols drawn from the visible world:

> There is a path . . .
> Which leads unto that living chrystal fount
> Who drinks thereof the world doth nought account
>
> . . . .
>
> This pearl of price, this tree of life, this spring
> Who is possessed of, shall reign a king.
> (p.220)

Earthly fountains, pearls, trees, springs, and kings were indeed vanities when compared to the heaven they figured, but they were not so thoroughly contemptible that the poet refused to use them and chose to express her view of heaven only in religious abstractions. The gap between worldly and divine things had been bridged by the divine significance that God had imparted to the sensible world. Much the same may be said of Bradstreet's verses on the burning of her house in which both earthly vanity and divine permanence were figured as houses:

> Thou hast an house on high erect,
> Framed by that mighty Architect,
> With glory richly furnished,
> Stands permanent though this be fled.
>
> (p. 293)

Other Puritans saw and uttered the same set of correspondences. Edward Johnson likened the relation between John Eliot and Christ to that between tenant and landlord; the Natick Indians, into whose language Eliot translated the Bible, had been unable to worship Christ, an inability which Johnson figured as their "blind hearts" unable to see God and Christ. Eliot was a light sent by God to give them back their sight. Ministry was, of course, the work of the shepherds, a basic metaphor capable of a few thousand variations, most of which the Puritans found time to cast into poetry. Religious errors, since they deprived men of the Beatific Vision, "blind men damningly" (pp. 149–150, 173).

In the mind of Roger Williams, the symbolic correspondences between Indians, devils, and ravens were so obvious that he could rely on his audience to understand that the following stanza expressed the Christian's conviction that even Indians serve God's providence:

> Gods providence *is rich to his,*
> Let *none* distrustful *be*;

25

In wilderness, *in great* distress
These Ravens *have fed me.*[14]
The yearnings of man's soul could be figured in physical terms.

Man's *restlesse soule hath restlesse eyes and ears*
Wanders in change *of sorrows, cares and fears,*
Faine would it (Bee-like) *suck by the ears, by the eye*
Something that might his hunger satisfie.

(p. 88)

Indeed, spiritual hunger and satisfaction often led the Puritans
to figure spiritual states in images unambiguously sensual. Allan I.
Ludwig has devoted a section of his book on the Puritan gravestones to a discussion of their "erotic symbolism."[15]

Such erotic figures for spiritual matters pervade Puritan writing
as well. In *The Soules Union with Christ* (1638), Thomas
Hooker enfigured this spiritual union:

> He is so joined unto the Lord, that he becomes one
> spirit: as the adulterer and the adulteress is one flesh. . . .
> Thus the soul settles itself upon Christ, hoping, expecting,
> longing, desiring, loving, embracing.

Once that union has taken place, Hooker develops the metaphor
in more explicitly erotic terms:

> The soul is satisfied with Christ, and the riches of his
> grace; the believer doth repose his confidence wholly
> thereupon: *Prov.* 5. 19. that which makes the love of a
> husband increase towards his wife, is this, *He is satisfied*
> *with her breasts at all times,* and then he comes to be
> ravished with her love: if a husband hath a loose heart,
> and will not content himself with the wife of his youth,
> but hath his back doors, and his goings out; this makes a
> breach of matrimonial affection; but when he is satisfied
> with her breasts, he is ravished with her love: so hope hath
> an expectation of mercy, and is satisfied therewith; the
> will closeth Christ, and it is fully satisfied with him.

The use of physical, earthly, often sensual imagery to enfigure the invisible things of God was so common among Puritans and so taken for granted that even the soul's marriage to Christ in the conversion experience could be discussed in language from Yankee negotiations over dowries. In *The Soules Benefit from Union with Christ* (1638), Hooker could move easily from a discussion of the delights of marriage with Christ to this canny reflection about the dowry of that marriage, salvation: "This now is the dowry of a Christian, the Lord Jesus Christ is no bad match, you must not think you could have done better."[16] Hooker had ample biblical precedent for precisely this kind of language, and nothing in Puritanism inhibited his following it, deliberately setting out to "stir the sensual man" in order to stir the spiritual. We have already seen that for Richard Steere salvation was figured as a courtship ritual: God sends before His coming suitor's gifts, "Gracious Ernests of his future Love" (line 259). These gifts "Excite our Appetites, to Taste / Of those Celestial feasts of Love and pleasure" (lines 511–512) in a heaven where God eternally "feasts / Our Ravish'd souls with Symptoms of his Love" (lines 449–450).[17] Samuel Willard made more explicit the correspondence between spiritual and physical ravishment: "If we Love him as we aught, he is our all. . . . If we do not come to enjoy him, and lie in his Embraces, we do not come with a right design, nor can we expect to profit."[18] The Puritan love of God was a passionate love, and often figured in sensual images.[19] The system of correspondences between the physical world and the spiritual, perceivable in both the Bible and nature, encouraged the Puritan writer to explore the multiple resonances of his imagery, to figure spiritual love by physical.

God Himself had bridged the gap between physical and spiritual, not only in the Incarnation, but also in His creation of a symbolic world and in His explication of that world in the Bible. In their own poetry, then, the Puritans had ample precedent for the use of sensuous and even sensual imagery to figure both physical and spiritual experience, for the appeal to the sensuous and sensual in man in the illustration of both human experience and religious doctrine.

The final negative assessment of Puritan poetry, that it was not and could not be symbolic, is somewhat more difficult to examine than the earlier three. Most readers can agree that the mere existence of Puritan art forces one to revise the generalization that the Puritans produced no art, that imagistic poems about nature and human experience qualify the generalization that Puritan poetry consisted only of "religious abstractions," and that the abundance of sensuous and sensual appeals clearly indicates that the Puritans did not in practice avoid such appeals. But any discussion of symbology must begin with an attempt to identify symbol and to separate it, if possible, from other forms of figuration. Wellek and Warren, beginning a chapter that attempts to do just that, admit that the terms image, metaphor, symbol, and myth "overlap."[20] Rather than go through the interesting but peripheral history of scholars' attempts to define and separate these terms, we can begin to understand the Puritans' practice of symbolism by examining an important definition of symbolism that does not illuminate their poetry and by suggesting a more general definition that does.

In distinguishing *figura* proper from other forms of figuration, Erich Auerbach noted that it "differs from most of the allegorical forms known to us by the historicity both of the sign and what it signifies." Most allegories represent an abstraction, say justice or courtesy, by a sign, say Artegall or Calidore. But a "*figura* is something real and historical that announces something else that is also real and historical." It differs from symbol, according to Auerbach, in that symbol has thaumaturgical aspects that *figura* lacks. "Symbol figures the power or person of a deity: to act upon the

symbol is conceived as tantamount to acting on the thing symbol-
ized, and consequently magical powers are imputed to symbol."[21]

If we insist on this definition of symbol, the Puritans had none.
Though they believed in God-wrought miracles, they had no means,
other than humble prayer, of bringing them about. They would
have considered the making and manipulation of magic symbols
utter idolatry, as would most Christians. Indeed Auerbach gave
no examples of this type of symbol. Instead he focused on *figura*,
which lacks magical power and is confined to predicting one
worldly event through another. These definitions may be adequate
to biblical exegesis in which *figura* operates along a chronological
axis more than an ontological. Figures of the Old Testament are
fulfilled in the New. But such definitions are of less use in discussing religious literature in which worldly images, operating
along an ontological axis, figure divine events without having a
magic power over them.

For such figures we must turn to a more literary set of definitions, in which the symbol is neither more nor less magic than
language itself. An image, according to I. A. Richards, is "a
mental event peculiarly connected with sensation."[22] It may appeal to far more senses than five, and is more a function of anam-
nesis than of direct perception. If one uses an image as a vehicle
by which to figure a tenor, he creates a metaphor, both terms of
which are stated. The tenor may be abstract or concrete; either
courage or Ulysses may be a lion. In allegory, the tenor is usually
an abstraction, an idea, figured by a sign that has no reality except
as a representation. (It is impertinent, for example, to ask what
Calidore did for a living before he became the Knight of Courtesy.)
A particular kind of image, the symbol differs from metaphor and
allegory in at least two ways, neither of them thaumaturgical. First,
unlike the allegoric vehicle, the symbol is real and important: it
has identity as a presentation as well as a representation, according

to Wellek and Warren; "it demands attention . . . in its own right."[23] Ursula Brumm phrased the distinction similarly: "The symbol is characterized as belonging primarily to the world that is apprehended, the allegory to the interpretation that is intended. . . . The symbol is a part of the world which has been singled out and ascribed a meaning."[24] Second, unlike the metaphor, symbol depends less on the ingenuity of the poet than on a relation or a significance inherent in the symbol itself: "The Greek verb, which means to throw together, to compare, suggests that the idea of analogy between sign and thing signified was originally present." This is particularly true of religious symbols, which are based upon an intrinsic relation between the sign and thing signified.[25] Because he presumes that the relation is intrinsic, that the meaning of the symbol is in the symbol itself, the symbolist rarely states both terms of his figure, and we may use the short-hand distinction that a symbol is a metaphor with a suppressed (unstated) tenor. Such intrinsic relations usually depend upon a cosmology in which concrete entities themselves have multiple significances; that cosmology is usually external to the work in which the symbol appears, and must be made available to the reader if the symbol is to be understood. Burns's metaphoric rose, then, lacks the intrinsic symbolic significances of the rose in Dante's *Paradiso*, significances with which a complex religious tradition had invested the latter. When Blake wished to go beyond that tradition, he had to create his own cosmology and to place his "sick" rose in a new symbolic universe.

For the Puritan, however, the world in which he lived was symbolic. Things meant. Moreover, the symbolism was complicated: no one-to-one correspondence between sign and thing signified reduced the Puritan world to tidy allegory. The things of this world were rich in multiple meanings. Explication of those meanings could be found in the Bible, which served the Puritan both as a key to the created universe and as a discourse on method. By following the symbolic methods of the biblical writers, he could apply his own powers of reason and perception to the sensible world and find there incomplete but reliable knowledge of its Creator. Puritan poets *saw* symbols in the Bible and the world. From these sources they derived not only most of their symbols, but the symbolic method itself, the lens through which they perceived and expressed their own experience. Not ornaments retrospectively imposed upon a simple narration, the Puritans' symbols were central to their writings because they were central to their lives.

Death required some summary of those lives, some statement of their meaning. It required an act of faith on the part of the living, who recorded that faith in hundreds of symbols of death and resurrection that Puritan artisans carved on gravestones for two centuries. Some were naturalistic figures for man's mortality: skeletons, hourglasses, skulls, picks, shovels, and coffins required and require no explication. Human experience made clear their intrinsic relation to the thing signified. Other symbols, such as rings and bells, were part of the burial service. Winged death's heads above hourglasses, skeletons about to snuff out candles or about to hurl arrows all figured the triumph of physical death. Other symbols had multiple meanings. A tree cut down by a hand from heaven might signify no more than the cutting off of human life. But trees dead in winter bloom again in spring and figure resurrection, a correspondence augmented by the Tree of Life in Eden. Puritan reliance on conventional religious symbolism is evident in the following epitaph, placed beneath the figure of a tree:

> But whilst you sleep the lamb on Calvery slain
> Feeds the young branches which shall sprout again.[26]

31

Surely more than naturalistic imagery, this collection of symbols
points to meanings beyond the literal, and is clear only to one
familiar with biblical symbolism. Much the same may be said of
other symbols common on Puritan gravestones: the Palm of Victory
(Psalms 92:12 and Revelation 7:9); the Crown of Righteousness
(2 Timothy 4:8, 1 Peter 5:4, and James 1:12); and numerous
carvings of flowers to which man's life is likened in Job 14 and
Isaiah 40:6. The hope of resurrection was often figured by juxta-
posing symbols of death and life—a skull pierced by a living tendril,
a coffin encircled by a vine, a cinerary urn bursting with flowers
—or by showing the soul, figured in effigy or as a bird, released
from the mouth of death and winging its way toward heaven.[27]

Symbolic perception and utterance pervaded Puritan literature
as well. Samuel Danforth II, in his "Ad Librum" (pp. 485–488)
from the *New England Almanack* for 1686, justified his *"Harmless Astronomy,"* not by arguing that it would help farmers get
better harvests or that astrology could tell one anything about
astral influences on natural phenomena, men, or nations, but by
arguing that he and others should study the heavens as symbols
made for man by the Creator. Danforth apologized for retaining
"The *Names* impos'd by old Idolatry / On Months and Planets"
(lines 31–32) and carefully distinguished himself both from the
natural astrologer, who claims to describe the actual influences of
planets upon natural disasters, such as storms and plagues, and
from the *"Judicial Astrologer"* (line 62), who claims to describe
their influence on persons and peoples. Danforth admitted the
limits of his method but cited biblical precedent for it (e.g. Genesis
1:14). In *Earth Felicities*, Richard Steere had urged his readers
to enjoy the beauties of the sensible world because they mirrored,
however dimly, the beauties of God and heaven and because contemplation of them would raise one's affections to their Maker.

Danforth, however, emphasized that the creatures were intrinsically symbolic:

> Theyr dayly Influences to define
> Infallibly is far beyond the Line
> Of finite Skill; so likewise to deny
> *Theyr Great Dominion*, is to defie
> The sacred Oracle [the Bible] itself, besides
> Each dayes Experience in *Winds* and *Tydes*.
>   (lines 36–41)

A key for the symbolic interpretation of the world, the Bible asserts correspondences that are confirmed by our own observation. Natural facts have spiritual significance, even as they would for Emerson.[28] Again, things mean: they are real in themselves and are invested with meaning by God:

> Theyr Maker made them *signs* and why I grow
> Except to *signify*; Then men may *know*
> By Observation and Experience
> *What 'tis they signify*, (In my poor sense).
>   (lines 42–45)

Significance is in the objects of the poet's perception; his task as poet is to see and utter it so that other men may know the meaning of their world. In the action of the welkin

> Th' Eternall Power and Godhead are
> To Observation Super-Ocular
> Clearly apparent, Here I find the clew
> Of Heavenly Manufacture which doth shew
> The way unto the Labarynth Divine
> Where the Eternall Glory's brightly shine.
>   (lines 69–74)

Tracing out the meaning of such clues required close adherence to the observable fact. Using the cosmos as metaphor, Milton could afford to be somewhat indifferent to the Copernican revolution. It did not matter much whether Satan invaded a Copernican or Ptolemaic solar system:

> Thither his course he bends
> Through the calm Firmament; but up or down
> By centre, or eccentric, hard to tell.[29]

But Danforth had to choose between the Ptolemaic view and the arguments of Copernicus and Brahe. Once he decided that the latter view was correct, he had to say so.

> Yet think not that I'l give my Affidavit
> Each star shall prove as Ptolemy would have it;
> I know the contrary.
> (lines 49–51)

Danforth's symbolic practice cohered with his statements of theory. The universe that figured God's will in the Old Testament was clearly Copernican.

> In Joshuah's *Solstice* at the Voyce of man
> The *Rapid Sun* became *Copernican*.
> (lines 77–78)[30]

To be sure, God could make the sun do anything He wished and was no more limited by the Copernican world view than by the Ptolemaic. The only important difference between the poet whose world serves him as a source for humanly manipulated metaphors and the poet whose world is invested with symbolic significance (however multiple) by God is that the latter attributes far more reality to the observable fact and alters his poetry to fit it. He believes that the significance lies in the symbol itself, not just in his own mind or words. For that reason he sees poetry less as controlled artifact than as an expression of observed truth. He does not create symbols; he sees and utters them.

That some saw these symbols more clearly than others and

that Puritans recognized and admired this ability are evident from Francis Drake's elegy on the pastor and poet, Jonathan Mitchell. Now that Mitchell is no longer able to clarify the symbolism of the universe, the poet and reader must *"Confess the World* a Gordian Knot *agen"* (p. 458). Mitchell, like many ministers, had been able to see and explain the significance of human experience. Winthrop's snake, the hailstorm that broke the windows of Sewall's house, the spring that delighted Anne Bradstreet were all real in themselves and yet possessed of a significance beyond themselves. In this respect, as we shall see later, they were no different from the symbolic objects, persons, and events through which God had revealed Himself in the Bible. They were part of a clear and unified view of human life and of its significance. For Grindall Rawson, young John Saffin, Jr. who had died of smallpox was a flower, an Israelite, a skull on Golgotha, a crucified Christian on Calvary, Moses ascending Mount Nebo to look into the Promised Land (pp. 476–477). All these resonances of the horror and promise of death are brought together in his elegy, not as ornament, but as observation and expression.

For Anne Bradstreet, houses and birds, for example, had a real and important existence of their own. But they figured religious ideas, persons, and events that were equally real and ultimately far more important. When Bradstreet wrote of "my clay house mol'dring away" (p. 294), she was of course referring to her body through the conventional symbol. When she lamented the burning of her house, the house was real and its destruction painful. She could, of course, remind herself that it was only a "vanity," but even such vanities were not entirely contemptible. Indeed, the heaven that would replace them was figured as another house

on high erect,
Framed by that mighty Architect,

35

With glory richly furnished
Stands permanent though this be fled.
(p. 293)

The Philomel of "Contemplations" was an earthly bird whose song no doubt delighted Bradstreet in England. But it figured both a psalmist, who "The dawning morn with songs . . . dost prevent [anticipate]" in praising God (Psalms 119.147), and the freedom of the unbodied soul. A conventional symbol, the bird figured the soul in "As Weary Pilgrim" in which the soul leaves "his silent nest" to "soar on high among the blest" (pp. 294–295). In "The Flesh and the Spirit," the Spirit rejects the "silver, pearls, and gold" (p. 214) of earth as "trash" (p. 217). The Spirit much prefers heaven, where the walls "are made of precious jasper stone; / The gates of pearl" and the streets of "transparent gold" (p. 217).

Clearly the difference between those precious objects that the Spirit rejects and those that it seeks is the difference between image and symbol. Like the "crystal river . . . / Which doth proceed from the Lamb's throne" (p. 217), the second set of objects is desirable because these objects figure heaven. "The Vanity of All Worldly Things" hinges on the same contrast, the same reversal. Having rejected "pearl and gold" as vanities, the speaker seeks the "living chrystal fount" near which she will find "this tree of life, this spring" (pp. 219–220). To be sure, pearls were contemptible when compared with God or heaven. Taylor wrote: "Were all the World a sparkling pearle, 't would bee / Worse than a dot of Dung if weighed with thee [God Himself]."[31] But God had created these earthly symbols and had invested them with a symbolic significance which man could hardly scorn. Indeed, the Puritan never scorned the objects themselves except from the imagined point of view of the soul in heaven or of God Himself. In her meditations, then, Anne Bradstreet, an orthodox Puri-

36

tan, could delight in the spring both for its own sake and for its significance as "a lively emblem of the resurrection."[32] No conflict divided the two.

Even for Roger Williams, seemingly the *ne plus ultra* of Puritan *contemptus mundi*, "the dungheap of this earth" had much to say of its Maker. In his *Key into the Language of America*, Williams described a world alive with symbolic significance: "The *Sun* and *Moon*, and *Stars* and *seasons* of the year do preach a *God* to all the sons of men, that they which know no letters, do yet read an *eternal Power* and *Godhead* in these" (p. 94). Even the humblest of objects figured forth their Creator:

> *Every little Grasse doth tell,*
> *The sons of Man, there God doth dwell.*
> (p. 150)

Since he saw the world in these terms, Williams wrote poems containing ravens, suns, shields, and fish, which meant considerably more than a nonsymbolic interpretation would suggest. His poetry should lead one to believe that, even when Williams advised Winthrop to "abstract yourself with a holy violence from the dungheap of this earth,"[33] he was writing symbolically. And symbols, as we know, have multiple meanings.

How well the Puritan poets made lasting art from a world rich in multiple meanings is a matter to be examined in extended discussions of individual poets and poems. But that both their world and their poetry did in fact contain symbols is evident. In order to read Puritan poetry, then, we need neither suspend our disbelief forever and completely nor learn to love Mather's gangrenous wit or Wilson's tedious anagrams. We need only bring to our reading some knowledge of the natural and human world that lived, and lives, in their poetry. Like ours, perhaps even more intensely than ours, it was a symbolic world.

From our examination of primary sources, of Puritan writing practice, we are left with considerable evidence that the critical generalizations purporting to describe Puritan poetry need to be revised. Such evidence indicates that the American Puritans were not hostile to all forms of art, certainly not hostile to the art they produced; that their writings were often inspired by the sensible world, a world they rendered in concrete images; that they often used sensuous and even sensual language to illustrate spiritual states and religious doctrine; and that they believed symbols capable of bridging the gap between the visible world of creation and its invisible Creator. Taylor was exceptional, then, primarily in that he was an exceptionally good poet; it is easy enough to find exceptions to previous critical generalizations without consulting Taylor, though his poetry does of course contain exceptions to them all. But we must revise these earlier generalizations, not simply dismiss them. The disparity between the descriptions and the facts of Puritan poetry can be explained in part by saying that nineteenth-century critics judged Puritan poetry by standards that we have discarded; that since more recent critics were writing books on other subjects, they chose to repeat these generalizations without examining their source; that the corpus of Puritan poetry available to the scholar not sitting amid the great manuscript collections has only recently increased to include many of the better poets; that the early bias of scholars toward the intellectual history of this period led them to dismiss belletristic concerns; that subsequent literary scholars followed the methods and limits set by such historians; and that therefore Puritan poetry has been less disparaged after examination than dismissed without it. These statements are individually true but collectively incomplete. They do not account for the Puritan poetics from which many critics deduced their descriptions of Puritan poetry, poetics that often seems inimical to the production of poetry. There seems at present a disparity between Puritan poetic practice and the poetics Puritan theology appears to imply. Any attempt to describe Puritan poetry accurately should examine that disparity, should account not only for those poems that still speak to the modern reader but also for the constellation of ideas and attitudes that informs them.

II

Ars Poetica

No one dreamed what a luxurious garden of flowers and spices had grown up in the turnip patch of the Puritan fantasy. . . . He [Edward Taylor] would surely have aroused the ire of his fellow theologians, who would have condemned his rich sensual imagery and his radical spiritualization as the latest form of idolatry.

URSULA BRUMM

Go to then; When thou settest thyself to meditate on the Joys above, think on them boldly as Scripture hath expressed them; Bring down thy conceivings to the reach of sense.

RICHARD BAXTER

Figures must be allowed to the Scriptures as well as to other writings, else God had not spoken in our mode, and this way is not to obscure, but illustrate, and also to move the affections.

SAMUEL WILLARD

The world and the creatures therein are like a book wherein God's wisdom is written, and there must we seek it out.

ALEXANDER RICHARDSON

Pleni sunt coeli et terra gloria tua.

Papist liturgy

No PURITAN has left us an *ars poetica*. It is, moreover, difficult to see a pattern of explicit poetics emerging from their scattered comments (always made in passing in works devoted to other subjects) on the nature and function of poetry. John Cotton declared that a man may be said to commit sin "when he imagineth, deviseth, plotteth sin, as a Poet his fictions" and seven pages later in the same work urged his readers "to turn Poets of righteousness, it is the seed of God that sets you awork." The English Puritan Richard Baxter, who wrote poetry, ended his *Saints' Everlasting Rest* with a poem from Herbert's *The Temple.* Jonathan Mitchell expressed his belief in the important religious function of poetry in his commendatory preface to Wigglesworth's *Day of Doom*:

> A Verse may find him who a sermon flies,
> Saith Herbert well. Great truths to dress in Meter
> Becomes a Preacher, who men's Souls doth prize.

Poetry has a salvific function and is therefore part of God's ministry on earth. It becomes a preacher, not merely to write poetry, but to write it carefully and well:

> No cost too great, no care too curious is
> To set forth Truth and win men's Souls to bliss.

Wigglesworth had done this, and Mitchell commended his poetry, not as a recreation, but as readings of the utmost importance:

> In costly Verse, and most laborious Rhymes,
> Are dish'd up here Truths worthy most regard:
> No Toys, nor Fables (Poets' wonted crimes)
> Here be, but things of worth, with wit prepar'd.

For Baxter and Mitchell, both writing at midcentury, poetry could be salvific and was therefore important, so important that poetry-writing was part of the original curriculum of Harvard.

For one of their eighteenth-century successors, John Bulkley, poetry was a recreation for the idle hours of lesser men. His preface to Roger Wolcott's *Poetical Meditations* was an embarrassed "*Apology* for the manner in which this *Worthy Person* has given us the *Ensuing History*, in Composing which he has Diverted

some of his *Leisure Hours.*" Wolcott's poetry was really metrical
history and therefore worth reading. Not central to the man's life,
it was merely a diversion for his "*Leisure Hours.*" Wolcott was,
moreover, an exception to the rule that "the *Accomplished Poet*
and the *Great Man* are things seldom meeting together *in one Person.*" For another eighteenth-century American Puritan, poetry
was an appropriate pastime for a minister but dangerous if taken
too seriously. In his *Manductio ad Ministerium* (1726), Cotton
Mather recommends Virgil as a guide to manners and Homer
as a guide to morals, arguing that, though a pagan, Homer has a
great deal in common with the Puritans: "He commonly pro-
pounds *Prayer* to Heaven as a most necessary Preface unto all Important Enterprises . . . and he never speaks of any *Supplication*
but he brings in a Gracious Answer to it. I have seen a Travesteer-
ing *High-Flyer,* not much to our Dishonor, Scoff at *Homer* for
this; as making his Actors to be like those whom the English call
Dissenters." Though he considers the poetry of Homer and Virgil
important enough to defend (and that of Ovid important enough
to decry), Mather advises his candidate for the ministry not to
take poetry too seriously. Mather suggests that he write an oc-
casional "*Epigram*" because "it may a little sharpen your *Sense,*
and polish your *Style,* for more important *Performance*s." Though
he might "make a little *Recreation* of *Poetry,*" he is solemnly
warned: "Be not so set upon *Poetry,* as to be always poring on the
Passionate and *Measured* Pages. Let not what should be *Sauce*
rather than *Food* for you, Engross all your Application. Beware
of a *Boundless* and *Sickly* Appetite, for the Reading of the *Poems,*
which now the *Rickety* Nation swarms withal: And let not the
Circean Cup intoxicate you. But especially preserve the *Chastity*
of your Soul from the Dangers you may incur, by Conversation
with *Muses* that are no better than *Harlot*s." Though Mather's
warnings continue, these examples are sufficient to indicate that

by 1726 Mather could recommend poetry only as a pastime, not as an important part of a minister's or a Christian's life. When poetry became important, it became dangerous, and Mather—his own informed enjoyment of poetry notwithstanding—warns his ministerial candidate against it as strongly as Jonathan Mitchell had earlier urged his "Preacher" toward it.[1]

As these examples suggest, scattered Puritan comments about poetry neither add up to any coherent poetics nor illuminate Puritan poetic practice. To understand the ideas and attitudes that obtain in Puritan poetry, then, we must turn to aspects of Puritan thought that, though not explicitly literary, have literary implications. Having done so, some earlier critics concluded that Puritan thought was inimical to the production of lasting art and poetry. We now know, however, that such art and poetry exist and that their existence and nature contradict both earlier critical generalizations and those expectations engendered by our present view of Puritan poetics. Earlier scholarship suggests several solutions to this problem. One might conclude that different "Puritans" believed different things and that Perry Miller's "monolithic" New England mind was a brilliant synthesis achieved only in Miller's own mind and a misrepresentation of a "pluralistic" reality.[2] Or one might posit imagistic, symbolic art as a psychic need so deep and powerful that no amount of cultural iconoclasm could obliterate it entirely. Allan I. Ludwig has argued eloquently that the existence of such art in "iconophobic" New England must be attributed to "a burning need for imagery. It is a need so engrained that even when the mind dreads imagery for fear of idolatry, religious art endures. The New England Puritans found their need for imagery so great that not even their storied fear of idolatry could come between them and the thousands of stone images they carved and rooted in the hilly New England landscape for a period of some 165 years." Later, Ludwig extended his explanation to

43

include two other cultures that exemplified the same paradox: "Nothing testifies more to the need for symbols than the suppressed iconophobia of the Hellenistic Jews, the early Christians, and the American Puritans. All three, to judge from their literature, were aware of the dangers of idolatry and all three have subsequently been found to have had a wealth of religious art no matter what the intellectual elite of the time might have thought about imagery."[3] In these cultures, intellectual prohibitions were no match for psychic needs.

This argument is useful as far as it goes. But in light of the Puritan attempts to resolve or at least record their every thought and experience, to make sense of their lives, and to search the chaos of experience and history for some perceivable order, it seems unlikely that they would simply carry the contradiction unexpressed throughout one hundred years of tacit inconsistency. They may very well have found their psychic needs overpowering their intellectual prohibitions: that process may well have been the root cause of their art. But they would certainly have attempted to rationalize the process, to make some sense of it, to make it part of a complex but consistent world view. We may wish to deem their entire intellectual history one long rationalization of dimly recognized psychic needs, but if we are to understand the Puritans' conscious motives for writing the poetry they did, we must examine that rationalization. We must read carefully the Puritans' statements concerning those ideas and systems that seem inimical to the production of poetry: their fear of graven images, their Ramism, their *contemptus mundi*. And we must examine other traditions, hitherto largely ignored, in which they also participated: the belief that the sensible world was a book written by the finger of God and that man could read something of God in it—a belief systematized in a kind of typology, whose adepts read the world as type and therefore spiritualized all images, and expressed in a kind of meditation called "meditation from the creatures," in which men used verbal images drawn from objects in the sensible world to raise their apprehensions and affections to God.

The fear of graven images was an obsession with the Puritans. Like most of their obsessions, however, it resulted, not in the childish dogmatism imputed to them by nineteenth-century commentators, but in a consistent system of clear, taut, definitions and distinctions. One distinction that Puritans did not make was that between material and mental idols. John Cotton, for example, argued that the Second Commandment "forbiddeth not only bodily Images (graven or molten or painted) but all spiritual images also."[4] A verbal idol, such as might be found in poetry, would be as great a sin as a material idol carved in stone. For that reason, Puritan poetry was clearly influenced by the fear of idolatry; to understand the poetry, we must examine the fear. We have seen that Puritan poets did in fact write and read image-filled poetry. We need to know why they felt they could. We need to know how they defined and recognized an idol.

Cross-references and marginal explications in the Geneva Bible afford us a clear answer. Though set from different type, the editions of the Geneva Bible published in London in 1582, 1601, and 1616 were identical in text, cross-references, and marginal explications. A Puritan using any of these editions would have read in Exodus 20:4–5 the familiar prohibition of idolatry:

> Thou shalt make thee no graven image, neither any
> similitude *of things* that are in heaven above, neither that
> are in the earth beneath, nor that are in the waters under
> the earth.
> Thou shalt not bow down to them, neither serve them:
> for I am the Lord thy God a jealous God, visiting
> the iniquity of the fathers upon the children, upon the
> third *generation* and upon the fourth of them that hate
> me.

In this phrasing of the admonition, man is forbidden both to *make* images and to *worship* them; though juxtaposed, the two are kept separate. In a marginal note to Verse 4, however, the editors referred the Puritan reader to Leviticus 26:1 and Psalms 97:7, in both of which the two prohibitions are phrased as one:

> Ye shall make you none idols nor graven image, neither rear you up any pillar, neither shall ye set any image of stone in your land to bow down to it: for I am the Lord your God.

In uttering the prohibition more succinctly, the Psalmist defined idolatry as the *worship* of graven images: "Confounded be all they that serve graven images, *and* that glory in idols." In these referents, idolatry was defined as the *worship* of idols, not merely the copying of natural objects. In an explanatory note to Exodus 20:5, moreover, the editors wrote: "By this outward gesture all kind of service and worship to idols is forbidden" and in a marginal note on the word "jealous" as used in Deuteronomy 5:8 (to which the reader was referred by a marginal note next to Leviticus 26:1), the editors explained that God was jealous "of his honor, not permitting it to be given to other." Now, there are other passages in the Bible to which the editors could have referred, passages in which the force of the prohibition is on the mere making of images, rather than the worshipping. That they did not, that they chose passages defining idolatry as the worship of images indicates that they defined and recognized idols according to their usage. An idol was not merely a copy of some material form; it was an object of worship. A Puritan needed only his Geneva Bible to enable him to make that distinction.

That Puritans did in fact make the distinction is evident in both their definitions and recognitions of idols. In 1642, John Cotton limited his definition of idols to images used in worship. In 1648, the Puritan Divines gathered at the Westminster Assembly agreed that the *Shorter Catechism* represented their beliefs. It represented American Puritan beliefs as well. American Puritans, gathered at the Cambridge Synod of 1648, asserted in the preface to their *Cambridge Platform* that the confessions of faith and the longer and shorter catechisms of the Westminster Assembly expressed "not their judgments only, but ours also." They gave their "professed and hearty assent and attestation" to "the public confession of faith, agreed on by the Reverend assembly of Divines at Westminster." And the *Cambridge Platform* was in turn approved by the Reforming Synod at Boston, in 1679; it remained the basic statement of New England Puritanism until the adoption of the *Saybrook Platform* in 1708 in Connecticut. Few documents, then, are so representative of the enduring core of Puritan belief as the *Shorter Catechism*. To the question *"What is forbidden in the second commandment?"* the *Catechism*'s answer was, "The second commandment forbiddeth the worshipping of God by images or any other way not appointed in his word." This same distinction informs *A Testimony from the Scripture against Idolatry & Superstition* by Samuel Mather (1626–1671), in which Mather makes two distinctions concerning the prohibition of graven images:

> 1. *That it is not meant of Images for Civil use, but for worship; thou shalt not bow down to them, nor serve them.* For the Civil use of Images is lawful . . . but the scope of the Command is against Images in State and use religious.
> 2. Neither yet is it meant of all Images for religious use, but *Images of their own devising,* for God doth not forbid his own institutions, but only our inventions.

Mather's distinctions are precise and clear. Only images used as objects of worship and religious images devised by man are forbidden.[5]

In September of 1655, Michael Wigglesworth recorded in his diary his determination to thank God for His mercies by erecting a pillar: "In memorial of his former mercies received in answer to prayer and of all his goodness hitherto I will erect EBENEZER, A pillar to the praise of grace."[6] Wigglesworth was going to rear up a pillar, and a pillar with religious significance at that. Surely he had read Leviticus 26:1; yet, in a journal packed with the tortured self-flagellation of a New England conscience unchecked by any sense of proportion, Wigglesworth calmly and guiltlessly proposed to set up a pillar. He even provided a sketch of this unmetaphorical pillar. Why wasn't it an idol? It was not an idol because he had not reared it up in order "to bow down to it" (Leviticus 26:1). It was not an object of worship. The same definition is implicit in William Bradford's description of the maypole at Merrymount. With references to pagan acts of worship, Bradford described Morton and his followers "quaffing and drinking . . . drinking and dancing . . . dancing and frisking . . . as if they had anew revived and celebrated the feasts of the Roman goddess Flora, or the beastly practices of the mad Bacchanalians." Because it had become an object of worship for these idlers, it was an "idle or idol maypole."[7]

It is clear, then, that the Puritan imagist feared only one kind of image, an image demanding worship, an image of God. Though hundreds of symbolic images appear on Puritan gravestones, images of God the Father and of Christ are conspicuously absent. Ludwig has observed that "only one direct representation of God the Father is known to exist in New England" (the Charles Bardin stone, carved late in the eighteenth century in that hive of heresy, Rhode Island, and identified by the Tashjians as a representation of Moses). In Catholic Ireland, scenes from the Passion were often cut on gravestones, and Christ was pictured directly, but no such scenes appear in New England.[8]

In the only systematic and comprehensive exposition of seventeenth-century American Puritan theology—Samuel Willard's *Compleat Body of Divinity in Two Hundred and Fifty Expository Lectures on the Assembly's Shorter Catechism*—Willard defined idolatry, not as the making or copying of any image, but as the making and worshipping of an image of God: "It is a madness and wickedness to offer at any Image or Representation of God: How many solemn cautions did God give his people against this by Moses, besides the express forbidding of it in the second Command; and God declares it to be a thing *Idolatrous*." Preaching in the late seventeenth century, Willard summed up the prohibitions of his predecessors. An idol was differentiated from a harmless image by its usage. If one sacrificed to an image, undertook to "offer at" it, it became an idol. Any direct representation of God Himself as a person would require worship and would therefore be an idol. To worship such an "Image of God," rather than God Himself, wrote Willard, would be "highly to dishonor him, and provoke him to Jealousy."[9] For the Puritans, not only the worship of a false god, but even a direct representation of the true God, such as appeared in Catholic and Anglican churches, was idolatry, and Cromwell's Puritan armies righteously destroyed them. Images of God's creation, however, linked to Him by His own word in Scripture, were clearly not forbidden. As we shall see when we examine the Puritans' attitudes toward the created world and the proper religious use of it, such images were encouraged. The coexistence of Puritan fears of idolatry with imagistic gravestones and poetry, then, derived neither from a paradox nor from the Puritan ability to hold in suspension ideas that really contradicted each other. Rather, it derived from a distinction quite clear to the Puritans but lost for a time among the moderns who study them.

Another allegedly baneful influence on Puritan poetry was the pervasiveness in Puritan culture of the rhetorical system of Peter Ramus. Ramist Puritans allegedly separated dialectic from rhetoric, defined the latter merely as the ornamentation of self-evident truths, and considered poetry only a subset of rhetoric in which one applied ornaments more heavily than in prose. A Ramist poem, then, consisted of a central axiom bejeweled with tropes and figures chosen by the poet according to no particular rule. Such poetry was appliqué work, its decorations adventitious, and its function trivial. Though several have agreed that Ramism stultified Puritan poetry,[10] critics have been unable to agree upon the exact literary implications of Ramism. In 1939, for example, Perry Miller declared that the metaphysical style of such as Donne and Andrewes "is to be linked to the Aristotelean logic and rhetoric," that "the theory of the metaphysical sermon is to be found in an adaptation of Aristotle to the needs of the preacher." He attributed "the opposing style, the Puritan form," to the influence of Ramus, and asserted that a Ramist poet would ornament his poetry with imagery that was merely decorative. Less than a decade later, however, Rosemond Tuve argued that Ramus, not Aristotle, lay behind the metaphysical style and that Ramism had effected the replacement of merely decorative imagery by the more functional metaphysical conceit.[11] Such contradictions derive less from critical misreading than from ambiguities in the Ramist system itself.

Ramus—with some assistance from his disciple, Omer Talon, whose *Rhetoric* was written as a companion volume to Ramus's *Dialectic* and was rewritten by Ramus after Talon's death—divorced rhetoric from dialectic. (He did so only in theory and argued that the two must always be united in practice.) From the time of the Greek Sophists, dialectic and rhetoric were intertwined, and the traditional five-part rhetoric comprised a fairly complete education, according to Father Walter Ong: "In antiquity a boy

was given a foundation of general information on all possible subjects (*inventio*). He was taught to use this material in composition
(*dispositio*), his mnemonic skill was developed (*memoria*), together with his literary style (*elocutio*) and his oral delivery
(*pronuntiatio*).These five activities added up to a rather complete education program extending over a good number of years."[12]
Ramus greatly simplified all this. Since he wanted rhetoric to be
completely separated from dialectic and since invention and dispo-
sition (or judgment) threatened to overlap with dialectic, Ramus
decided that they were really a part of dialectic and not the concern of the rhetorician. Memory he identified with judgment on
the basis that judging things properly helps one to remember
them. That left within the purview of rhetoric only elocution, or
striking expression, and pronunciation, which was ignored in Ramist writings though presumably taught orally. Ramist rhetoric,
then, was striking expression, which, Ong has pointed out, "was
conceived largely as 'ornament' or 'garnishing.' " Though Ramists attempted to dichotomize this category into "trope" and
"figure," their division was hardly consistent or discrete: "in the
Ramist view trope is always some sort of metaphor, and figure is
anything else that strikes one as unusual." The Ramist rhetorician
concerned himself with ornamenting the truths that he had found
and organized as part of dialectic. It was as simple as that.

It may in fact seem childishly simple. The recognition that it
was so is one of Ong's significant contributions to our understanding of Ramism. Ramus and his followers were teaching children,
boys in their early teens. We can understand much of the vague-
ness and formulaic oversimplification of Ramist rhetoric by considering the audience to which it was directed. In early Greek
education—upon which Ramus based his own system—dialectic
was taught before rhetoric. Indeed, as Ong has observed, "common sense would dictate" this order. Yet "Ramus taught rhetoric

as a one-year course before dialectic," a course "comparable to a grade school or junior-high-school subject in America today." As part of the *trivia*, rhetoric was "the business of youngsters"; Talon was "quite representative of the general Renaissance pattern" in his insistence that in teaching rhetoric "one must have regard for the 'tender' years of his pupils." Rhetoricians were aware that such regard often necessitated simplification and distortion of their subject: Melanchthon defended his accepting the "view that dialectic and rhetoric differed in that the former presented things in a naked state, whereas the latter clothed them with argument" by arguing that, "although many persons objected to it, it was one which little boys could understand." Limited to the understanding of little boys, Ramist rhetoric "maintains the low theoretical level enforced on the subject (in postclassical times) by its place in the lower reaches of the curriculum, and evinces no real understanding of the semantic importance of metaphorical or of any similar processes." We may be sure, then, that when Talon wrote in 1545 that "just as wisdom treats of the knowledge of all things, so rhetoric treats of ornamentation and striking expression," he meant exactly that. Though later critics have argued that Ramists—when they wrote of "ornamentation"—had in mind something more intellectually respectable than mere appliqué work, Ong has convincingly demonstrated that they did not, that such Ramists as Bilsten or Alsted defined "rhetoric quite flatly as 'the art of expressing oneself ornately.' "[13] Clear enough to a child, this definition and the maxims surrounding it have proved puzzling to adults who, by failing to consider Ramus's audience, have brought to the study of his system far more intelligence and sophistication than the system will bear.

Convinced that cached within the childish maxims of Ramist handbooks was an adult rhetoric, Perry Miller and Rosemond Tuve have attempted to draw it forth, only to come up with contradictory versions of it. Later critics have recognized that Ramism implied no single cogent rhetoric. Wimsatt and Brooks, for example, have noted that

> the Ramist reshuffling of . . . ancient rhetoric . . . was a
> procedure of highly ambiguous import. It might mean,
> on the one hand, that a person decided: "Invention and
> disposition, the two substantial sinews of argument, are
> really parts of logic. Rhetoric in fact is mainly logic.
> What good rhetoric wants is a severe and honest style of
> adherence to argument. The elocution is the trimmings
> —or the clippings. Save them who will." This in fact
> was the kind of 17th-century thinking represented in . . .
> the plainish, anti-metaphysical, anti-baroque style
> which in England would appear in pulpit eloquence, in
> the scientific writing of the Royal Society, and even in
> literary prose, for instance, in the lucidly conversational
> idiom of Dryden.

Though the plain style of these examples depended on many more influences than Ramist method, it is clear that an adult writer could use his early training in Ramism as a base on which to develop a plain style of writing.

> But at the same time, a person caught in the consequences
> of Ramist rhetoric and logic might conceivably entertain a
> different train of reflections, somewhat as follows: "The
> art of rhetoric, as distinct from philosophy and science,
> has after all been always a matter essentially of style.
> Leaving the content and structure of argument, therefore,
> to the logician, the scientist, the theologian, let me discuss
> rhetoric in its pure form, that of the figures and tropes." [14]

Such a person might well move from Ramist maxims to the development of a florid style, as did Ramus himself and the Puritan Stephen Gosson whose attack on poetry is far more ornate than Sidney's defense of it. If one believed that all figuration was ornament for a truth that could exist just as well, be just as true, without the garnishing, one's figures were likely to be adventitious.

In theory, then, Ramist method encouraged no particular style to the exclusion of all others. Those trained in its rhetoric could grow up to write metaphysical high style, Puritan plain style, or anything between these extremes. What was true of prose influenced by Ramism was true of poetry as well. The man who considered his writing essentially dialectic would seek to express plain truth: the man who considered his writing essentially rhetoric would seek to ornament his writing with figures and tropes. Though Perry Miller has argued that the Ramist necessarily considered poetry a subset of rhetoric, and though Roy Harvey Pearce has just as confidently asserted that "Ramist logic . . . made dialectics one with poetics," Ramus was not so sure. In Talon's *Rhetoric*, poetry was treated as a part of rhetoric on the grounds that "it is speech which is out of the ordinary in that, as sound, it attracts attention." Yet later Ramus decided that poetry was a "separate art, like medicine."[15] Just as it had implied no single rhetoric, so Ramist theory implied no single poetics. Poetry was under no theoretical compulsions that would identify it as peculiarly Ramist.

In practice the same amorphousness of Ramist influence is evident. Father Ong has noted that "Ramists did not write . . . much poetry at all," and from the study of practicing poets influenced by Ramist thought no consistent pattern emerges: Ramism influenced diverse poets, good and poor. Among major poets influenced by Ramism, Perry Miller listed Philip Sidney, who wrote into his *Arcadia* the figures from Temple's commentary on Ramus; Christopher Marlowe, who portrayed Ramus's death in *The Massacre at Paris* "in terms which make clear his intimate knowledge of the doctrine"; and John Milton, who rewrote Ramus's *Dialecticae*. Among poor poets influenced by it, Ong mentioned the Jesuit scientist Ruggiero Boscovich, whose five-thousand-line poem entitled *The Eclipses of the Sun and Moon* explained Newtonian physics, and Paolo Lucini, who wrote a three-thousand-line paraphrase of Newton's *Opticks*.[16] Neither Ramus nor his successors, then, wrote deeply and consistently about poetics; nor was any inevitable effect wrought by Ramism upon the poetry of all influenced by it.

Nevertheless, one literary implication of Ramism is quite clear. For the Ramist, rhetoric was trivial; rhetorical garnishing was decoration, fit for children or for the idle hours and mental relaxation of men. If poetry was merely a subdivision of rhetoric, then "poetry was appliqué work of the worst mechanical sort."[17] Had the Puritan poet considered his figures merely decorations, the products of his own mind and imagination, he would have considered them and his poetry trivial. But for the Puritan such figures and symbolic correspondences were not created by the rhetorician and therefore part of *elocutio*; they were created by God and found in the world by the poet. If they were to be put into a Ramist classification at all, then, they would be classified under *inventio* as part of dialectic. For the Ramist, *inventio* (coming from *in venire*) meant to "come upon," "discover," or "lay open to view"; it is not well translated if we take it to mean "invent" in the sense of "create" or "make."[18] Although the Ramist system implies no particular poetics to the exclusion of all others, it clearly obtains in the poetics of the Puritans, who considered their poems descriptions of God's world, not creations of the poet's fancy. Though Anne Bradstreet's poetry, for example, evinces skill and a deep concern with her art, it was designed neither to demonstrate that skill nor to assert her role as a maker of verse, but to respond to glory of God immanent in the created world and seen, not made, by the poet. Her words to her children might well have been addressed to all readers of her poetry: "I have not studied in this you read to show my skill, but to declare the truth, not to set forth myself, but the glory of God."[19] Puritan poetics dealt with perception and articulation rather than with the poet's creation, and the common notion that Puritan poetry was merely rhetorical decoration applies more to the sugared clichés of eighteenth-century American poets than to the poetry of the seventeenth-century Puritans, whose figures, as we shall see, were part of their dialectic, part of their perceived world.

Whether a poet considers his figures and symbols ornaments of his own creation or intrinsic parts of the world he describes depends upon whether he considers the sensible world intrinsically symbolic. In working out their own view of the sensible world and of its role in soteriology, the Puritans had to consider two potentially contradictory traditions. One traditional view of the sensible world was that it was evil, delusory, a prison for the spirit of man. The other was that the sensible world was the good creation of a good God, a symbolic message from God to man, to be read for its revelation of its Maker. Some who held the former view traced the cause of this wretchedness to the creation, others to the Fall, at which the world itself or man's perception of it became depraved, totally separate from God, from all goodness. Several heretical Christian sects exemplified extreme forms of this view. The Gnostics, as we have seen, attributed the creation of the sensible world to a decidedly inferior, and, in some accounts, evil deity named Ialdabaoth, whom the Jews mistakenly worshipped as Yahweh. They believed that all things visible, including the sun and stars, were the creation of this evil spirit and that, among earthly things, only the soul of man had any goodness. Manichaeans believed that God created and ruled only half the universe, the good half; the good principle was embodied in spirit. The other half was, of course, created and ruled by the Devil, whose evil principle was embodied in matter.

Among medieval Christians, this attitude (often without the concomitant metaphysics) was revived by several dualistic sects, of which the Cathari afford us a representative example. Exhibiting a dualism and otherworldliness in comparison with which the Puritans seem libertine, the Cathari began to make their influence felt in the 1140s. Measures taken against them indicate the strength of that influence. Anathematized by the Third Lateran Council in 1179, they represented the extreme form of dualism against which the church struggled throughout the papacy of Innocent III (1198–1216). To some extent, they occasioned the founding of the Dominican and Franciscan orders, which attempted to combat dualism, as did a crusade begun against the Cathari in 1209 and the Fourth Lateran Council, called in 1215 to establish clear definitions of orthodoxy and heresy. The reason for all this orthodox furor was, according to Donald R. Howard, "the pessimistic side of their doctrine, their conviction that matter is evil and the soul a prisoner in an evil body." This belief "led them to deny those Christian dogmas which involved world and flesh—the Incarnation, the sacrament of the mass, the virgin birth—and led them even to repudiate procreation: they thought birth itself an evil, since it imprisoned the soul in matter." For the Cathari, the moral imperative of this dualism was clear enough: the best way to spend one's life was in the *endura*, suicide by starvation.[20]

Less extreme than Catharism was the belief expressed in ecclesiastical treatises on "contempt of the world" written in Europe from the twelfth century to the seventeenth. So coherent and recognizable was this tradition of *contemptus mundi* that when Lothar of Segni (later Pope Innocent III) wrote in 1195 a work entitled *De miseria humane conditionis*, scribes added a prefix intended to indicate the genre of the work, a prefix by which this classic has since come to be known, *De contemptu mundi*.[21] Whatever the reasons for its influence (most commentators begin their discussions of it by stating that the work has no literary merit), Lothar's treatise was of profound and enduring significance. Over five hundred extant manuscripts preserved in libraries throughout Europe testify to the value placed on the work in its own time. It was quoted by Chaucer and by the author of *Piers Plowman*. In England in the sixteenth century it was made available in two translations, one of which went through five editions in the decade following its publication in 1576, and in a poetic synopsis written by the Puritan Stephen Gosson. It is clear from the *topoi* of their numerous poems on the vanity of worldly things that the American Puritans were familiar with the recurrent themes of the tradition, if not with the work itself. Lothar brought together the conventional themes of traditional *contemptus mundi*. In such chapters as "Of the Miserable Entrance upon the Human Condition," "Of the Vile Matter from which Man is Made," and "On the Putrefaction of the Dead Body," he wrote of the corruption of nature, especially of the human body, the pain of its birth, diseases, and death:

> I shall try to make my explanation clearer and my treatment fuller. Man was formed of dust, slime, and ashes; what is even more vile, of the filthiest seed. He was conceived from the itch of the flesh, in the heat of passion and the stench of lust, . . . born only to die. He commits depraved acts by which he offends God . . . and vain acts by which he ignores all things important, useful, and necessary. He will become fuel for those fires which are forever hot and burn forever bright; food for the worm which forever nibbles and digests; a mass of rottenness which will forever stink and reek.

This loathsome body imprisoned the soul of man, who longed for death and release: "Surely he does not want to be let out of prison who does not want to leave his body, for the body is the soul's prison."[22] He lamented the mutability and the vanity of earthly things, and evils in the social order. And he gave descriptions of the Day of Judgment and the punishments of hell, contrasting the insignificance of human life with the eternal consequences that follow from either contemning the world or loving it.

The poetic implications of such a world view are clear enough. Had the Puritans' *contemptus mundi* been as simple and extreme as that of the Gnostics, Manichaeans, and Cathari, they could not have celebrated the beauty of the natural world, seen it as the good gift of a loving God, read it for some revelation of His will, and used images drawn from it to figure spiritual states and heavenly delights. Had they been able to write poetry at all, they could have written either poetry comprising only religious abstractions or Swiftian denunciations of a filthy world figured forth in scatological imagery. Secular poetry would have been both meaningless and sinful; sacred poetry of a concrete or symbolic sort would have been impossible. We know, however, that the Puritans did write both secular and religious poetry. They found their rationale for doing so in other religious traditions they were heir to: a tradition in which the created, sensible world was a book written by God as a message, a revelation to His creatures; the tradition of structured meditation first codified by Loyola and made acceptable to Protestant sensibilities in the writings of such Puritans as Thomas Taylor and Richard Baxter; and the branch of that tradition called "meditation from the creatures," of which the American Puritans could have read in Thomas Taylor's *Meditations from the Creatures* but probably did read in Baxter's *Saints' Everlasting Rest*, in a section entitled "heavenly contemplation assisted by sensible objects."

Even Lothar's *contemptus mundi* was qualified. In the prologue to *De miseria humane conditionis*, a *tour de force* of pessimism on the wretchedness of man's world and the depravity of man, he expressed to Pope Celestine III (his immediate predecessor) his desire to write another treatise in which he would "describe also the dignity of human nature; so that, as in the present work the proud man is brought low, in that the humble man will be exalted." In the work itself he equated evil, not with the material world, but with human error, held the natural wisdom of pagan authors in high repute, argued that man's perception and reason, though dimmed by sin, could still lead him to understand part of God's truth.[23] Unlike the Gnostics, Manichaeans, and Cathari, but like Augustine, Lothar believed that the creatures of the sensible world, however mutable and physically corrupt, were good, the creations of a good God, not of an inferior deity like Demiurgus or an evil one like Ialdabaoth.[24]

Other medieval writers addressed themselves to the religious uses of the sensible world. St. Francis and Alain de Lille emphasized the goodness of creation and the revelations it offered of a truth beyond itself. On the significance of creatures, Alain wrote:

> Omnis mundi creatura
> Quasi liber et pictura
>   Nobis est speculum.
> Nostrae vitae, nostrae mortis
> Nostri status, nostrae sortis
> fidele signaculum.[25]
>
> [Every creature in the world
> Like a book and a picture
>   Is a mirror for us.
> A faithful hint ("small sign")
> Of our life, our death
> Of our portion, our lot.]

Richard of St. Victor made more explicit both the author and the function of the creatures' significance:

> Universus enim mundus iste quasi quidam liber est digito
> Dei scriptus, hoc est, virtute divina creatus, et singulae

creaturae quasi figurae quaedam sunt, non humanae placito
inventae, sed divino arbitrio institutae ad manifestanda, et
quasi quodammodo significanda Dei invisibilia.

(PL 96, 723B)

[For this whole world is rather like a book written by the
finger of God, that is, created by divine power, and the
individual creatures are like figures, not invented by the
whim of man, but established by the divine will, to show
forth, and as it were in a certain way to signify, the
invisible things of God.]

God had invested the world with meaning; its significance was
perceived, not created, by man. John Scotus made explicit the implications of the former statements when he urged the devout
Christian to use his senses in his quest for salvation, to recognize
the harmony of the perceived world and the Bible:

Sensu corporeo formas ac pulchritudines rerum percipe
sensibilium, et in eis intelliges Deum Verbum. . . . Dupli-
citer ergo lux aeterna se ipsam mundo declarat, per Scrip-
turam videlicet et creaturam.

(PL 122, 289C)

[Perceive by your bodily sense the forms and beauties of
sensible things, and in them you will discern God the
Word. . . . Therefore in a double way the eternal light
declares itself to the world, namely through Scripture
and creation.]

And Pseudo-Hrabanus explicitly noted the symbolic significance
of individual creatures:

Singulae creaturae e diversis proprietatibus, habitudinibus
et respectibus consideratae sunt signa libri, seu facies
quaedam, dictas res spirituales repraesentantes . . . sunt . . .
divino arbitrio institutae ad manifestandum invisibilem
Dei sapientiam et operum ejus alta et spiritalia mysteria.[26]

[Individual creatures—viewed according to their diverse
properties, qualities, and respects—are images of a book;
or if you will they are forms representing the said spiritual
realities which were established according to the divine
will to reveal the invisible wisdom of God, and the
profound and spiritual mysteries in His works.]

This symbolic significance imposed upon man a moral imperative.
Man had to read the invisible mysteries of God in His visible works.
God had intended him to do so, had so instructed him, as Bernard
of Clairvaux had noted, in the Bible:

> Invisibilia Dei, Apostolo teste, a creatura mundi, per ea
> quae facta sunt, intellecta conspiciuntur. Et est velut
> communis quidam liber, et catena alligatus, ut assolet,
> sensibilis mundus iste, ut in eo sapientiam Dei legat
> quicunque voluerit.
>
> (*PL* 183, 565 C)
>
> [As the Apostle testifies, the invisible things of God are
> seen and understood, since the creation of the world, from
> those things which have been made. And this sensible
> world is, as it were, a book open to all, tied with a chain
> as is customary, so that in it, whoever may wish to may
> read the wisdom of God.]

That the world was a book written by God to be read by man
was as much a commonplace among the Puritans of the seventeenth
century as it had been among the Catholics of the Middle Ages.
Though their Calvinist belief in a sovereign God might imply to
a modern reader the concomitant nominalist belief in an unintelligible multiverse, Puritans clearly believed that God had created
an intelligible universe. Now Thomists believed that God was
essentially rational and therefore necessarily created both a rationally intelligible universe and rational creatures to perceive it.
Puritans put no such limits on the sovereignty of God. Essentially
indescribable, God had freely chosen, in an act of loving conde-

scension, to take on the attribute of reason and so to create an intelligible universe, not from necessity, but from His desire to accommodate the finite nature of man. God had revealed Himself through His creatures, and man was under a moral imperative to seek his God through the creatures. Their Bible told them as much: "Forasmuch as that, which may be known of God, is manifest in them: for God hath showed it unto them. For the invisible things of him, that is, his eternal power and Godhead, are seen by the creation of the world, being considered in *his* works to be the intent that they should be without excuse" (Romans 1:20; Geneva Bible, London, 1582). The Puritan understanding of this admonition is clear in the writings of Alexander Richardson and Samuel Willard. Richardson, an English Puritan minister, wrote that man learned by the creatures of God "to see his order in them." Born without knowledge of the creatures or their order, man yet possesses natural "faculties" by which he may seek out that order. "And this teacheth man thus much, that he is to seek out, and find this wisdom of God in the world, and not to be idle; for the world, and the creatures therein are like a book wherein God's wisdom is written, and there must we seek it out."[27]

In his systematic exposition of American Puritan belief, Samuel Willard provided the theological rationale for such ascents from the creatures to the Creator as those practiced by the speakers of Richard Steere's *Earth Felicities, Heavens Allowances*, and Samuel Danforth II's "*Ad Librum.*" "God being the great and ultimate Object of Religion," wrote Willard, "the knowledge of him is the *first* thing necessary to be sought after." The first source of such knowledge, the first medium through which "God would reveal himself to us," is the created world, which both demonstrates God's existence and begins to lead us to Him. "The works of *Creation* do undeniably prove the Being of God. . . . The things that are made lead us by the hand to him that made them." Admittedly, that part of God's nature reflected to the understanding of man through the creatures does not compass God, is not His essential Glory but only, as in the promise to Moses, his "back-parts":

> This Incomprehensible Being hath made such discoveries of himself in his Back-Parts, as present him a suitable Object for Faith to rest upon. There are some precious rays of the Divinity, that irradiate us by way of reflection; by which we may so far acquaint ourselves with God, as may make us happy. God is called a *Sun*, (Psal. 84.11). Now if we fix our eyes directly on the body of the Sun, it will wholly dazzle us; but if we look on the reflected light or beams of it, we are safe, and it is comfortable; and so it is here. The Divine perfections are irradiated upon our Understanding through a dark glass . . . which displays of himself to his Creatures, God is pleased to call *his back-parts* . . . because they fall short of the plenary discovery of his Native Excellency, in the immediate unreflected manifestations of it. . . . His knowledge of himself, and that knowledge of him which he imparts to us, are infinitely disproportionable.

Yet even the little knowledge of Himself which God imparts to us through the two revelations, Nature and Scripture, is completely sufficient to our earthly needs and to our salvation. Willard saw God's refusal to reveal more of Himself as an act of love, an accommodation to the finite nature of man. He cited Exodus 33:20 —"Thou canst not see my face: for there shall no man see me and live"—and concluded that "in these Backparts is contained all that we can stand in need of. Let us but read over all those Glorious Golden Letters, in which the Name of God is displayed, in his Word and Works, and lay by them the slate of the Believer, lay all of his wants open, take the full account of all that can be thought of requisite to his everlasting Beatitude, and we shall find that nothing is here wanting to answer it to the outside, and beyond that."

Through his reading of the world and the Bible, therefore, the Puritan could discover all that he needed to know of God, indeed all that he possibly could know this side of heaven. He could read "the name of God" in His "works" as well as in the Bible. And he could be sure that his perception and reason were giving him accurate, though incomplete, knowledge of God's nature and His expectations of man. Like Steere, Willard believed that faith only confirmed and extended the findings of human reason. "Because Heaven's mode and way is not known unto us, therefore he speaks to us in the language or manner of Earth." It pleases God "to fit his discovery of himself to us to our manner of entertaining it, . . . and by such a way we come to see something concerning him who is himself invisible: and this tells us how useful or necessary reason is to Faith; it being an instrument which is used to convey the discoveries of God unto it; and therefore Faith doth not relinquish or cast off reason; for there is nothing in religion contrary to it, though there are many things that do transcend, and must captivate it."[28]

In his attitude toward the religious significance of the created world and the reliability of man's faculties in perceiving that significance, Willard was hardly a lone rebel or a cloistered scholar working out in his study sophisticated heresies that would have shocked the average Puritan. His words were spoken as sermons to the congregation at Old South Church in Boston. Had they found his views unorthodox, they could have admonished him, sent letters to other pastors in order to determine his orthodoxy, and finally have voted to replace him. Many other congregations had taken these steps against ministers rash enough to depart, however slightly, from the views of their parishioners. That they did none of these things indicates that Willard's views were to a great extent accepted by the members of his congregation, that they saw the relation between the creatures and the Creator much as Willard did.

It was a view quite conducive to the production of religious poetry, poetry which predicated in human terms spiritual truths beyond the experiential ken of living men. As Allan Ludwig has noted, Willard's notion of what men may predicate about God is even more univocal than the Thomist theory of proportionality. All monotheistic religions must steer a middle course between two extremes in their descriptions of God. If one can speak of God *univoce*, if words applied to God retain their ordinary meanings (i.e. mean exactly what they mean when applied to man), then God, though comfortingly understandable, loses His transcendence and becomes little more than a perfect man. If, on the other hand, a religion contends that any predications about God must be made completely *aequivoce*, that terms applied to God have none of their ordinary meaning, God retains His transcendence but loses His intelligibility and becomes completely ineffable, unlimited but un-recognizable and hardly a suitable object of faith and worship.

Aquinas feared that the belief in univocal predication would lead to complete anthropomorphism and a loss of God's transcen-dence, that the belief in equivocal predication would lead to unin-telligibility and, finally agnosticism. He therefore attempted to resolve the dilemma by steering a masterful if impenetrably com-plicated course between two simple extremes. Aquinas began by pointing out the inadequacy of the *via negativa* descriptions of God. Where Pseudo-Dionysius, for example, could content him-self with pointing out that God was not corporeal, Aquinas ob-served that such a statement implied, not that God *lacked* the perfections of the body but that He infinitely transcended them and was not less than a body, but infinitely more than corporeal. Most descriptions used in the *via negativa* were implied in God's Being, and a laborious listing of them was therefore unnecessary. Still other attributes of God, such as His goodness and wisdom, could not be described through the *via negativa*. The denomination of

66

"good" or "wise" was, as Copleston noted, "predicated affirmatively and directly of the divine substance." Do such predicates apply only to creatures, in which case our statement that "God is good" is false? Or have we emptied those predicates of their ordinary meanings, in which case the statement is meaningless?

Characteristically, Thomas chose neither: he "distinguished." He argued that although our concepts of goodness and wisdom are drawn from the creatures, they apply to the Creator as well, but in an analogical sense which is neither univocal nor equivocal, but somewhere between them. Both symbolic and propositional descriptions of God depend on some *likeness* between Creator and creature. For Aquinas this likeness or analogy is one of "proportion" or "proportionality." For example, the resemblance between the number 8 and the number 4 is one of proportion (a proportion described as 2 or $\frac{1}{2}$ depending upon the operation performed). The resemblance between the proportions of 6 to 3 and 4 to 2 is one of proportionality, a resemblance of two proportions to one another. When we say "God exists" we are speaking of an ill-defined but real analogy of proportion. We mean that *our* existence is in some respect like His, though (as with all analogies) it is in many respects different. The two existences are relatively the same, though simply different. When we say "God thinks" we are speaking of an analogy of proportionality in that there is some likeness between God's relation to His intellectual activity and man's relation to his intellectual activity. We may also use analogy symbolically, speaking of God as a "Sun" and meaning that what the sun is to the bodily eye, God is to the soul. Though Aquinas's system may be more subtle than this reduction of it, we need not be concerned to duplicate it here, for two reasons. First, even at its most complex, it retained a univocity that made possible propositional and symbolic predications about God in terms of His creatures. Second, the Puritans—perhaps because it was popish or perhaps because they thought theology should be simple enough for the comprehension of every man—do not seem to have followed out its implications. Samuel Willard wrote of God that "His knowledge of himself, and that knowledge of him which he imparts to us, are infinitely disproportionable." The likeness between God and His creatures was not one of proportion or proportionality.

Faced, as was Aquinas, with the problem of steering some middle course between univocal anthropomorphism and equivocal agnosticism, the Puritans rejected complicated resolution in favor of simple paradox. Duns Scotus had set the precedent for their *via media* in his "middle opinion, that it is compatible with the simplicity of God that there should be some concept common to Him and to the creature, but this common concept is not a generically common concept." Scotus asserted that God and the creature were completely different in the real order—he was no Spinoza—but he believed, in Copleston's words, that "God is knowable by man in this life only by means of concepts drawn from the creatures, and unless these concepts were common to God and creatures, we should never be able to compare creatures with God as the imperfect with the perfect: there would be no bridge between creatures and God. Even those masters who deny univocity with their lips, really presuppose it." Scotus concluded that "*esse*, existence, belongs primarily and principally to God in such a way that it yet belongs really and univocally (*realiter et univoce*) to the creature; and similarly with goodness and wisdom and the like." Though from God's point of view, in the real order, no similarity may have been necessary, yet in order to treat on man's level, God had created a real similarity.[29] In their own view of the relation between the creatures and the Creator, the New England Puritans were as univocal as Scotus: the "good" man differed from the "good" God only in the degree, the imperfection of his goodness;

the bright Sun differed from God in the imperfection of its brightness.

On this simple distinction, the Puritans worked their own subtleties and qualifications. First they insisted, as we have seen in Willard, that their statements about God could neither compass Him nor say anything of His essence. Such statements applied only to what Willard called his "irradiations" or "back-parts" or communicable glory—human predicates or attributes (such as goodness, rationality, the brightness of a Sun) that God had chosen to take upon Himself so that He could be understood, to a limited but sufficient extent, by His creatures. But within the limits set by these qualifications, the Puritans could—for all practical purposes —read their world and Bible for reliable, accurate, and sufficient knowledge of God; they could be sure that such knowledge as God chose to impart through these media was understandable in human terms, that their passionate love for an anthropomorphic God was neither sin nor delusion. They could legitimately ascend from predications about His creatures to predications about Him Who had invested those creatures with meaning in order to make possible just such an ascent. Things not only meant; things meant God and salvation. Such was the Puritans' view of their world and its Maker.

Living in a symbolic world, the Puritans found types, or symbols, in both their Bible and their own experiences. Samuel Mather had argued that man could not *make* types: "It is not safe to make any thing a Type merely upon our own fancies and imaginations; it is *God's* Prerogative to make *Types*."[30] But no commandment forbade man to *see* types, and Puritans saw them in their world as well as in their Bible. Though Perry Miller and Ursula Brumm have asserted that Edwards was original in extending the typological method from biblical exegesis to a reading of the spiritual significances of the sensible world, it is clear that this method had been practiced by medieval writers and the Puritans of the seventeenth century. They, like Edwards after them, saw "the natural world (the only one accessible to human comprehension)" as "the image of and the key to the transcendent world of religion, which could thus be understood indirectly." Like him, and like their medieval predecessors, they believed that "the things of the world are ordered [and] designed to shadow forth spiritual things." Like Edward Taylor, they saw "the world slickt up in types / In all Choise things chosen to typify."[31]

In 1674, Joshua Moody, assistant pastor at the First Church, preached the election sermon in Boston, using the common figure of human existence as a war and finding in the technical commands of the parade ground and in the movements and accoutrements of battle a wealth of spiritual significance put there by God. He explained the figurative method as the best way to speak of God in the language of men, as indeed the way that God Himself chooses: "As for my manner of speaking in the using of many Metaphorical Expressions, and Allusions unto the Calling, Postures, and motions of Soldiers . . . I conceive a man should take Measure of his theme to cut out his Language by, and make it up something according to the mode of his Auditory." Since his theme was the spiritual significance of secular callings, Moody was careful to point out that God was constantly "spiritualizing all our Employments" and that his own use of figures was not presumptuous creation, but merely an explication of God's method: "From the King upon the Throne to the Hewer of wood and drawer of water, the Lord is in his Word teaching us by such familiar and known *metaphors* taken from those Callings that we are versed in."[32] For Moody as for the others, the transcendent God had condescended to treat on man's level, had chosen to be immanent in the world in forms that man could understand. Though they steered a middle course between complete anthropomorphism and complete unintelligibility, the Puritans steered rather closer to the former than has been commonly believed. The world they inhabited, no less than the Bible from which they tried to draw the pattern for the perfect church and society, was a communication from God, to be studied closely and explicated accurately. Though its abuse could lead them from Him, its proper religious use was a "plain man's pathway to heaven." It offered the plain poet a world rich in intrinsic symbols, correspondences, and significances that were not decorations but necessary parts of the truth he attempted to tell.

One way in which the Puritan used the world in his quest for heaven was in religious meditation. Norman Grabo has recognized that "the art of Puritan devotion was basically a method for channeling emotion into verbal structures—a poetic method."[33] Meditation was a central concern for English and American Puritans throughout the seventeenth century, and the meditational handbooks used by the Puritans dealt with the essentially literary problem of using verbal methods to arouse and express emotion. So close were meditation and poetry in the Puritan mind that Bradstreet entitled one of her best long poems "Contemplations," Pain entitled his only extant poems *Daily Meditations*, and Edward Taylor referred to the poems written at monthly intervals for over forty-four years as "Preparatory Meditations." To understand Puritan poetry, and the attitudes toward the world, imagery, and language that inform it, we must examine this system of ideas and attitudes that stood so closely and clearly behind it.

Histories of Catholic meditational practices and of Puritan meditation after Baxter have been well told and require no detailed repetition here. Until the beginning of the seventeenth century, most works on meditation were written by Catholics and brought into England by the Jesuits. From these early writings on, the function of meditation was to arouse the affections, to bring the Christian into more intimate emotional relation with his God. In his *Introduction to the Devout Life*, St. Francis de Sales defined meditation: "when we think of heavenly things, not to learn but to love them, that is called to meditate: and the exercise thereof, Meditation."[34] St. Ignatius Loyola provided a relentlessly structured method for the arousal of this love in his *Spiritual Exercises*. The "exercitant," as Loyola called the person meditating, was to exercise in sequence three faculties of his soul—memory, understanding, and will. Subject matter for the meditation—e.g. doctrine, scriptural incident, or some object with spiritual significance—was called up by memory, and one first attempted to get as detailed and vivid an apprehension of it as he could using only his memory and imagination. Then one exercised one's understanding, or reason, upon the image or proposition supplied by memory until, after thorough intellectual examination, the work of understanding was complete. Only then did the exercitant judge the subject and submit it to his will and affections, which were moved to great joy or sorrow. Meditation drove dogma into imagination, enlivened doctrine into thoroughly apprehended truth.

Among Puritans this formerly Catholic method of spiritual exercise received surprisingly quick and wide acceptance. Answering in 1589 the charge (by the Jesuit Robert Persons) that the English had no devotional writers, Edmund Bunny contended that the Reformers were reading handbooks of meditation. By 1628 they were writing them. In that year, the English Puritan minister Thomas Taylor published his *Meditations from the Creatures*, "as it was preached in Aldermanbury": "I thought fit to afford a little help, to lead up careful Christians into this mount of Meditation: in which mount God will be seen." Though "the Lord himself, his Word and Decrees, are the principal object of ordinary Meditation," Taylor wishes to extend traditional meditation to include among its objects images drawn from the sensible world. He suggests that "so are his works and execution of his decrees a fit object," and cites the example of David, who "acknowledgeth himself occupied in contemplation of the heavens and stars . . . that he is led to God by them." The relationship between God and the world, then, is not dualistic but hierarchical. God is an author, and the world is His book, to be read by man and not despised, mistrusted, or ignored. "The world is his book; so many pages, as so many several creatures; no page is empty, but full of lines; every quality of the creature, is a several letter of this book, and no letter without a part of God's wisdom in it."

If the world itself is metaphorical, then "the voice of the Creatures is not to be banished out of the church," and ministers must be metaphorical in their conceivings and their preachings: "If all Scriptures be profitable to teach and improve, then those that teach divine things from natural." Such teaching was, of course, metaphorical, but the method itself had biblical sanction, since "the Prophets and Apostles, and Christ himself were most in this kind of instruction, by Parables and Similitudes: therefore Ministers and Pastors may do the like."

In focusing on the metaphorical nature of the physical world and the metaphorical language of the Bible, Taylor was moving toward an understanding of meditation as a literary, as well as a religious, exercise. And he knew it. Discussing metaphorical predications about the nature of God, he clearly moves into the realm of literary criticism: "Hands and fingers are ascribed to God metaphorically. And here the heavens are called not the works of his hands, but his fingers: to note his singular industry, his exquisite workmanship and art, and also special love and care." For Taylor, then, meditation from the creatures lifted one's thoughts and affections to God, not by denying the physical world, but by reflecting on it in words, by translating God's physical metaphors

73

into verbal metaphors. The world was a text, a system of metaphors, a language, a voice, and Taylor concluded his treatise with a Latin tag: "Vox Dei est in omnibus, per omnia, de omnibus et ad omnia, loquens nobiscum semper et ubique." In the third edition (London, 1632) of this popular book, he provided his own translation: "The voice of God in all the creatures and by them all speaketh unto us always and everywhere." The sensible world was a voice to be heard, a book to be read, and meditation was a verbal, a literary, method of practicing one's religion.[35]

For the Puritans who later came to America, as for Thomas Taylor, meditation was a verbal method of taking a truth from the physical world or of giving life to a truth already understood intellectually by driving it home to the affections. In *The Soules Preparation for Christ* (London, 1632), Thomas Hooker defined meditation: "It is a settled exercise for two ends: first to make a further inquiry of the truth: and secondly, to make the heart affected therewith." That Hooker's meditative technique was metaphorical is clear from his examples: "It is with meditation as it is with usurers that will grate upon men, and grind the faces of the poor, and suck the blood of the needy, they will exact upon men. . . . So doth meditation, it exacts and slayeth the soul of a poor sinner, you have committed adultery in a corner but you shall not carry it away."[36] For Hooker, the language of meditation was concrete, imagistic, and metaphoric because this kind of charged language would affect the heart. It was not only possible for meditation to use such language, linking the invisible things of God with the visible things of this world, the holy practice of meditation with the cruelty of usurers; it was necessary; it was commanded.[37]

Early in his career, for example, young John Cotton wrote that "a man that is enlightened with the knowledge of God's will, and the mystery of Salvation; may lawfully in his meditations make use of diverse Creatures or Things, that are apt and fit to represent Spiritual things unto him."[38] And in 1648 the *Shorter Catechism* of the Westminster Assembly—a work that exerted a pervasive influence among American Puritans—made the practice of meditation a duty, a necessary part of preparing oneself for the Lord's Supper. But the most pervasive influence on Puritan meditational practices and the poetry they informed was a book published in England in January 1649/50, Richard Baxter's *The Saints' Everlasting Rest*, a work so influential among Puritans that until recently scholars assumed that it was the first Puritan treatise on meditation and ignored its predecessors.[39]

Well qualified to succeed in making acceptable to his fellow Protestants Catholic methods of devotion, Baxter had sided early with the Puritan cause and had served as a military chaplain in the Parliamentary armies during the Civil War. Though he contributed to the Restoration, he turned down the bishopric that would have been his reward and suffered sufficiently under Charles II and James II to qualify for popular investiture as a living Protestant martyr. In 1659, he was to publish *A Key for Catholicks, to open the jugling of the Jesuits*, a work which would have cleared him of the charge of being soft on Catholics, had anyone thought to make it.[40] His *Saints' Everlasting Rest* appeared almost exactly one year after the execution of Charles I. Nine editions in twelve years bespeak a ready audience. Called by one scholar "one of the most popular Puritan books of the entire seventeenth century," and the major book of a man whose "various works were common to the libraries of both New England and the southern colonies,"[41] Baxter's enormous tome was intended as a guidebook for the Puritan's journey to heaven. The most important part of that journey was meditation; hence the most important part of Baxter's book was "The Fourth Part. Containing a Directory for the getting and keeping of the Heart in Heaven: By the diligent

75

practice of that Excellent unknown Deity of *Heavenly Meditation.*
Being the main thing intended by the Author, in the writing of
this Book; and to which all the rest is but subservient." In this
section of one of the most popular and influential of Puritan books,
Baxter repeated several themes in Thomas Taylor's *Meditations
from the Creatures* and brought together most of the attitudes
that made Puritan poetry possible and informed his own poetry—
the positive approach to the sensible world, the recognition that
though the senses were potentially dangerous they had their part
in worship, the rationale for the use of sensuous imagery drawn
from the creatures to describe the invisible things of God, and a
complex but consistent statement of the uses and limits of language
in meditation.

Baxter began by insisting on the centrality of meditation to the
holy life: "All that I have said is but for the preparation to this:
The Doctrinal part is but to instruct you to this: the rest of the
uses are but introductions to this." Primary among "Some Ad-
vantages and Helps for raising and Affecting the Soul by this
Meditation" were the senses and their objects. Baxter's detailed
discussion of them made explicit many of the complex but consistent attitudes implicit in Puritan poetry:

> Why sure it will be a point of our Spiritual Prudence,
> and a singular help to the furthering of the work of Faith
> to call in our sense to our assistance: if we can make
> friends of these usual enemies, and make them instru-
> ments of raising us to God, which are the usual means of
> drawing us from God, I think we shall perform a very
> excellent work. Surely it is both possible and lawful, yea,
> and necessary too, to do something in this kind: for God
> would not have given us either our Senses themselves, or
> their usual objects, if they might not have been service-
> able to his own Praise, and helps to raise us to the appre-
> hension of higher things.

Though they recognized the potential dangers of the senses, Puritans could use them in religious meditation and therefore in the literature that recorded that meditation. Like all things worldly, the senses trapped men who thought that there was nothing beyond them, but they, again like all things worldly, had a proper use. Indeed, even God used them when revealing Himself to man through Scripture:

> And it is very considerable how the holy Ghost doth
> condescend in the phrase of Scripture, in bringing things
> down to the reach of sense; how he sets forth the excel-
> lencies of Spiritual things in words that are borrowed
> from the objects of sense; how he describeth the glory of
> the New *Jerusalem*, in expressions that might take even
> with flesh itself: As that the Streets and Buildings are
> pure Gold, that the gates are Pearl. . . . That we shall eat
> and drink with Christ at his Table in his Kingdom: that
> he will drink with us the fruit of the Vine new; that
> we shall shine as the Sun in the Firmament of our Father:
> These with most other descriptions of our Glory are
> expressed, as if it were the very flesh and Sense; which
> though they are all improper and figurative, yet doubt-
> less if such expressions had not been best, and to us neces-
> sary, the Holy Ghost would not have so frequently used
> them.

Baxter's tone here was insistent; he realized that he had to make his case, to assure his readers that he was not urging them to become merely men of sense. But he did make the case, as the many examples of sensuous expression of spiritual truths (examined in Chapter 1) testify.

For Baxter, then, as for the American Willard, God had condescended to treat on man's level in His use of figurative language, and that condescension compelled an appropriate response from man:

He that will speak to man's understanding; must speak
in man's language, and speak that which he is capable
to conceive. And doubtless as the Spirit doth speak, so
we must hear; and if our necessity cause him to conde-
scend in his expressions, it must needs cause us to be low
in our conceivings.

Indeed, the central and defining event in Christianity, the Incarnation of the invisible God in visible man was, like creation
and all other metaphor, God's act of making part of Himself available to the understanding of man:

It is one reason of Christ's assuming and continuing our
nature with the Godhead, that we might know him the
better, when he is so much nearer to us: and we might have
more positive conceivings of him, and so our minds might
have familiarity with him, who before was quite beyond
their reach.

Baxter was, of course, aware of the dangers of idolatry (to which
he asserted the Catholics had fallen) and of the limits of language.
He realized that an anthropomorphic view of God and heaven
was a psychic necessity, not a metaphysical fact:

But what is my scope in all this? is it that we might think
Heaven to be made of Gold and Pearl? or that we should
picture Christ, as the Papists do, in such a shape? or that
we should think Saints and Angels do indeed eat and
drink? No, not that we should take the Spirit's figurative
expressions to be meant according to strict propriety: or
have fleshly conceivings of spiritual things, so as to believe
them to be such indeed: But this; to think that to conceive
or speak of them in strict propriety, is utterly beyond our
reach and capacity: and therefore we must conceive of
them as we are able; and that the Spirit would not have
represented them in these notions to us, but that we have
no better notions to apprehend them by; and therefore

that we can make use of these phrases of the Spirit to
quicken our apprehensions and affections.

Correspondences between the invisible things of God and the visible things of earth exist by fiat of God and can be expressed only through some form of figuration. Though these figures do not express God and heaven as such are known by God Himself and by those saints who are with Him in heaven, they do express as much of the beatific vision as man on earth can and needs to know. Limited and potentially dangerous, they are hardly to be scorned by mortal man.

In Baxter's prose, then, we find the theological rationale for the figures that constitute so much of Puritan religious poetry. We find here the explicit statement of the attitude that enabled Puritan poets to delight in the sensible world, to state its vanities only in comparison with the joys of God and heaven, and to use the former to figure the latter. Even God had taken upon Himself the attributes of man, and though to afford a direct picture of Him would certainly have been idolatrous, as both Baxter and Willard had warned, nevertheless, man could understand and speak of and love God as anthropomorphically as God had "accommodated" His revelations to the temporary, earthly understandings of His creature. Having justified the uses of figuration to describe things spiritual, Baxter concluded: "The like may be said of those expressions of God in Scripture, wherein he represents himself in the imperfections of creatures, as anger, repenting, willing what shall not come to pass, &C." They are "improper, drawn from the manner of man," but "we can see no better yet."[42]

Baxter made explicit the Puritan attitudes toward the sensible world, the religious use of images drawn from it, and the limits and necessity of figurative language based on that imagery. As our examinations of Puritan poetry and of Puritan writings on the religious significance of the sensible world have shown, these attitudes were far more pervasive and uniform than a doctrinaire pluralist would expect. Though the Puritans neither wrote an explicit *ars poetica* nor, like Blake and Yeats, constructed their world view in order to provide symbols for poetry, their world view was positive, symbolic, and therefore far more conducive to the production of poetry than the world view imputed to them in popular critical generalizations. The poetics implicit in their prose writings avoided the worship, not the perception of images. Based on the belief that the world was the gift of a loving God, it comprised many paeans to the beauty and abundance of the natural world, a world perceived both as an *a fortiori* argument for the beauty and goodness of God and as a God-wrought system of symbols intended to lead man to heaven. Puritans believed that meaning resided in the symbolic world itself, and their poetics has far more in common with the Latin concept of the poet as *vates* ("seer"), one who sees and says the truth, than with the Greek concept of the poet as *poeta* ("maker"), one who creates verbal artifacts. We may use the critical tools provided by the New Critical view of the poem as verbal artifact in our reading of Puritan poetry; but it is clear that the making of such artifacts was not their intention when they wrote it: their avowed task was simply to say, to utter, the metaphoric truth they saw.

The sensible world, the senses, the words used to arouse and describe the meanings and affections appropriate to them—all were limited but necessary; all had their parts to play in salvation. Though not the ultimate object of man's love, they were created by God out of His love for man in order to give him a suitable object for his earthly love.

Nowhere is that earthly love clearer, and nowhere is the distance between the Puritan and the Gnostic or Manichaean or Catharist dualist greater than in their attitudes toward the death of the body. The Cathari, for example, believed that the proper duty of man on earth consisted of the *endura*, suicide by starvation. But the Puritans were clearly not half in love with easeful death. Though neoplatonic in some respects, they saw the body as something more than the prison from which the soul should happily escape at its first opportunity. Samuel Willard wrote of death: "It makes a separation between the soul and body. This is the very nature of it, and is in itself a misery; and for that reason the Godly themselves have a natural reluctancy against it; they would not pass through it if they could go to heaven without it." The terror inherent in that "reluctancy" is clear from the work of David Stannard, who has recently presented considerable evidence "that the Puritans were gripped individually and collectively by an intense and unremitting fear of death."[43]

Puritan poets, like all Puritans, knew that they had to face that terror. They knew that part of their work in this world was to wean their affections from the unmixed love of it. But they also knew that this world was God's metaphor for His communicable glories and that another part of their duty was to see and utter that metaphor, to use the figural value of this world to turn their attention and affections to the next.

III

Anne Bradstreet and the Practice
of Weaned Affections

I have not studied in this you read to show my skill, but
to declare the truth, not to set forth myself, but the glory
of God.

The spring is a lively emblem of the resurrection.

Were earthly comforts permanent, who would look for
heavenly?

ANNE BRADSTREET

THOUGH her fellow Puritans both in England and America
thought Anne Bradstreet an excellent and orthodox poet,
commentators in the nineteenth century so thoroughly established
the generalization that Puritan theology vitiated poetry that some
twentieth-century critics have often praised her poetry by impugn-
ing her orthodoxy or praised those poems that apparently have
least to do with religion. In his prefatory commendation to the
Boston edition of her poems, her fellow Puritan John Rogers
praised the power of her art:

> Thus weltring in delight, my virgin mind
> Admits a rape; truth still lyes undiscri'd,
> Its singular, that plural seem'd, I find,
> 'Twas Fancies glass alone that multipli'd;
> Nature with Art so closely did combine,
> I thought I saw the Muses trebble trine,
> Which prov'd your lonely Muse, superior to the nine.

Less enthusiastically, but still with no hint that her poetry contradicted her orthodoxy, Cotton Mather wrote in 1702 that "her
poems . . . have afforded . . . a monument for her memory beyond

82

the stateliest marbles." By the nineteenth century, however, it was widely believed that Puritans could not have written lasting poetry. Evert and George Duyckinck turned to the one extant poem by Anne's father, Thomas Dudley, for a verse to "exhibit the severity of his creed and practice." His daughter's poems they considered more domestic than religious. At best and "with a little more taste" she "might have been a happy describer of nature for she had a warm heart and a hearty view of things." As it was, however, she "writes as if under bonds to tell the whole truth, which she does without any regard to the niceties or scruples of the imagination." Bradstreet was a minor domestic poet whose Puritanism was apparently quite beside the point.[1]

That her Puritanism ruined her poetry was the central judgment of Moses Coit Tyler in 1878. The "narrow and ferocious creed" which destroyed the poetry of such as Michael Wigglesworth severely limited that of Anne Bradstreet: "Literature, for her, was not a republic of letters, hospitable to all forms of human thought, but a strict Puritan commonwealth, founded on a scheme of narrow ascetic intolerance, and excluding from its citizenship some of the sublimest, daintiest, and most tremendous types of literary expression."[2] That her poetry broke free from the restraints of her Puritanism and recorded her rebellion has been the conclusion of some subsequent critics. Stanley Williams wrote of her poetry to her husband: "The warm, human lines seem to snap the chains of current poetic theory; for the moment seventeenth-century American verse ceases to be the prisoner of religion." And Ann Stanford asserted that her heart "rebelled" at something in Puritan dogma, that "it is this clash of feeling and dogma that keeps her poetry alive," and that "no better description could be found for the poetry of Anne Bradstreet" than the Lawrencian concept of duplicity, "a tight mental allegiance to a morality which all their passion goes to destroy."[3]

Others have either based their readings upon the quiet recognition of her orthodoxy or vigorously defended it. Samuel Eliot Morison, writing before the picture of Anne Bradstreet-as-poetic-rebel had been drawn, could quietly state that "her art was not an escape from life, but an expression of life. It was shot through and through with her religious faith." The endurance of her poetry "was proof, if it were needed, that creative art may be furthered by religion." But Robert Richardson had to argue insistently, and persuasively, that Bradstreet wrote "from what might be called the Puritan sensibility" and that in her "Contemplations" Bradstreet "has reached that ideal but rare state of Puritan consciousness, a carefully reasoned and emotionally convincing resolution of the problem of how to live in the world without being of it." For Richardson, Bradstreet's poetry records not the poet's resistance to Puritan dogma but her struggle toward and attainment of the moral imperatives of that dogma. And William J. Irvin has argued, in reading the "Contemplations," that "one should see . . . the entire emotional structure of the poem, as well as the epistemological one, as part of the Puritan psychology."[4] But we need not examine further the fairly simple question of whether Bradstreet happened to believe in the general framework of theological attitudes that —pluralist arguments about specific matters of church polity notwithstanding—we still label "orthodox." She did. We need to examine the more subtle question of what she, as practicing poet, made of her theology. We need to examine where experientially her religion took her and where poetically she took her religion.

Though the question of Bradstreet's orthodoxy, then, has been argued in some detail, and though her poetry has attracted more critical attention than that of any other Puritan poet save Taylor,[5] no one has yet examined the ways in which her Puritanism illuminates not only the substance of her poems but also their imagery, structure, and dynamics. In Bradstreet's work, theology became poetics as well as poetry, and the complex of attitudes examined in Chapter 2 has as much to do with Anne Bradstreet's poetic uses of the natural world as with her purely religious uses of it.

Her attitude toward the things of this world was certainly orthodox enough. Like Augustine,[6] the Puritans considered the creatures of the sensible world the creations of a good and provident God. Since the sensible world depended for its existence and continuance upon the *concursus Dei*, the sensible world was essentially good, and man was to love it. As Perry Miller has recognized, the real danger besetting the Puritans in their relation to the world was not Gnosticism but pantheism: "always they verge so close to pantheism that it takes all their ingenuity to restrain themselves from identifying God with the creation." That ingenuity remains manifest in Puritan statements that, though the world itself is temporally good and is ordered by God for the good of man, it is not ultimately good: compared with its Creator it is empty and cannot satisfy man's restless soul. Though man is permitted, indeed required, to love the world, then, he must "wean" his affections from the unmixed love of it if he is to pass from this world to the next. The man who cannot do so gives to the creature a complete love rightfully belonging to the Creator and therefore commits idolatry.

Puritan preachers distinguished clearly between proper and idolatrous love of the creature: "He doth not forbid mercy or love to Beasts or Creatures, but he would not have your love terminated in them, bounded in them, he would not have you rejoice or delight in the Creature, before you have part in the Creator, for if you affect these things for themselves, the love of God is not in you." Commanded to love the world with weaned affections, the Puritan struggled, not to work up a little love for himself and his farm, pets, children and wife, but to accept in the love of God the fact that all these things were transitory, to wean his affections from them so that he could without rancor bid goodby at death to things he loved all too well. In *The Soules Justification* (London, 1638), Thomas Hooker explained that one should love the creatures as well as God: "Will you love your friends that are dear unto you, or your Parents that do provide for you, or your wife that is loving and merciful to you? you will love these, as there is good cause you should." Love of God should differ from love of the creatures only in degree, and Hooker concludes merely that one should "love Christ more than all these." The Puritan's struggle was to wean his affections from the unmixed love of such creatures, to convince himself that finally the world he loved was subordinate to its Creator. Though the beauties of the world were the creations of God, the command was clear: "Get thy heart more and more weaned from the Creature, the Creature is empty, it's not able to satisfy thee fully, nor make thee happy."[7]

That the command to love the world with weaned affections did not prevent the Puritans' loving the world is evident in much Puritan literature and can be exemplified, for our purposes, in two otherwise dissimilar sources, Cotton's sermon on calling and Sewall's *Phaenomena quaedam Apocalyptica*, a pamphlet explicating in tireless detail the prophecies in Revelation. Cotton urged his hearers, not to forsake their "natural" and "civil" lives in order to perfect their spiritual lives, but to live both fully. In an illuminating allusion to Paul and Augustine, Cotton described the "natural life" as "that, by which we do live this bodily life, I mean, by which we live a life of sense, by which we go through all conditions, from our birth to our grave, by which we live, and move, and have our being. And now both these a justified [elect] person lives by faith." Leaving aside the difficult questions of intention and audience, we may be sure that Cotton alluded to the description of God as One in Whom "we live, move, and have our being," (Acts 17:28) which Augustine repeated in his *Confessions*: "in Thee we live and move and have our being." His allusion linked living the natural life in the world to living in God. For Cotton, then, the natural life, the life of sense, was also a part of God, a way of serving Him, an expression of faith. Sewall's love of the sensible world and his belief in the intrinsic harmony of this world and the next are rendered more imagistically than Cotton's. In a pamphlet "devoted," as Miller wrote, "to rendering mystical visions into dull prose," Sewall took sudden leave of his dullness to sing a hymn to the sensuous beauties of Plum Island and to its fitness as a place for the work of redemption:

> As long as *Plum Island* shall faithfully keep the commanded post; Notwithstanding all the hectoring Words and hard Blows of the proud and boisterous Ocean . . . As long as Sea-Fowl shall know the Time of their coming, and not neglect seasonably to visit the Places of their Acquaintance: As long as any Cattle shall be fed with the Grass growing in the Meadows, which do humbly bow down themselves before *Turkey-Hill*; As long as any Sheep shall walk upon *Old Town Hills*, and shall from thence pleasantly look down upon the River *Parker*, and the fruitful Marshes lying beneath; As long as any free and harmless Doves shall find a White Oak, or other Tree within the Township, to perch, or feed, or build a careless Nest upon; and shall voluntarily present themselves to perform the office of Gleaners after Barley-Harvest; As long as Nature shall not grow Old and dote; but shall constantly remember to give the rows of Indian Corn their education, by Pairs: So long shall Christians be born there; and being first made meet, shall from thence be Translated, to be made partakers of the Inheritance of the Saints in Light.[8]

Loving Plum Island with weaned affections would not keep one from his inheritance.

Bradstreet's prose statements place her within the tradition of orthodox Puritans who loved the sensible world but knew that it could not compare with its Maker. In her "Meditations Divine and Moral" she used the conventional figure of weaning to describe the process through which the Christian, who loves the things of this world, learns ultimately to give them up for the joys of the next:

> Some children are hardly weaned; although the teat be
> rubbed with wormwood or mustard, they will either wipe
> it off, or else suck down sweet and bitter together. So is it
> with some Christians: let God embitter all the sweets of
> this life, that so they might feed upon more substantial
> food, yet they are so childishly sottish that they are still
> hugging and sucking these empty breasts that God is
> forced to hedge up their way with thorns or lay affliction
> on their loins that so they might shake hands with the
> world, before it bid them farewell.[9]

For Bradstreet, then, the things of the world were good and wholesome in their place and for a time. They become a hindrance to growth in God only when loved foolishly, when clung to as if there were nothing beyond them. Her attitude toward the things of this world was clearly orthodox.

What we need to realize now is that her far more complex attitude toward the religious and poetic uses of the sensible world was also orthodox, that Puritan orthodoxy was conducive to the production of poetry, and that Bradstreet's poetry is illuminated by an understanding of the theology which structured the experiences her poetry expressed. As we saw in Chapter 2, Puritan preaching and precedent sanctioned certain uses of the sensible world. Bradstreet, as a Puritan poet, could celebrate the world, could use images drawn from it to figure spiritual states and truths, even in poems on its ultimate vanity, and could ascend from love of the creatures to love of the Creator through her contemplations of the former.

✗ Though delight in the beauty of the world pervades much of her poetry, Bradstreet (unlike the Romantics and several of her fellow Puritans) wrote no poems intended simply to celebrate the sensible world. But neither is her poetry a collection of religious or philosophical abstractions: never her ultimate goal, the sensible world was always her point of departure; it was where she began. In such beginnings we find her celebrations of the natural world, her sense of herself as a fellow creature:

> Some time now past in the autumnal tide
> When Phoebus wanted but one hour to bed,
> The trees all richly clad, yet void of pride,
> Where gilded o'er by his rich golden head.
> Their leaves and fruits seemed painted, but was true,
> Of green, of red, of yellow, mixed hue;
> Rapt were my senses at this delectable view.
>
> (p.204)

Now neither the senses nor the objects that delighted them were at all evil, and Bradstreet would later in the same poem salute the sun as a fellow creature: "Hail creature, full of sweetness, beauty, and delight" (p. 206). But Bradstreet was no Walt Whitman, no H. D.; such was her Puritan habit of mind that she could never rest content with the image itself. For her the image shadowed forth its Maker; its goodness and beauty constituted an *a fortiori* argument for the goodness and beauty (predicated univocally) of God, and in the stanza just after her celebration of "this delectable view" she immediately thought of its *glossa*, or spiritual interpretation:

I wist not what to wish, yet sure thought I,
If so much excellence abide below,
How excellent is He that dwells on high,
Whose power and beauty by his works we know?
Sure he is goodness, wisdom, glory, light,
That hath this under world so richly dight;
More heaven than earth was here, no winter and no night.

(p. 205)

Imbued with divine meaning, the world was to be not only appreciated but understood. Man was to make sense of his earthly experience in the service of his religion.

As Bradstreet made explicit in her "Meditations Divine and Moral," the world was to be used: "There is no object that we see, no action that we do, no good that we enjoy, no evil that we feel or fear, but we may make some spiritual advantage of all" (p. 272). One valid use of the sensible world was figuration. Images could figure, as they had in Scripture, purely human experiences: "We read in Scriptures of three sorts of arrows: the arrow of an enemy, the arrow of pestilence, and the arrow of a slanderous tongue. The first two kill the body, the last the good name; the two former leave a man when once he is dead, but the last mangles him in his grave" (p. 278). They could figure the spiritual states of man: "We often see stones hang with drops not from any innate moisture, but from a thick air about them; so may we sometime see marble-hearted sinners seem full of contrition, but it is not from any dew of grace within but from some black clouds that impends them, which produces these sweating effects" (pp. 280–281); and "As man is called a little world, so his heart may be called a little commonwealth" (p. 286). They could figure man's quest for salvation: "The hireling that labours all the day comforts himself that when night comes he shall both take his rest and receive his reward; the painful Christian that hath wrought hard in God's vineyard and hath born the heat and drought of the day, when he perceives his sun apace to decline and the shadows of his evening to be stretched out, lifts up his head with joy, knowing his refreshing is at hand" (p. 273); and "We see in orchards some trees so fruitful that the weights of their burden is the breaking of their limbs, some again are meanly loaden, and some have nothing to show but leaves only, and some among them are dry stock; so it is in the church, which is God's orchard" (p. 286), and Bradstreet's different types of trees become different types of Christians.

Images in the perceived world figured even the "irradiations," the communicable glories of God, Who is portrayed in Bradstreet more as a wise and loving parent than as the celestial lunatic so often foisted off on the Puritans by their modern detractors: "A prudent mother will not cloth her little child with a long and cumbersome garment. . . . Much more will the allwise God proportion His dispensations according to the stature and strength of the person He bestows them on" (p. 279); and "A wise father will not lay a burden on a child of seven years old which he knows is enough for one twice his strength; much less will our heavenly Father (who knows our mold) lay such afflictions upon his weak children as would crush them to the dust, but according to the strength he will proportion the load" (p. 280). Indeed, Bradstreet insisted that man's relation to God was familial, even physical: "Lord why should I doubt any more when Thou hast given me such assured pledges of Thy love? First, Thou art my Creator, I Thy creature, Thou my master, I Thy servant. But hence arises not my comfort, Thou art my Father, I Thy child; 'Ye shall be My sons and daughters,' saith the Lord Almighty. Christ is my brother, I ascend unto my Father, and your Father, unto my God and your God; but lest this should not be enough, thy Maker is thy husband. Nay more, I am a member of His body, He my head" (p. 250). Lower world and higher were linked by figuration; God's investing the lower world with such divine meaning was an act of love.

One last example illustrates the habit of mind that informed Bradstreet's perception and her poetry. Even the wheeling of the seasons manifested to her the facts of her religion, had been intended by God to manifest them: "The spring is a lively emblem of the resurrection: after a long winter we see the leafless trees and dry stocks (at the approach of the sun) to resume their former vigor and beauty in a more ample manner than what they lost in autumn; so shall it be at that great day after a long vacation, when the Sun of righteousness shall appear; those dry bones shall arise in far more glory than that which they lost at their creation, and in this transcends the spring that their leaf shall never fail nor their sap decline" (p. 279). Bradstreet was aware that such figuration did not imply complete metaphysical identity and was able, as this example shows, to turn dissimilarity to figurative advantage: the resurrection of the body into heaven was after all, a more perfect spring than spring itself. But throughout her prose and poetry she was concerned with figuration, not as a verbal trick the limitations of which gave her opportunity to display her ingenuity, but as a basic principle operative in her perceived universe. She lived in a world in which several orders of reality now often separate—the worldly or earthly or natural or sensible, the biblical, and the eschatological—were the harmonious creation of a single God and were held together by Him in a web of intrinsic correspondence. The worldly season, spring, was intended by God to figure forth both Christ's resurrection in the Bible and the resurrection of the saint after death. Perceptive Christian that she was, Bradstreet could hardly have thought of one without immediately thinking of the other two, not because of a tidy list such as those offered in typological dictionaries, but because of a pervasive habit of mind that lay behind both Puritan poetry and the typological dictionaries. In Puritan poems, symbolic correspondences occur, not at the level of trope, but at the level of perception.

The relevance of this habit of mind to our understanding of Puritan poetry becomes clear if we consider the well-known critical dictum of Allen Tate that good poetry possesses a characteristic that he named "tension," a word formed by "lopping the prefixes off the logical terms *ex*tension and *in*tension."[10] "Tension," wrote Tate, was the coherence of all denotative meanings no matter how far one chose to extend them, the coherence of all connotative intensional meanings, and the coherence of the one set of meanings with the other. In our attempt fully to understand a poem, we must explore both the intensional and extensional meanings of its imagery. In order to understand Bradstreet's poetry, we need to be aware of the implicit symbolism that pervades it.

Three poems afford us a clear example of the way her symbols link the different orders of reality, the way earthly experiences resonate with biblical and eschatological significances. In her "Contemplations" Bradstreet described the sun in the figure of the Bridegroom, a figure taken from the nineteenth psalm of David. But Bradstreet developed the figure far more than the psalmist had, and her description of the sun and earth in spring centered on marriage and impregnation:

> Thou as a bridegroom from thy chamber rushes,
> And as a strong man joys to run a race;
> The morn doth usher thee with smiles and blushes;
> The Earth reflects her glances in thy face.
> Birds, insects, animals with vegative,
> Thy heat from death and dullness doth revive,
> And in the darksome womb of fruitful nature dive.
>
> (pp. 205–206)

That both sun and bridegroom were equally real to Bradstreet is evident in "A Letter to Her Husband, Absent upon Public Em-

ployment," in which she likened her own bridegroom to the warm
and fecund spring sun, now absent in winter:

> I, like the Earth this season, mourn in black,
> My Sun is gone so far in's zodiac,
> Whom whilst I 'joyed, nor storms, nor frost I felt,
> His warmth such frigid colds did cause to melt.
> My chilled limbs now numbed lie forlorn;
> Return, return, sweet Sol, from Capricorn;
> In this dead time, alas, what can I more
> Than view those fruits which through thy heat I bore?
> (p. 226)

If the warming sun is like a bridegroom, her own husband partakes
of the warmth and fertility of the sun, and both can be seen and
figured in terms of sensual love and the production of children.
For the Puritans, moreover, the sun was frequently used as an
admittedly imperfect figure for God, and Christ was of course
the bridegroom, come to marry His church and her saints. Death
was a spiritual marriage. It is appropriate, then, that in "As Weary
Pilgrim," written only three years before her death, she figured
her approach to death as the approach of a bride to her wedding.
Her grave is "the bed Christ did perfume," which shall receive
her withered and "corrupt" body only to yield forth "a glorious
body" on the day when "soul and body shall unite / And of their
Maker have the sight." Because of this promise, a song of age and
death could become a song of love and approaching union: "Lord
make me ready for that day, / Then come, dear Bridegroom,
come away" (pp. 294–295).

In "As Spring the Winter Doth Succeed" (p. 256), the revivification of nature, the return of her husband and Christ's love, her
recovery from physical illness and from doubt about her election,
and the biblical pilgrimage through the valley of Baca (Psalms
84:5–6) all resonate through a single set of coherent images:

My sun's returned with healing wings,
My soul and body doth rejoice,
My heart exults and praises sings
To Him that heard my wailing voice.

. . . .

O hath Thou made my pilgrimage
Thus pleasant, fair, and good,
Blessed me in youth and elder age,
My Baca made a springing flood.
(p. 256)

Sun God bridegroom husband and Christ, and spring health re-
union and confidence of election—these image clusters were linked
in the poet's perception of the created universe. Once we understand that such linkings take place in the human imagination
rather than in some adventitious and rigid typological dictionary,
once we see that we too call a charitable person a Good Samaritan,
a sanctimonious hypocrite a Pharisee, a traitor Judas, because that
is how we see them, because that in our perceived world is what
they are, we are ready to read the poetry of Anne Bradstreet, to
appreciate both the rendered experiences and the verbal correlatives
she found to express them, and to participate, however partially,
in the consciousness that created that poetry.

Vanity was one of the most common themes of Bradstreet's
poetic career. The vanity of all earthly things, the imperative that
man wean his affections from the things of this world may seem
less than ideal as a theme for poetry. Allen Tate has shown us the
dangers of what he called "the angelic imagination" of Poe, who
allegedly "circumvented the natural world" and refused "to see
nature," who immersed himself in "a subjectivism which denies
the sensible world," which operates "at a high level of abstraction,
in which 'clear and distinct ideas' only are workable."[11] Quite
apart from the debatable proposition that Poe exemplified the "angelic" rather than the "symbolic" imagination is the more certain

proposition that the author who rejects the reality of the sensible world and the figurative validity of images drawn from it must either agree with Rimbaud, Mallarmé, and Stevens that language itself can be or create reality (a secular version of the Christian doctrine of *logos*) or must content himself with a literature of "real" abstractions, a literature in which the sensible world functions only to destroy itself so that Eiros and Charmion or Monos and Una can get together and talk about it, functions only as a conversation piece for retrospective spooks.

As an orthodox Puritan, Bradstreet could not adumbrate the French symbolists by arguing that her words created meaning; the meaning of the sensible world was in the things of the sensible world themselves. It had been put there by God before all time; it was seen and uttered by the poet. To follow the latter course she would have to ignore the tradition that the world was a message sent to man from God; she would have to ignore Paul's admonition in Romans 1:20 to seek the invisible things of God through the visible things that He made; she would have to ignore Calvin, Richardson, and the preachers of her own time among whose sermons one finds statements similar to those quoted from Willard in Chapter 2. It was, of course, possible though unlikely for a Puritan poet to take this latter course: I know of only one who did so (Michael Wigglesworth). And he wrote terrible poetry. In writing on the vanity of earthly things from the point of view of one intent on weaning her affections from them, Mistress Bradstreet was courting poetic disaster.

The poetics that enabled her to avoid such disaster is revealed quite clearly in one of her most carefully wrought poems, "The Vanity of All Worldly Things." As reference to the tenth satire of Juvenal and to Samuel Johnson's imitation of it indicates, the theme is hardly original, but Bradstreet's treatment of it is quite original and distinctly Puritan. Having demonstrated with some ferocity that all human wishes are vain, Juvenal suggested a presumably valid wish, a wish that was not vain: "Ask for a stout heart that has no fear of death, and deems length of days the least of Nature's gifts; that can endure any kind of toil; that knows neither wrath nor desire, and thinks that the wars and hard labours of Hercules are better than the loves and banquets of Sardanapalus."[12] He recommended the Stoic solution of banishing vain wishes for pleasure, riches, love, and honor, of ceasing to wish for them. Though Johnson's stoicism was Christian, it was stoicism nonetheless. Finding his desire for pleasure thwarted again and again, the reader was advised by Johnson to stop desiring pleasure.

Bradstreet's poem begins within this tradition. After an initial statement that no one can find "on brittle earth a consolation sound," the speaker dismisses the consolations offered by honor, wealth, pleasures, and beauty.

> What is't in honour to be set on high?
> No, they like beasts and sons of men shall die,
> And whilst they live, how oft doth turn their fate;
> He's now a captive that was king of late.
> What is't in wealth great treasures to obtain?
> No, that's but labour, anxious care, and pain.
> He heaps up riches, and he heaps up sorrow,
> It's his today, but who's his heir tomorrow?
> What then? Content in pleasures canst thou find?
> More vain than all, that's but to grasp the wind.
> The sensual senses for a time they please
> Meanwhile the conscience rage, who shall appease?
> What is't in beauty? No that's but a snare,
> They're foul enough today, that once were fair.
>
> (p. 219)

So far the poem represents a rejection of earthly vanities, but the grounds for that rejection are somewhat unusual. Worldly pleasures are rejected, not because they are evil, or demean man, or bring about damnation, not because they are illusory, but because they are transient, because they do not last. A person set on high in honor will find his privileged position and the joys of it cut short by death. Political reversals may cut short the joys of king-ship. The wealthy person may lose his money or die without heirs. Pleasures, like the wind, cannot be made to stay. Sensual pleasures please, but only for a time. (Here Bradstreet loaded the case some-what, since the conscience would presumably rage only at forni-cation or adultery, not at love between husband and wife.) And beauty withers with age and disease. Earthly joys are vain, then, because they do not endure, and Bradstreet's statement of vanity, though it contains allusions to Ecclesiastes, differs from that of Solomon[13] who had tasted the joys of life and found them wanting, not merely transient. The statement that youth, for example, is vain because it does not last is less an indictment of youth than of old age. In this poem, earthly joys are vain because they are de-ficient as pleasures.

For one whose statement of vanity is based on such a criterion, the stoic solution of ceasing to desire satisfaction is ludicrous be-cause such a cessation is against the nature of man and therefore impossible:

> What is it then? to do as stoics tell,
> Nor laugh, nor weep, let things go ill or well?
> Such stoics are but stocks, such teaching vain,
> While man is man he shall have ease or pain.
>
> (p. 219)

Since man was built to seek joy, the stoic center of indifference is impossible. Like Richard Steere, then, Bradstreet rejected the stoic solution as fit perhaps for "stocks" but not for human beings. Man will seek lasting satisfaction, but will not find it in this world. This rejection of stoicism is the turning point of the poem. The speaker continues to seek "that *summum bonum* which may stay

my mind" (p. 220) and finds it in heavenly joys which are figured
as lasting versions of those earthly joys rejected in the first section
of the poem:

> It brings to *honour* which shall ne'er decay,
> It stores with *wealth* which time can't wear away.
> It yieldeth *pleasures* far beyond conceit,
> And truly *beautifies* without deceit,
> Nor strength, nor wisdom, nor fresh youth shall fade,
> Nor death shall see, but are immortal made.
> This pearl of price, this tree of life, this spring,
> Who is possessed of shall reign a king.
> Nor change of state nor cares shall ever see,
> But wear his crown unto eternity.
> This satiates the soul, this stays the mind,
> And all the rest, but vanity we find.
>
> (p. 220, italics added)

In this poem, one is led to heaven by his desire for earthly joys,
a desire unsatisfied on earth, not because the things of earth are
bitter, delusory, or sinful, but because, though sweet, they do not
endure. Heaven in this poem consists of earthly joys uninterrupted
by pain, change, and death.

Once we understand this we are in a position to read other
poems that hinge on the same distinction between the ultimate
value of earthly things (they are worthless compared to the joys
of heaven) and their immediate value (they are made by God to
delight men and to whet men's hunger for heaven). In one of her
prose meditations, Bradstreet made this distinction explicit: "All
the comforts of this life may be compared to the gourd of Jonah,
that notwithstanding we take great delight for a season in them
and find their shadow very comfortable, yet there is some worm
or other, of discontent, of fear, or grief that lies at the root, which
in great part withers the pleasure else we should take in them,
and well it is that we perceive a decay in their greenness, for were

earthly comforts permanent, who would look for heavenly?" (pp. 288–289). The figure of the gourd of Jonah is well chosen. When Jonah, outraged at the Lord's having dragged him to Nineveh to prophesy the destruction of the city and then having made a fool of him by deciding not to destroy it, prayed for death, the Lord made life more pleasant for him by causing a large-leaved plant to grow up and give him shade. Jonah was exceeding glad of the plant and enjoyed it for a full day before the Lord, to help him wean his affections from immoderate love of the creature, sent a worm to wither the plant. The point of this story for us is that the plant was the good gift of a good God to a man whom God intended to enjoy it. It functioned to lead Jonah back to the love of God by way of love of the creature, and its function required that it not last. Because the delights of earth are used by God to remind man of the delights of heaven, the Puritan poet could use images of the very objects she rejected to figure the joys she sought.

Nearly all of her poems on vanity hinge on just such a progression. They take love of the creature for granted, and become the poetic exercise through which the poet argues herself from that penultimate love to the ultimate love of the Creator. "My straying soul," wrote Bradstreet, "is too much in love with the world" (p. 257). That soul must wean its affections from the transient delights of this world in order to partake of the lasting delights of the next. For that reason, the Spirit in "The Flesh and the Spirit" rejects the "pearls, and gold" (p. 214) of this world in order to fix her attention upon heaven with its "gates of pearl" and streets of "transparent gold" (p. 217). In "Upon the Burning of our House," the temporal house taken away by God is mourned in quiet understatement. "My pleasant things in ashes lie," observes the speaker; then she addresses the burned house:

> Under thy roof no guest shall sit,
> Nor at thy table eat a bit.

> No pleasant tale shall e'er be told,
> Nor things recounted done of old.
> No candle e'er shall shine in thee,
> Nor bridegroom's voice e'er heard shall be.
> In silence ever shall thou lie.
>
> (p. 293)

But such reflections are "vanity," and the speaker, faced with the grim fact of the destruction, begins "my heart to chide" with harsh questions and commands:

> Didst fix thy hope on mold'ring dust?
> The arm of flesh didst make thy trust?
> Raise up thy thoughts above the sky
> That dunghill mists away may fly.
>
> (p. 293)

She compares her love for her house and her pain at its passing to Christ's love for man and His suffering on the cross; this comparison is a terribly powerful argument for the ultimate triviality of the house. It enables the speaker to achieve the perspective she seeks. Raising her thoughts, then, from such "dunghill mists" as the memory of a well-loved house, she finds "above the sky" the promise of heaven, figured appropriately as a house:

> Thou hast a house on high erect,
> Framed by that mighty Architect
> With glory richly furnished,
> Stands permanent though this be fled.
>
> (p. 293)

Again the heaven the poet seeks is figured by images drawn from the earth she must ultimately leave and differs from it chiefly by being a better, that is a "permanent," version of it. The balanced imagery and the clear progression indicate that in Bradstreet's poetry a Puritan habit of mind became a subtle and powerful poetic strategy.

Before discussing the ways in which Bradstreet's recognition of
the poetic and religious uses of the creatures illuminates several of
her other poems—notably those to her husband and her elegies on
the deaths of her grandchildren—it is worth noting how often her
poetry expresses a harmonious interplay between the worldly concerns of the poet as creature and the spiritual concerns of the poet
as Christian, an interplay likely to be ignored in a discussion which
emphasizes, as mine does, the poems on vanity. Where the poems
on vanity center on the next world and contributions of the creatures
to the Puritan's understanding of and progress toward it, these
poems center on the next world and contributions of providence
toward the temporal satisfaction of earthly desires. In "Upon
Some Distemper of Body," the God praised is One "Who sendeth
help to those in misery" (p. 223). Since the misery derives both
from physical illness and from concomitant doubts about her election, the provident God has seen to both and is thanked for both:

> He eased my soul of woe, my flesh of pain,
> And brought me to the shore from troubled main.
>
> (p. 223)

In a poem of gratitude "For Deliverance from a Fever," Bradstreet told of her fear, when ill, that she was not elect:

> Beclouded was my soul with fear
> Of Thy displeasure sore,
> Nor could I read my evidence
> Which oft I read before.
>
> (p. 247)

In terror the poet cried out, as she should have, for God to spare
her soul "though flesh consume to naught," but again God linked
physical with spiritual deliverance, "spared my body frail," showed
"to me Thy tender love, / My heart no more might quail" (p.
247). Again and again God is thanked for His earthly gifts and
petitioned for others:

My wasted flesh Thou didst restore,
My feeble loins didst gird with strength.
(p. 248)

. . . .

My feeble spirit Thou didst revive,
My doubting Thou didst chide,
And though as dead mad'st me alive,
I here a while might 'bide.
(p. 249)

Instead of praising some neoplatonic God for revealing to her the vanity of earthly things, Bradstreet sang hymns of praise and gratitude to an anthropomorphic God Who often answered petitions for such worldly gifts as health and long life. She gave thanks "For the Restoration of My Dear Husband from a Burning Ague" (p. 261), for "My Daughter Hannah Wiggin Her Recovery from a Dangerous Fever" (p. 262), for "My Son's Return out of England":

In sickness when he lay full sore,
His help and his physician wert.
When royal ones that time did die
Thou healed'st his flesh and cheered his heart.
(p. 263)

She petitioned Him for the safe return of her husband from England (pp. 265–266 and pp. 267–268), and gave thanks for letters from him and finally for his safe return (pp. 269–270). As these examples indicate, God often abetted Bradstreet in her love of the creature even as He had brought Jonah back from his angry prayers for death by sending him a creature to love.

Such a love and use of the creatures lies behind and illuminates Bradstreet's poems to her husband and her elegies on her grandchildren. In both sets of poems, love of the creature is taken for granted as a God-wrought part of human nature and is considered

a part of love of God. We have already seen that Bradstreet saw
and expressed the intrinsic correspondences between loving a creature such as the Sun, which in Psalms 19:5 is likened to a bridegroom, loving Simon, her earthly bridegroom, and loving God,
who is both the Sun of Righteousness (Malachi 4:2) and the bridegroom of His faithful (Matthew 2:5, Mark 2, Luke 3, Revelation 18:23). Her love for her husband should, according to Puritan creed, be less intense and lasting than her love for God and
would end with her death, with her marriage to God. But during
her life that love was, doctrinally as well as symbolically, part of
the evidence of her election. Puritan ministers, as Edmund Morgan
has noted, preached that conjugal love "was a duty imposed by
God on all married couples. . . . If a husband and wife failed to
love each other they disobeyed God." As Benjamin Wadsworth
warned his congregation, a person who had too thoroughly weaned
his affections from his spouse, was not holy but wicked. The wife,
for example, "who neglects to manifest real love and kindness" is
"a shame to her profession of Christianity; . . . she . . . not only af-
fronts her Husband, but also God . . . by this her wicked behaviour."
In Puritan sermons, moreover, "the relation between husband and
wife furnished the usual metaphor by which the relationship between Christ and the believer was designated."[14] In symbol and in
doctrine, then, Bradstreet's loving her husband was linked to her
loving God.

In "To My Dear and Loving Husband," Bradstreet wrote of
a real human love carefully subordinated to but completely in
harmony with love of God:

> If ever two were one, then surely we.
> If ever man were loved by wife, then thee;
> If ever wife was happy in a man,
> Compare with me, ye women, if you can.
> . . . .

Thy love is such I can no way repay,
The heavens reward thee manifold I pray.
Then while we live, in love let's so persevere
That when we live no more, we may live ever.

(p. 225)

Commenting on the closing couplet, Ann Stanford has written: "There are two possible interpretations of these lines: first, she may mean that they may have children, who will produce descendants, so that they may live on in their line. This is similar to the idea of some of Shakespeare's sonnets, for example. Second, it may mean that they will become famous as lovers, and live in fame. This would hardly seem to be a good Puritan idea, but the Cavalier idea of immortality through fame is not one Mistress Bradstreet would scorn."[15] No one knows what Anne Bradstreet might have thought of this "Cavalier idea," since she never discussed it. She mentioned Sidney's fame in her epitaph on him but dealt more with the moral example of his life and, repeatedly, with the tragedy of his death than with the conventional consolation that his name would be remembered. Nowhere did she make Shakespeare's claim that her verse would live "so long as men can breathe and eyes can see," and nowhere did she ask that any but her immediate family remember her. Her closing lines, then, might have had the meanings Stanford imputed to them if they had been appended to Donne's "The Canonization," but Bradstreet's poem does not prepare us for such an interpretation.

Instead, the lines immediately preceding the closing couplet express the hope that her husband will receive from "the heavens" a meet reward for his love. The last two lines, then, clearly express the hope that, by persevering in their love in a characteristically Puritan way, by loving each other as God has commanded them but not letting an immoderate love of the creature idolatrously supercede their love of God, they will live forever in

GOD'S ALTAR

heaven. They will love just "so"; they will "so persevere" that
their love will serve God as He intended that it should. Wife
and husband will, when they die, be taken up to heaven where
they will "live ever," neither through the biological immortality
conferred by their descendants nor through the fame conferred by
future lovers who have canonized them for their love, but through
the immortality conferred by God on His elect. Whatever its effect
on modern readers, Bradstreet's closing couplet surely meant this
to her fellow Puritans, especially to her husband for whom the
poem was written. Simon Bradstreet—the son of a nonconformist
minister and himself an A.B. and A.M. from Emmanuel College,
Cambridge, the training ground for most of the first-generation
New England ministers—was no doubt alert to the religious allusions of Anne's verse. Writing for such an audience, she could
afford to use understatement in matters of religion.

In "A Letter to Her Husband, Absent upon Public Employment," for example, earthly love is figured through the images
and language of divine love. We have already seen the associations
called up in Puritan religion and in Bradstreet's poetry by the sun,
its fertilization of the earth in spring, and the bridegroom. If we
add to these the associations engendered by Christ's parable (Matthew 22:2–14) identifying those whom God's love bids enter
heaven with the wedding guests of a king, we can appreciate the
richness of Bradstreet's language:

> My head, my heart, mine eyes, my life, nay, more,
> My joy, my magazine of earthly store,
> If two be one, as surely thou and I,
> How stayest thou there, whilst I at Ipswich lie?
> So many steps, head from the heart to sever,
> If but a neck, soon should we be together.
> I, like the Earth this season, mourn in black,
> My Sun is gone so far in's zodiac,
> Whom whilst I 'joyed, nor storms, nor frost I felt,

His warmth such frigid colds did cause to melt.
My chilled limbs now numbed lie forlorn;
Return, return, sweet Sol, from Capricorn;
In this dead time, alas, what can I more
Than view those fruits which through thy heat I bore?
Which sweet contentment yield me for a space,
True living pictures of their father's face.
O strange effect! now thou art southward gone,
I weary grow the tedious day so long;
But when thou northward to me shalt return
I wish my Sun may never set, but burn
Within the Cancer of my glowing breast,
The welcome house of him my dearest guest.
Where ever, ever stay, and go not thence,
Till nature's sad decree shall call thee hence;
Flesh of thy flesh, bone of thy bone,
I here, thou there, yet both but one.

(p. 226)

Though the biblical referents are too numerous to catalog, the progression of attitude in this poem, and the use of the language of religious love to express a love that remains primarily earthly deserve some comment. It is clear from the beginning that Simon is not God, not even her God. He is her "magazine of *earthly* store." Yet their love becomes, in the powerful central section of the poem, a similitude of the love between God and man. Simon's going southward to Boston, like the sun's going southward to Capricorn, or God's withdrawing His love, brings on a winter. When that love was present, winter melted to spring; the Sun, like a bridegroom, rushed from his chamber to make the earth fertile; so Simon sired Children, made them in his own image and likeness, "true living pictures of their father's face." Like the sun's, the bridegroom's, God's, their love brings about creation. Her heart becomes "Cancer," or the place of the summer zenith of the Sun, the guest chamber Christ sought at Passover, the banquet hall to which the king of the parable called his guests, the heaven to which God calls His elect, a place of eternal welcome and love where one may "ever, ever stay." All these images connote perfection, eternity. Then, having modulated from the opening, in which their love is her "earthly store," to a central section filled with images of God, salvation, and eternal joy, the poem modulates again, this time back to the recognition that both are subject to "natures's sad decree." But in that central section, the joys of human love were figured in a complex of perfectly coherent images linking the love of the earth and the sun (figured elsewhere in Puritan poetry as the love of Tellus and Apollo), wife and husband, man and God.

Such coherent resonances of symbolism exemplify both the verbal realization of Puritan love (which was human as well as spiritual, for one's spouse as well as one's God) and the verbal realization of such criteria as Tate's theory of "tension," the coherence of all denotations and connotations of one's imagery. Since literature records significant human experience and since criticism records the attempt to understand literature, it is not surprising that a fine poem lives in all three worlds. What is surprising is that Bradstreet has said so much in so quiet a voice, has spoken through such quiet understatement. If one does not listen carefully, one may translate a moving expression of the essential univocity of love—love of God is univocally human love—into a Cavalier convention about the immortality conferred by fame. I do not mean to imply that understatement is a dominant standard of value or that Bradstreet's love and poetry are somehow better than the overstated love and poetry of, say, Walt Whitman, who bared his omnivorous breast and embraced the universe with pantoscopic ardor. Both are fine poets. I mean only to state that Bradstreet's characteristic mode is understatement, and that to understand her, we must listen carefully.

This is especially true of her poems on the deaths of her grand-children. Perhaps such understatement led Hyatt Waggoner to conclude that "Puritan poetry in general tends to find this world so radically imperfect as not to be worth saving or grieving for." Of Bradstreet's poem on the burning of her house, he wrote that "the conflict of values was almost completely suppressed, but the same theology may be seen at work, denying the significance of a conflict actually felt. . . . Except for one line, we have to *guess* that the poet felt grief at the loss of her worldly goods."[16] Roy Harvey Pearce took the same tack in his reading of Bradstreet's poems on the deaths of her grandchildren: "She would give the impression that her acquiescence in God's dealing with her has been achieved without much effort. She rests assured in the inevitability of her all too human fate."[17] Both men criticized Bradstreet's poems of acceptance and would have preferred verbal correlatives for anguish. Before examining the poems themselves, we need to recognize that this type of argument has been made and answered before, most decisively in Brooks and Warren's *Understanding Poetry*.

In their discussion of Ben Jonson's elegy "On My First Son," Brooks and Warren answered Elizabeth Drew's criticism that "somehow the emotion is weakened by the obvious artfulness of it. The poet can think too cleverly about the situation to carry conviction." Suggesting as a parallel Milton's intricate Petrarchan sonnet "On His Blindness," a carefully wrought poem in which the emotional shock Milton felt is understated, Brooks and Warren answered that Jonson's poem is a "mature effort to make sense of an emotional shock" and that, had he chosen to dwell only on his grief, he might have produced a poem as unarguably wretched as James Russell Lowell's "After the Burial." An intellectual descendant of the Puritans, Lowell, too, was faced with the death of a child and was offered, as was Bradstreet, the consolations of faith. Unlike Bradstreet, he wrote the poem of struggle, of fully stated grief. "In the breaking gulfs of sorrow," he expressed in thirteen pounding quatrains the "sweet despair" of the flesh as the father gazes at "the thin-worn locket / With its anguish of deathless hair," remembers the "touch of her hand on my cheek" for which he "would give all my incomes from dreamland," gazes at "that little shoe in the corner, / So worn and wrinkled and brown" and tells the part of his mind which has tried to comfort him that "that little shoe . . . with its emptiness confutes you, / And argues your wisdom down." No one has to guess at the speaker's grief: it drenches us. Yet his is clearly an inferior poem. Its hackneyed imagery, pile-driver rhythms, and self-indulgent repetitiveness take us nowhere, tell us nothing. Without depth or control, the poem is an amplified verbal correlative of uncontrolled screaming, and as Brooks and Warren quite rightly argue: "The purest and most instinctive expression of emotion is a scream, and a scream is not poetry."[18]

Now poetry does not operate at the level of critical generalization, and the mere facts that the mode of statement urged on Bradstreet by Pearce and Waggoner usually results in bad poetry and that the mode of understatement and control practiced by Bradstreet has in the past characterized some fine poetry by such as Jonson and Milton are not offered as evidence for the excellence of her verse. They are offered merely to counter the assumption that we may dismiss Bradstreet's poems because she does not scream. That assumption is also a critical generalization and, as we have seen, not a very good one.

To understand Bradstreet's elegies, then, we must look closely both at the text itself and at its historical context. One of her characteristic elegies is "In Memory of My Dear Grandchild Elizabeth Bradstreet, Who Deceased August, 1665, Being a Year and Half Old":

Farewell dear babe, my heart's too much content,
Farewell sweet babe, the pleasure of mine eye,
Farewell fair flower that for a space was lent,
Then ta'en away unto eternity.
Blest babe, why should I once bewail thy fate,
Or sigh thy days so soon were terminate,
Sith thou are settled in an everlasting state.

By nature trees do rot when they are grown,
And plums and apples thoroughly ripe do fall,
And corn and grass are in their season mown,
And time brings down what is both strong and tall.
But plants new set to be eradicate,
And buds new blown to have so short a date,
Is by His hand alone that guides nature and fate.

(p. 235)

The tone of this poem is carefully controlled. Rosemary Laughlin has noted that the stanzaic form itself is difficult and intricate: "the rhyme scheme is *ababccc*, with the last line an alexandrine." The six pentameter lines center on earthly, temporal matters, "while the alexandrines effect a contrast of the eternal with the transient." It is clear from the pentameter lines of the first stanza that Bradstreet loved the child and joyed in her presence. Her question—"why should I once bewail thy fate, / Or sigh thy days were so soon terminate"—indicates that to do so was her natural reaction to the child's death. Rosemary Laughlin has observed that even the prosody suggests grief: "The slow alexandrines might also suggest that resignation to God's will was a heavy thing for the poet to bear, especially since the slight irregularity of the meter produces a somewhat tortured hesitation."[19] Her grief, then, is present in the poem and requires some controlling if the poem is not to lapse into sentimentality.

But it is controlled; that resignation is achieved. Through the intricate rhyme scheme, through the closing alexandrines, through the internal rhyme on "blown" and "alone" that doubly knits together the last two lines of the closing triplet, Bradstreet achieved the sense of distance and order that enabled her to make some sense of the emotional shock, to avoid merely wallowing in grief as Lowell would two centuries later. Her argument for resignation is sane and convincing, granted her premises. If one happens to believe in God and heaven, and feels certain that one's grandchild has been taken by God to heaven, wailing and sighing because one misses the child and begrudges God the joys of her presence are not only inappropriate but selfish, self-indulgent. Why should one wail? Having stated in Stanza 1 the argument that the child's death is providential and therefore not to be mourned, the poet supported the argument in Stanza 2 by giving evidence that God had in fact taken the child, that her death was not merely in the order of nature. In the order of nature, trees, plums, apples, corn, and grass die in old age, after maturity. For a creature to die young, then, God must providentially intervene in the order of nature, must suspend it, not merely allow it to function through the *concursus Dei*. All the evidence indicates that God, who controls both "nature and fate," has done so in taking the child so early. The closing lines, then, are not a sudden abdication to the will of God by a rebellious poet:[20] they are rather the best argument that can be made, the best consolation for the survivors— that the child's untimely death is a clear act of providence, not merely a regrettable part of the order of nature. Those who truly love the child will of course miss her, but they should be consoled that she was singled out by God for an early entrance into heaven.

If we consider the contexts of this elegy, we shall find more evidence that its tone is one of willed resignation and we shall be better able to understand the *donnée* from which Bradstreet's elegies proceeded. One context can only be called that of human expectation. The assumption that an elegist should work toward expressing grief, rather than begin with it and try to resolve it, seems to me wrongheaded. Whether or not there *are* human givens, we tend to live as if there were and to assume that grief at the death of one we love is one of them. Indeed, part of the grisly humor in Arthur Kopit's *Oh Dad, Poor Dad, Mamma's Hung You in the Closet and I'm Feelin' So Sad* is that Jonathan feels compelled to explain to us that his mother's having killed his father, had Dad stuffed, and hung Dad in the closet, makes him sad. Another context is that of the Puritan attitude toward love of the creatures. We have already noted Perry Miller's observation that the Puritan theology bordered on pantheism, on the identity of the sensible creation with God; the numerous exhortations of Puritan ministers to wean one's affections from the immoderate love of one's family, for example, presupposed the very love they sought to moderate. We have already seen that Bradstreet's meditations and poetry were full of concern for creatures, of petitions for the health, safety, and continued earthly life of herself and her family, and of hymns of thanksgiving for the continued life of her husband and for his love of her, a love commanded by God. Love of one's family and resistance to and grief at their deaths were to be expected among Puritans. But a willed resignation to those deaths was also expected.

Contained in a private autobiography written for his son, Thomas Shepard's description of his wife's death makes painfully clear both his grief and his determination to accept his wife's death: "He took away my most dear precious meek and loving wife. . . . In it the Lord seemed to withdraw his tender care for me and mine, which he graciously manifested by my dear wife; also refused to hear prayer, when I did think he would have hearkened and let me see his beauty in the land of the living, in restoring her to health again." Like Bradstreet, Shepard had petitioned God for earthly favors, for the return of a spouse to health. But God had ignored him, "taking her away in the prime time of her life when she might have lived to have glorified the Lord long." Shepard made explicit the sense of loss that Bradstreet had understated: for him "this loss was very great; she was a woman of incomparable meekness of spirit, toward myself especially and very loving." She had read over Shepard's notes for his sermons, had shared his life, and had told him when she first became ill "that we should love exceedingly together because we should not live long together." But in her final delirium she had not recognized her husband, but had prayed to Christ. Whatever the effect of this information on a modern sensibility, it is clear that Shepard did not turn to Promethean defiance. He argued himself toward acceptance: "I am the Lord's, and he may do with me what he will. . . . Thus god hath visited and scourged me for my sins and sought to wean me from this world, but I have ever found it a difficult thing to profit ever but a little by the sorest and sharpest afflictions." In 1663, his wife had been quite ill, and though Shepard found "the affliction . . . very bitter," he was able to say at last: "I had need of it for I began to grow secretly proud and full of sensuality delighting my soul in my dear wife more than in my god whom I had promised better unto." So now, after his wife's death, he had finally won his way to a willed resignation: "This made me resolve to delight no more in the creature but in the Lord."[21] Shepard had meditated his way from a real grief to an equally real acceptance. As a meditative Puritan poet, Bradstreet might well be expected to follow this movement from grief to resolution in the elegy we have just examined.

Bradstreet's other elegies follow the same movement. Her elegy on her granddaughter Anne Bradstreet begins, not with the easy acceptance imputed to her by Pearce, but with grief:

With troubled heart and trembling hand I write,
The heavens have changed to sorrow my delight.
(p. 236)

That grief is mitigated somewhat by the realization that on this earth joy simply does not last: "Was ever stable joy yet found below?" The child, though beautiful, was fragile "as a withering flower . . . as a bubble, or the brittle glass, / Or like a shadow turning as it was" (p. 236). The failure to accept the frangibility and transience of earthly joy is not heroic but foolish:

More fool then I to look on that was lent
As if mine own, when thus impermanent.
(p. 236)

And persistence in grief or defiance of providence is selfish, for though her grandmother is bereaved, the child is happy:

Farewell dear child, thou ne'er shall come to me,
But yet a while, and I shall go to thee;
Mean time my throbbing heart's cheered up with this:
Thou with thy Saviour art in endless bliss.
(p. 236)

From an earth where joy is never stable, the child has been taken to a heaven where "bliss" differs from earthly joy only in that it is "endless," uninterrupted by imperfection or time, by pain or death. Faced with the absence of a child so taken, the adult survivors are faced with the choice described in her elegy "On My Dear Grandchild Simon Bradstreet" (p. 237). They can either be "mute" toward a providential act the purpose of which passes their understanding, or they can "dispute." The first choice requires trust, that temporary suspension of curiosity that we can manage only toward those we love and believe in. One whose love of and belief in God are not sufficient to enable him to trust in God, to suspend

115

his curiosity about God's motives and methods, can refuse to face the facts of God's will which for the Puritan were the facts of life, death among them. He can, like Ahab, Manfred, and the unnamed quester in Frost's "The Most of It," demand that the universe give some account of itself. Such demands, however, are unlikely to be answered in any satisfactory detail, and the Puritans, who were not Romantics, never glorified them, always tried to argue themselves into the acceptance of what pagans called fate, what they called God's will, what we might call the facts of life. Bradstreet wrote:

> With dreadful awe before Him let's be mute
> Such was His will, but why, let's not dispute.
> (p. 237)

Resigned to death and parting as necessary parts of her life in the world of time, Bradstreet could bid farewell to the child, taking comfort in the belief that he was translated to a world where joys were endless:

> Go pretty babe, go rest with sisters twain;
> Among the blest in endless joys remain.
> (p. 237)

In heaven God provided, not the revelation that earthly joys were not worth desiring, but joys more satisfactory as joys, because they were perfect and because they lasted.

In her "Meditations Divine and Moral," Bradstreet made explicit the attitude implicit in her poetry: she stressed to her son the necessity of trusting in God, even when no human sense can be made of His providential dispensations, of believing without seeing: "There is nothing admits of more admiration than God's various dispensation of His gifts among the sons of men." By human standards, some are treated well, some horribly. "And no other reason can be given of all this but so it pleased Him whose will is the perfect rule of righteousness" (pp. 281–282). At times God's will remains inscrutable and His actions against all reason. Though Bradstreet wrote to her children that she was tempted "many times by atheism" (p. 243), she resisted such an answer and argued that when God has temporarily veiled His face and "we cannot behold the light of His countenance, . . . when He seems to set and to be quite gone out of sight, then must we needs walk in darkness and see no light; yet then must we trust in the Lord and stay upon our God, and when the morning (which is the appointed time) is come, the Sun of righteousness will arise with healing in His wings" (p. 282). For Bradstreet, then, resignation to the will of God required a difficult and conscious act of her own will; to believe what one had not yet seen was something to be struggled for and achieved. All her elegies begin with her intense grief at the death of her grandchildren, then discipline that grief by moving through a series of controlled arguments expressed in tightly ordered verse forms to a final willed and genuine resignation. Each poem is a part of the difficult process it records, a method for achieving the resignation it expresses.

It is appropriate that a poet who was able to figure the eternal things of God by the temporal things of earth, who considered earthly joys vain because they were transient and divine joys preferable because permanent—she wrote "were earthly comforts permanent, who would look for heavenly?" (p. 289)—and who steeled herself to accept the deaths of those she loved by reflecting that death was just part of this temporal world and that the children had gone to a world free of the pain of time, would write her greatest poem on the theme of time. Bradstreet's "Contemplations" (pp. 204–214) is a single, unified poem about the temporal and the eternal, about their intersection in man who must, like Browne's "amphibium," live in both worlds at once.

The poem begins completely within the world of time:

> Sometime now past in the autumnal tide,
> When Phoebus wanted but one hour to bed.
>
> (lines 1–2)

Though it is nearly winter and nearly night, the sensible world is beautiful in purely human terms: "Rapt were my senses at this delectable view" (line 7). The beauty of the sensible world, as we have seen before, is an *a fortiori* argument for the beauty, predicated univocally, of God:

> If so much excellence abide below,
> How excellent is He that dwells on high,
> Whose power and beauty by his works we know?
> Sure he is goodness, wisdom, glory, light,
> That hath this under world so richly dight;
> More heaven than earth was here, no winter and no night.
>
> (lines 10–15)

We know from the first stanza that both winter and night are near, but so fully is the world charged with the grandeur of God that the speaker has forgotten that temporarily, and finds herself in a natural world so thoroughly satisfying as to seem eternal. In the next two stanzas (Stanzas 3 and 4) the speaker begins her hymn to the beauty of nature, a beauty conferred on nature by God to figure forth His own beauty and to lead men to Him. Nature's beauty seems eternal: the "stately oak" seems limitlessly old:

> Hath hundred winters past since thou wast born?
> Or thousand since thou brakest thy shell of horn?
>
> (lines 20–21)

But in the alexandrine the speaker recognizes that the oak, though created by God to figure forth His own eternity is not God, is not itself eternal: "If so, all these as nought, eternity doth scorn" (line 22). So with the sun, which seems a God and is a God-wrought symbol for Himself, but which is not itself divine:

> Then higher on the glistering Sun I gazed,
> Whose beams was shaded by the leavie tree;
> The more I looked, the more I grew amazed,
> And softly said, "What glory's like to thee?"
> Soul of this world, this universe's eye,
> No wonder some made thee a deity;
> Had I not better known, alas, the same had I.
>
> (lines 23–29)

Again, the alexandrine serves to qualify the claims of divinity made for the creature in the pentameters. In the world of time, the sun seems but is not the Creator. In Stanza 5, the sun is likened, as in the nineteenth psalm of David, to the bridegroom who warms and makes fertile, an act of earthly creation. In Stanza 6 the sun is presented as a source of comfort and light for human kind and as the power that divides day from night and orders the circle of the seasons, but again the alexandrine functions to remind us (and perhaps the speaker) that the sun is, after all, only a "creature," though "full of sweetness, beauty, and delight" (line 41). In Stanza 7, the speaker returns to the argument of Stanza 2—that the beauty and glory of the sensible world have been created by God as an act of love toward His creatures, to show forth to them a metaphor for Himself that they can understand:

> How full of glory then must thy Creator be,
> Who gave this bright light luster unto thee?
> Admired, adored for ever, be that Majesty.
>
> (lines 48–50)

This first section of the poem, then, is a hymn to the communicable glory of the eternal God as that glory is reflected in the temporal universe. Neither a hymn to nature nor a hymn (based on analogy) to God Himself, it begins with the sensible universe and praises it as a suitable vehicle for the divine metaphor. Nowhere does it presuppose the analogical method of Aquinas and therefore claim to praise God Himself through the analog of the created universe; at all times the speaker is aware of the difference between the eternal God and the temporal vehicle He has chosen for His metaphor. Neither a Thomist nor a pantheist, the speaker is a careful Puritan who at all times has her theology well in hand.

In Stanzas 8 and 9, however, the tone changes. Her first impulse is to sing a song meet or appropriate to the poem of God's creation:

> Silent alone, where none or saw, or heard,
> In pathless paths I lead my wand'ring feet,
> My humble eyes to lofty skies I reared
> To sing some song, my mazed Muse thought meet.
> My great Creator I would magnify,
> That nature had thus decked liberally;
> But Ah, and Ah, again, my imbecility!
>
> (lines 51–57)

Though she can see the glory of God in the sensible world, she cannot adequately praise the Creator Himself. She sees that other creatures can:

> I heard the merry grasshopper then sing.
> The black-clad cricket bear a second part;
> They kept one tune and played on the same string,
> Seeming to glory in their little art.
> Shall creatures abject thus their voices raise
> And in their kind resound their Maker's praise,
> Whilst I, as mute, can warble forth no higher lays?
>
> (lines 58–64)

Why can nature, and even the lowest of creatures in it, sing praise of the Creator when man cannot?

The answer is clearly the central event that separated man from the rest of creation, the Fall. The answer is that these other creatures, having never fallen into disobedience, retain the pristine glory they had at their creation, while man has fallen below nature. The Fall, then, neither diminished nature nor man's perception of it: the Fall significantly altered man's relation to nature. Before the Fall, man had been lord of nature and it had served him: after the Fall, man was inferior in the natural order, unable to obey and praise God unconsciously, as all of nature still did. Since the poem records contemplations rather than structured argument, the speaker, without explicit transition, begins to trace man's fall into the consciousness of time.

Stanzas 10 through 17 are a retrospective view of man's history, a history characterized as a continuing descent from the primal perfection in which God created him. We see the Fall, the effect of which was to transform "glorious Adam," who was in Eden "made Lord of all" into the fallen man,

> Who like a miscreant's driven from that place,
> To get his bread with pain, and sweat of face,
> A penalty imposed on his backsliding race.
>
> (lines 76–78)

This event placed man in a new relation to nature and God, a relation different from that of the grasshopper and cricket. Where before, man had been the lord of all natural creatures, he now became inferior to them, at least in the order of nature.

Man's history after the Fall is one of long declension. Man's consciousness, his perception of the temporal world, causes him to become obsessed with time and affords him a specious glimpse of eternity:

> When present times look back to ages past,
> And men in being fancy those are dead,
> It makes things gone perpetually to last,
> And calls back months and years that long since fled.

> It makes a man more aged in conceit
> Than was Methuselah, or's grandsire great,
> While of their persons and their acts his mind doth treat.
>
> (lines 65–71)

But that mind merely enables man to view the long decline of his race. When Adam looked ahead upon "their long descent," he "sighed to see his progeny" (lines 108, 111). When the speaker looks back upon the Fall and subsequent decline, the history itself answers her question; it explains her inability to sing like the grasshopper and cricket.

Her question answered, the speaker turns in Stanza 18 from her historical reflections back to her observations of man and nature. Again, on its own terms, nature seems immortal and man an inferior and short-lived creature:

> When I behold the heavens as in their prime,
> And then the earth (though old) still clad in green,
> The stones and trees, insensible of time,
> Nor age nor wrinkle on their front are seen;
> If winter come and greenness then do fade,
> A spring returns, and they more youthful made;
> But man grows old, lies down, remains where once he's laid.
>
> (lines 121–127)

As the speaker realizes in the appropriately halting alexandrine, fallen man is lower than nature, judged only in terms of the temporal world. Her reaction is not to envy that natural world, which is timeless and seems eternal on its own terms, but to judge man and nature by a more cosmic set of terms, those of her religion:

> Shall I then praise the heavens, the trees, the earth
> Because their beauty and their strength last longer?
>
> (lines 135–136)

. . . .

Nay, they shall darken, perish, fade and die,
And when unmade, so ever shall they lie,
But man was made for endless immortality.

(lines 139–141)

Man lives in two worlds. In the natural world, the world of time, he is a frail and short-lived creature, fallen, no longer "lord of all" (line 73). In the timeless world of eternity, however, he can share with God joys that never fade; from this point of view the speaker can see that nature's apparent timelessness is only its lack of consciousness, that nature will die, never to rise again. As a part of the natural order, man is inferior; he has, after Adam, fallen below the other creatures and has steadily declined. As part of the supernatural order, however, he is superior to nature; he is immortal, and if elect, destined for endless joys of which nature can know nothing. If the poem were merely a rejection of the world, an expression of the unmitigated desire to flee the natural order for the supernatural, it could end here.

But the speaker is still on earth, is still a part of both orders. In Stanzas 21 through 33 the speaker expresses this double life, predicts the Romantic solution which would affirm the order of quasi-eternal nature and man's part in it, rejects that secular solution as an affirmation of man's death, and comes at last to her own Puritan resolution. At first, the natural order affords her real, though transient, satisfactions:

Under the cooling shadow of a stately elm
Close sat I by a goodly river's side,
Where gliding streams the rocks did overwhelm,
A lonely place, with pleasures dignified.
I once that loved the shady woods so well,
Now thought the rivers did the trees excel,
And if the sun would ever shine, there would I dwell.

(lines 142–148)

If these "pleasures dignified" would last forever, earth would be heaven, and man's double nature would be reconciled for him: the temporal world and the eternal would be one. In the alexandrine, the speaker makes her acceptance of this world ("there would I dwell") conditional upon an impossibility. The sun will not shine forever; man's place in the order of nature commits him to death.

Still, the natural world is a message sent by God to lead man to Him, and the speaker is right in supposing the river (in Stanzas 22 and 23) a symbol of man's route to heaven. But the fish within that river are, unlike man, unconscious. Symbolic characters figuring forth the eternal joys God has stored up for man, the fish themselves can neither partake of the joys they symbolize nor understand the message: "nature taught . . . you know not why, / You wat'ry folk that know not your felicity" (lines 168–169). The relation of the temporal world to the timeless is, in the mind of the speaker, not dichotomy but hierarchy, even as it was in the poems on vanity and death. Though her recognition of nature's transience is understated, it is always there, even in her most apparently Romantic celebrations of the natural order. Like Keats, the speaker has heard the voice of the nightingale and longed to join in its song:

> The sweet-tongued Philomel perched o'er my head
> And chanted forth a most melodious strain
> Which rapt me so with wonder and delight,
> I judged my hearing better than my sight,
> And wished me wings with her a while to take my flight.
> (lines 179–183)

Though several critics have referred to the "Contemplations" as a Romantic poem, and have made much of the similarities between Bradstreet's bird and Keats's (both are nightingales, for example),[22] their differences are more telling. Keats clearly considered the nightingale a messenger from an immortal world: "Thou

wast not born for death, immortal Bird!" ("Ode to a Nightingale" line 61). He considered flying away with it a death to the
world of time and an entrance into the timeless world of eternity.
Bradstreet's nightingale, like her trees and fish, is clearly terrestrial,
and the speaker considers joining it in flight only for "a while."
For the Romantic, moreover, affirming the order of nature and
himself as a part of it took the place of affirming God and the
supernatural order: nature offered man the same rewards that God
used to. In his "Prospectus," Wordsworth wrote that man, "When
wedded to this goodly universe" (*The Recluse*, line 806), would
find himself in "Paradise, and groves / Elysian, Fortunate Fields"
(lines 800–801), regions of the eternally blessed, worlds without time. In his *Dejection: An Ode*, Coleridge wrote that "wedding Nature to us gives in dower / A new Earth and new Heaven"
(lines 68–69).

For the Puritans, God, not man and nature, authored the eternal
"new heaven and a new earth" of Revelation (21:1). As the
speaker has already said, nature is mortal and shall "darken, perish,
fade, and die . . . But man was made for endless immortality"
(lines 138, 140). Her relation to the natural world is real, but
temporary and as such subordinate to her relation to the eternal
order of God. The point of man's apparent inferiority to nature
is not that he should strive to wed himself to nature. To do so
would be to affirm his own death since the things of nature die
forever: "when unmade so ever shall they lie" (line 140). The
point of that apparent inferiority is that from it he learn to look
elsewhere for his superiority. He must learn to look to his election.
Time is

> the fatal wrack of mortal things. . .
> But he whose name is graved in the white stone
> Shall last and shine when all of these are gone.
>   (lines 226, 232–233)

The "white stone" from Revelation 2:17 was identified with election in a marginal gloss in the Geneva Bible: "Such a stone signifieth here a token of God's favor and grace; also it was a sign that one was cleared in judgment." As Elizabeth Wade White has noted, these closing lines of the poem "firmly state the Puritan way of thought."[23]

That way of thought valued the sensible world as the earnest of a loving God, to be read for what it revealed of Him, to be used and loved while one abode in it. But the Puritan was not to become trapped in his love for this frangible and transient world: he was to wean his affections, to subordinate his love for this world to his love for its Maker and to prepare himself to leave these temporal joys for the eternal ones of heaven. In Stanzas 1 through 6 the speaker celebrates the beauty of God's metaphorical world. In Stanzas 8 and 9 she asks why man cannot praise God as nature does, and in Stanzas 10 through 17 answers that the Fall separated man from nature. In Stanzas 18 through 33 she returns from her historical reverie to her contemplations of man and nature and works out her resolution. Bradstreet's speaker moves from her contemplations on the happiness of the creatures, a happiness based on their ignorance of the time that traps them, to contemplations of the happiness of the elect, an eternal happiness based on wisdom, on the wise use of this temporal world. She neither affirms nor rejects the order of nature. Only the dead can be done with the things of this world. She lives in it, loves it, and prepares herself to transcend it when she fulfills her human identity as one of the elect.

This preparation, as we have seen, is the great theme of Bradstreet's poetry. The struggle to wean one's affections from the real and good things of this world, without ceasing to love them, be grateful for them, and understand them as transient earnests of eternal joys to come provided much of the theme and technique of her poems on vanity, on her love for her husband, on the deaths of her grandchildren, and on time itself. Like her fellow Puritans, Bradstreet had to steer a middle course between two sinful extremes: loving the creatures too little was an affront to God, Who had created them and commanded man to love them; loving them too much, without subordinating that love to the love of their Maker, was idolatry. Her poems were records of that middle course; they were prayers, religious acts, her version of the altar commanded in Exodus. God's altar was intended to lead man to heaven, but it was made of earth or stone. So Bradstreet's poetry was essentially about and part of her pilgrimage to heaven. The pilgrimage and the poetry necessarily took place on earth, among the things of this world.

IV
Gnostics and Naturalists

It is an extraordinary fact about the grave and substantial men of New England, especially during our earliest literary age, that they all had a lurking propensity to write what they sincerely believed to be poetry.
MOSES COIT TYLER

Learn what deceitful toys and empty things
This World and all its best Enjoyments be.
MICHAEL WIGGLESWORTH

The world's a well strung fidle, mans tongue the quill.
NATHANIEL WARD

The *Sun* and *Moon*, and *Stars* and *seasons* of the year do preach a God to all the sons of men.
ROGER WILLIAMS

THOUGH no Puritan poets fitted tidily into the narrow stereotype subsequently prepared for them by critics, Michael Wigglesworth and Philip Pain came close. Hyatt Waggoner has argued that Puritan poetry is characterized by a "very nearly Gnostic dualism of spirit and flesh, good and evil, God and the world," that "the Puritan poet placed very little value on 'the world's body,' " and that therefore Puritan poetry lacked imagery and consisted of little more than rhymed "religious abstractions," based on a theology that was "thoroughly world-denying."[1] In this estimate he elaborated on comments by Moses Coit Tyler, who had written of the Puritans' "unconscious Manichaeism" and Charles Feidelson, who had written that Puritan poetry was limited by "a conflict between the symbolic mode of perception, of which our very language is a record, and a world of sheer abstractions certified as 'real.' "[2]

Such descriptions apply to Wigglesworth and might well have been arrived at merely by considering him typical. As Edmund Morgan observed in the introduction to his edition of Wigglesworth's diary: "His diary is even more challenging than his verse to any liberal view of the Puritans. For the man that emerges here calls to mind those stern figures in steeple-crowned hats who represent Puritanism in popular cartoons. So closely does Michael Wigglesworth approximate the unhappy popular conception of our seventeenth-century forbears that he seems more plausible as a satirical construction than he does as a human being."[3] In their descriptions of a Puritan so obsessed with himself, with his own quest for salvation, that he suppressed or ignored all purely human experience, early critics accurately described, not the typical Puritan, but the atypical Michael Wigglesworth. Where Bradstreet and Shepard had reacted to the illness of their spouses with fervent prayers for their recovery to health, and had recorded that reaction, apparently because they thought it a significant part of their lives, Wigglesworth recorded of his wife's misery in labor only his own discomfort and a quick moral: "February 20 toward night being wednesday my wife began to travail, and had sore pains. The nearness of my bed to hers made me hear all the noise. Her pangs pained my heart, broke my sleep the most of that night, I lay sweating, praying, almost fainting through weariness. The next day the spleen much enfeebled me . . . and as sleep departed from mine eyes so my stomach abhorred meat." Father, mother, and child survived, allowing Wigglesworth to reflect: "If the dolours of child-bearing be so bitter (which may be only a fatherly chastizement) then how dreadful are the pangs of eternal death."

Again where Bradstreet and Shepard had bitterly lamented the deaths of those near to them and had had to argue themselves into acceptance, Wigglesworth reacted to his father's death by setting himself "to confess before the Lord my sins against him in want of natural affections to, and sympathy with my afflicted parents, in my not prizing them and their life which God hath graciously continued so long." Only after a paragraph on the effect his father's death was apt to have on his relations with God and a few sentences about his plans, not to be a better son but to be a better minister, does Wigglesworth record: "My Father died the first of october."[4] These are the words of a man who had weaned his affections all too well from love of the creature. His fear was not that his immoderate love for his family would bind him to this world but that he had failed to work up for his family the earthly love that God had commanded. This "want of natural affections" may explain Wigglesworth's reaction to the death of his first wife. As Richard Crowder noted: "Michael was crushed, but tried at once to make his sorrow a stepping stone to greater holiness." Now this is the correct Puritan reaction, but a comparison of Wigglesworth's account with Shepard's might well lead a modern reader to conclude that Michael leapt all too nimbly from the grief to the spiritual profit it afforded him. Such a reaction, however, would be both uncharitable and beside the point. Whatever Wigglesworth felt, it is what he considered important that he recorded. Clearly, he considered the moral, the doctrine, more important than its experiential effects. For that reason, even in Wigglesworth's private papers, we find much handily applied doctrine, little human experience.[5]

This same standard of value obtained in his poetry. Just as he had recorded, not his wife's virtues or the sorrow of her death, but the spiritual profit her death afforded him, so he advised the reader who had lost someone he loved:

> Thy Wife, or Child, or Friend,
> They were but blessings lent thee;

They were the Lords both first and last;
And doth this not content thee?
May not the Lord require,
When he sees fit, his own?
Thou may'st be thankful unto him
They were no sooner gone.[6]

Here we see little imagery, many abstractions, no prosodic subtlety, only rocking trimeters and tetrameters. The doctrine is the thing. For that reason, Bradstreet's human consolation—that the loved child is partaking of eternal joys—is absent, is replaced by the doctrinal explanation that the Lord owns everything, that man owns nothing and should therefore be grateful for whatever transient joys he gets. After all, it could have been worse.

This sterile little piece of rhymed doctrine is all too typical of Wigglesworth's verse. Even his most famous effort, *The Day of Doom*, is too often a collection of rhymed abstractions. In composing it, Wigglesworth seems to have rejected the sensible world and imagery drawn from it even as he rejected the classical Muses in his prefatory prayer. Except for some powerful apocalyptic imagery borrowed from the Bible, the poem proceeds through a series of drab arguments in which the damned present their cases in dry theological stereotypes and have them answered by an equally drab Judge. Such power as the poem retains for the modern reader derives from either his memories of the Bible, of Dante, of Milton, or from his own fears of the final conflagration and the possibility of judgment. The reader, not Wigglesworth, provides the natural imagery and the experiential drama of this poem. Its popularity among contemporary readers derived, I think, from its good moral tendency, from the orthodoxy of its doctrine, and from its simplicity, its availability to every reader. It had the theological directness of Billy Graham, the universal availability of Norman Vincent Peale, and a theme comparable in its universal importance to that of Erich Segal. Like them, it was popular. But from its popularity we need conclude neither that Puritan taste was any more demented than our own (Bradstreet and Herbert were also popular) nor that the poem had some great merit lost on modern readers. Even Cotton Mather, in his sermon at Wigglesworth's funeral, identified Wigglesworth's poetry as catechism and his audience as simple people and children: "He *Wrote* several Composures, wherein he proposed the edification of such Readers as are for plain Truths, dressed up in a *Plain Meter*. These Composures have had their Acceptance and Advantage among that sort of Readers; and one of them, the *Day of Doom*, which has been often Reprinted in both *Englands*, may find our Children till the *Day* itself arrive."[7] And as mere observation shows, it is all too obviously a collection of religious abstractions. If, as Wellek and Warren asserted, poetry requires "sensuous particularity" and "figuration,"[8] Wigglesworth's verse is rarely poetry.

One reason for its failure, and one difference between Wigglesworth and most other Puritan poets, is Wigglesworth's dismissal of the natural world, his inability to perceive, and hence to use, metaphor. First, Wigglesworth was an extreme literalist in his reading of the Bible. Anne Bradstreet recognized that "Ebenezer," the stone set up by Samuel in witness of God's assistance in his battle against the Philistines (I Samuel 7:12), had metaphorical as well as literal significance: she could therefore write of God's favors and her gratitude: "I have sometimes tasted of that hidden manna that the world knows not, and have set up my Ebenezer." But Wigglesworth followed the example of Samuel by planning to set up a literal physical pillar, described and drawn in his diary.[9] Second, unlike many of his fellow Puritans, Wigglesworth completely rejected the sensible world. Bradstreet wrote poems alive with the beauty and significance of the sensible world. Even her poems on vanity began with concrete delights and argued that they were temporary forecasts of heaven's delight, to be used wisely and ultimately rejected only so that one might have permanent and perfect versions of them. But for Wigglesworth, the sensible world was never used to figure heaven; it was merely vain and, to judge from his poetry, insignificant and potentially damning.

In his "Vanity of Vanities: A Song of Emptiness," the reader is called to

> Learn what deceitful toys and empty things
> This World and all its best Enjoyments be.
> (p. 107)

He is told that pleasure, far from being a temporal forecast of the eternal joys of heaven, is merely a source of temptation:

> what is Pleasure but the Devil's bait,
> Whereby he catcheth whom he would devour,
> And multitudes of souls doth ruinate?
> (p. 107)

In twenty-seven static quatrains, Wigglesworth listed all the possible worldly things that might please man, then said they were worthless—not ultimately worthless in comparison with their Maker, not transient, not literally empty but symbolically valuable—just simply worthless. Having gone nowhere, the poem ends where it began:

> Go boast thyself of what thy heart enjoys,
> Vain man! triumph in all thy worldly Bliss:
> Thy best Enjoyments are but Trash and toys;
> Delight thyself in that which worthless is.
> (p. 110)

From such a useless, pointless world, the speaker of Wigglesworth's poems looks forward to his release through death. Samuel

Willard may have written that death "makes a separation between
the soul and the body, . . . is in itself a misery; and for that reason
the Godly themselves have a natural reluctancy against it; they
would not pass through it if they could go to heaven without it."
And Anne Bradstreet may have prayed, "Lord . . . let me be no
more afraid of death," a succinct combination of the Puritan aspi-
ration toward weaned affections and the equally Puritan admission
that she was still afraid to die: this combination would recur in her
last poem, "As Weary Pilgrim," in which she prayed "Lord make
me ready for that day / Then come, dear Bridegroom, come
away," a prayer all the more touching because of the admission
that she was not yet ready to die and be married to Christ.[10] But in
"Death Expected and Welcomed" (p. 111) and in "A Farewell
to the World" (pp. 112–114), Wigglesworth's speaker is more
than ready. He is the Gnostic, the Neoplatonic Puritan of the
popular stereotype. For him, the sensible world is meaningless
and corrupt; the body is merely a prison for the soul. Separation
of body and soul is not the misery described by Willard but a
longed-for joy: "Farewell, vile Body, subject to decay," he exults,
"Thou shalt not henceforth be a clog to me" (pp. 113–114). For
him, only the abstractions of religious doctrine are real and important. Their experiential effects are carnal, worldly, fit subjects
for rigorous suppression, not glorification in verse.

That Wigglesworth's poetry rarely rose above versified doctrine
is evident from the one poem his chief advocate chose to resurrect.
In general, Richard Crowder described his poetry quite accurately:
"His subject matter was man's spiritual life. He tried to show
what one's attitude should be towards earthly existence, but gave
little concrete description of or advice about the conduct of daily
life." His "imagery was in fact quite bookish." The one complete
poem that Crowder exempted from this description is one first
published in the 1666 London edition of *The Day of Doom*, "I

Walk'd and Did a Little Mole-Hill View." Its references are to
images "from daily life," wrote Crowder: "More lively than certain other of the author's works, it shows a close observation of
nature that colors none of the other poems." Crowder has even
considered the possibility "that the poem was included in the London edition by error and is apocryphal," and O. M. Brack, Jr. has
argued that the London edition has no authority and that the poem
is probably not by Wigglesworth. But Brack adds that "these questions probably will never be answered with certainty," and the
poem itself is quite like others by Wigglesworth:

> I walk'd and did a little Mole-Hill view,
> Full peopled with a most industrious crew
> Of busie Ants, where each one labour'd more
> Than if he were to bring home Indian Ore.

So far, except for the incongruity that the ants inhabit a mole hill
instead of an anthill, this might be the beginning of a poem based
on observation of nature. That it is not, that it is merely an un-
original allegory based on the most conventional signs, becomes
clear in the next line:

> Here wrought the Pioneers, there march'd the Bands,
> Here Colonies went forth to plant new Lands.

Pioneers, colonies, and marching bands identify these ants as people, not ants. Were the poem really based on observation of nature,
the ants might have been allowed to dwell in an anthill. Wigglesworth's reason for transplanting them becomes clear when, in a
typical Wigglesworth touch, the ant colony suffers a judgment:
"there came an angry Spade, and cast / Country and People to a
Pit at last." Now we know that on the literal level that molehill
must have been in a garden, where ants would not have time to
build an anthill. Wigglesworth had to get them there to have a
pretext for their destruction. But literally one cannot destroy an

ant colony by throwing it into a pit; the ants simply crawl out; if buried, they simply dig out. No, if Wigglesworth ever saw an anthill, he must not have paid much attention to it. His ants were people, and dwelt in books.

Wigglesworth continued his walk and came upon a beehive, its inhabitants busily storing up earthly treasure "Until the greedy Gardener brought his smoke, / And, for the work, did all the workmen choke." Bees, like ants, are conventional signs for industry, and one could never tell from his description of them that Wigglesworth had ever looked at a bee. Having run through his two conventions, he provided their moral: "Lo here, frail Mortals may fit Emblems see / Of their great toil, and greater vanity." Imputing the defects of the poem to Wigglesworth's Calvinism, Crowder argued: "Granted the illiberal Calvinism on which the piece is based, this is, nevertheless, much better poetry than almost anything else Wigglesworth left behind."[11] One can agree that this poem is the best of Wigglesworth without agreeing that it is a good poem. Indeed, the avoidance of natural imagery in a poem which seemed to require it, the failure to tell what one saw in a poem introduced as one's contemplations while walking outside, indicates how thoroughly Wigglesworth ignored the sensible world and its figurative significance in his poetry. Insofar as anyone living in the seventeenth century could be a Gnostic dualist, he was. That dualism pervaded his poetry and wrecked it. We may apply to Wigglesworth, particularly to his "Molehill," the criticism that Larzer Ziff has applied to all Puritan literature: "In leaping from the literal over a vast range of expression to arrive at the allegorical, they were, in effect, dismissing a whole dimension of what we might today call external reality."[12] But we need not agree that Wigglesworth's Gnostic dualism was typical.

Indeed, only one other contemporary poet seems to have written any amount of poetry based on as complete a rejection of the world. But Philip Pain was not just another Wigglesworth. He remains interesting for our purposes because his poetry exemplifies the rejection of the sensible world so often imputed to (and so rarely found among) Puritan poets and because he himself may not have been a Puritan. Leon Howard has commented that Pain was probably educated "in the liberal piety of George Herbert. Meditations 30 and 32, for example, could hardly have been produced by one who had been brought up in strict conformity with the Westminster Confession, which had been accepted also as orthodox Congregational doctrine in the *Cambridge Platform* of 1648."[13] Though we know nothing of Pain's life, save that it ended in shipwreck shortly before his *Daily Meditations* were published in 1668, several of his poems could not have been written by an orthodox New England Puritan. In Meditation 30, he wrote:

> Sure every soul in this world hath its day
> Of grace, and if he will improve it, may.
>
> (p. 26)

Smacking as they do of unlimited atonement and universal conditional election, these lines are more likely to have been written by an Arminian Anglican than a Calvinist Puritan. I have found nothing like them in the poetry of Pain's Puritan contemporaries. In Meditation 32, Pain wrote that those in hell were there only because they had misspent their time on earth; all Puritan notions of "preparation" and covenant taken together do not add up to as complete an Arminianism as these lines express. For Pain, heaven was open to all: everyone was potentially elect. Actual election depended not on the will of a sovereign God but on the choice of mortal man. By the time of the Arminian Charles Chauncy (1705–1787), New England Congregationalists would have begun to believe such things. But in 1668, only Anglicans and Catholics did. It seems, however, that one could be a Gnostic dualist, could write "thoroughly world-denying" poetry, without being a Puritan.

Pain's poetry expresses an unqualified rejection of the world and a yearning for death, themes absent from the work of such Puritan poets as Wood, Johnson, Steere, and Bradstreet. As the subtitle of his book announces, Pain's meditations are all on "death and eternity." Expressed in abstractions, repetitious and static, Meditation 41 is typical:

> How eagerly doth vain man here pursue
> These worldly things, when his days are so few?
> His time is short, it's short, yea *short indeed*,
> That flies so swiftly from him, with such speed.
>   Lord, help me to consider that I must
>   Not here live alwayes, but return to dust.
>   (p. 29)

Never were transience and impending death made less interesting. Bradstreet had also reflected on the impermanence of earthly things, but her reflections were enlivened by a real relation to the sensible, transient world, by a belief that the lower world figured the higher, by a concept of heaven univocally predicated from the joys of earth. No such complexities enliven Pain's writings. He may utter the doctrine that "All creatures in their kinde sound forth the praise / Of their blest Maker" (p. 28), but that doctrine never became for him, as it had for Bradstreet, a poetics. He never made us see, perhaps because he never saw, the glory of God in His creatures.

His failure to see in the doctrine a foundation for symbolism was I think due to Pain's rejection of the sensible world, a rejection so thorough that in his closing poem Pain imputed to the "saints on earth" a longing for death that few, if we can believe their own writings, ever felt:

What makes the Saints on earth desire to be
Dissolved, and that blessed day to see?
What makes them whilst they're here below to groan?
Lord, they know that when they from hence do go,
On them a glorious Kingdom thou'lt bestow.

(p. 34)

Though the closing couplet is harmless cliché, the question is both poor theology and poor poetry. As we have seen from the reflections on death written by such Puritans as Willard and Bradstreet, the Neoplatonic thanatos of this passage is not particularly Puritan. And as we have seen and shall continue to see in our consideration of Puritan poetry, neither is Pain's poetic bungling. In this chapter I use the word "naturalist" merely as an opposite of Gnostic. A naturalist poet, then, is one capable of celebrating the beauties of the natural world, of using images drawn from it to figure spiritual states and theological doctrines, and of seeing and expressing its spiritual or cosmic or divine significance. He sees the sacred in the secular; he seeks and finds the supernatural significance of the natural. Where a Gnostic's poetry is apt to comprise only versified doctrine expressed in stock religious abstractions, a naturalist's will give us some sense of the experiential results of that doctrine expressed in metaphors and symbols that are grounded in our sensory experience.

Puritan New England produced more than her share of practicing poets, as Moses Coit Tyler recognized: "The Muse of New England, whosoever that respectable damsel may have been, was a muse by no means exclusive; such as she was, she cordially visited every one who would receive her,—and every one would receive her. It is an extraordinary fact about these grave and substantial men of New England, especially during our earliest literary age,

139

that they all had a lurking propensity to write what they sincerely believed to be poetry."[14] Not all of them were wrong.

"Poetry's a gift wherein but few excell," wrote Nathaniel Ward; "He doth very ill, that doth not passing well."[15] Even among the first generation of Puritan settlers were several who did "passing well." Ward himself, minister at Ipswich (or Aggawam) from 1634 to 1647, recognized both that the things of this world had a place in poetry and that poetry had an important place in the world, which was itself a poem:

> The world's a well strung fidle, mans tongue the quill,
>   That fills the world with fumble for want of skill,
> When things and words in tune and tone do meet,
>   The universall song goes smooth and sweet.
>
> (p. 367)

As Frost later recognized in "The Aim was Song," poetry fulfills part of the natural order of things.

Several Puritans did "excell" in the gift of poetry, in a variety of the traditional genres[16]—including epic, lyric, narrative, and elegy. Edward Johnson's *Good News from New England* (pp. 156–173) affords us a verbal correlative for the Puritan view of life as epic struggle. Though not published until 1648, it records the experiences and the significance of the Great Migration of 1630. Johnson sailed with the Winthrop party, probably aboard the flagship *Arbella*, and his lines on first sighting New England provide what Waggoner rightly found lacking in Thomas Tillam's "Uppon the first sight of New England"—"sight of the new land" and "insight into what the experience of sighting it must have been like." "We wonder," wrote Waggoner, "if it might have been saved as a poem if William Carlos Williams had guided the pen for just a line or two."[17] Perhaps Johnson's lines on his sailing with the Great Migration into Boston harbor in 1630 might have happened:

With hearts revived in conceit, new land and trees they eye,
    Senting the Caedars and sweet ferne from heats reflection drye,
Much like the bird from dolsome Romes inclos'd in cage of wyre,
    Set forth in fragrant fields doth skip in hope of her desire.
So leap the hearts of these mixt men by streights o'er seas inured,
    To following hard-ships wildernesse, doth force to be endured.
In clipping armes of out-strecht Capes, there ships now gliding enter,
    In bay where many little Isles do stand in waters Center.
Where Sea-calves with their hairy heads gaze 'bove the waters brim,
    Wondring to see such uncouth sights their sporting place to swim.
The seas vast length makes welcome shores unto this wandring race,
    Who now found footing freely for, Christs Church his resting place.

                                    (lines 172–183)

Abundant imagery, Homeric simile, sonorous assonant echoes, and
a recognition and rendering of cosmic significance combine here in
American epic poetry. Members of the Great Migration saw themselves as latter-day Israelites, a "wandring race" come at last to
the Promised Land. Johnson's *Good News from New England*
expresses both the minute details and the cosmic range of that
vision.

    In his description of the stormy ocean passage, we hear babies
crying for mothers too seasick to hold them, and see preachers
facing the storm as they had faced the repression from Archbishop
Laud:

At ships mast doth Christs Pastors preach, while waves like Prelates proud,
    Would fling them from their pulpits place as not by them allow'd.

                                    (lines 158–159)

But these people, weak and apparently insignificant, are on an er-
rand of cosmic importance, are the instruments of a God Who
will not allow their destruction:

But Christ as once, so now he sayes peace ye waves, and be still,
    For all their height they fall downe flat, obey they must his will.

                                    141

And now the Seas like medowes greene, whose ground and grass even are,
   Doth gently lead their ships as sheep from place to place afar.
                              (lines 162–165)

Later in this same poem Johnson described the abundance of summer in the new land:

   Bespread with Roses Sommer 'gins take place with hasty speed,
      Whose parching heate Strawberries coole doth moderation breed.
   Ayre darkening sholes of pigeons picke their berries sweet and good,
      The lovely cherries birds entice to feast themselves in woods.
                              (lines 258–261)

This stolid Puritan soldier could render both his delight in the fruitful natural world and his awe at the mystery of a New England winter, a season quite unlike anything experienced in England:

   Sharpe, sudden, yet with lightsome looks doth winters cold come in,
      With thicke, large Coat doth cloath the earth, both soft, smooth
                                             white and trim.
   The large tempestuous surges are bound in with frozen band,
      Where ship did anker, men doe walke, and carts as on the land.
                              (lines 282–285)

Johnson's epic can hardly bear comparison with Homer's or Milton's. But in his ability to make us see both the myriad of details and the cosmic panorama of New England history, as it was viewed by the people who lived it, Johnson was a writer of epic. And the prosodically impressive, imagistic, and vital poetry of Johnson comes closer to affording us an American epic than does either Timothy Dwight's *Conquest of Canaan* or Joel Barlow's *Columbiad*.

Before considering Puritan work in other genres, I wish to examine the casual classicism of Puritan poetry. Like most educated people of the Renaissance, the Puritans had a solid grounding in the classics. Had anyone taken their divinity seriously, the classical deities might have seemed false gods to the Puritan. As it was, however, the gods were so obviously not divine, so thoroughly identified with the natural world (their names were usually used only as shorthand designations for the natural objects or forces they metaphorically controlled) that only Michael Wigglesworth felt compelled to reject them, even as he had rejected nature. In his prefatory poem to *The Day of Doom*, he refused to invoke the Muses and argued:

> what a deal of Blasphemy,
> And Heathenish Impiety,
> In Christian Poets may be found,
> Where Heathen gods with praise are crown'd!
>
> (p. 20)

In his rejection of classicism, as in his complete rejection of the natural world, Wigglesworth was alone among Puritan poets. Other Puritans, though they made no attempt to revitalize the classics or adapt classical mythology as had Spenser and Milton, felt no particular aversion to the classical deities, who often appear in poems on the natural world. Such appearances, however, are not heavily allusive.

Samuel Danforth's almanac verse combines lyric and what might best be called a brief verse narrative of God's work in the world. It moves from the natural order to its supernatural significance. The minister at Roxbury included Nymphs, Phoebus, and Astraea in one of his almanac poems for 1647. The poem begins as a salute to spring and the greening of New England, itself a green plant transplanted and tended by God, and assisted by classical deities who seem to be more natural spirits of the place than subordinate gods:

> Awake yee westerne Nymphs, arise and sing:
> And with fresh tunes salute your welcome spring,
> Behold a choyce, a rare and pleasant plant,
> Which nothing but it's parallell doth want.

143

. . . .

> Bright Phoebus casts his silver sparkling ray,
> Upon this thriving plant both night and day.
> And with a pleasant aspect smiles upon
> The tender buds and blooms that hang theron.

"Astraea," a goddess of innocence and purity, "At this tree's roots
. . . sits and sings / and waters it" that it might grow strong, graft
onto itself other shrubs, and make them healthy. All these peoples,
figured as grafts onto the one true stock, will be brought to God
through New England; Danforth encouraged them to grow in
grace:

> Sprout forth, poor sprigs, that all the world may sing
> How Heathen shrubs kisse Jesus for their king.

(pp. 417–419)

Unlike the Romantics, Danforth's Puritans had gone into the
state of nature not to imitate the natural man but to convert him.
Danforth's poem, then, begins with his reading of the significance
of a New England spring and moves toward an expression of the
religious significance of New England history. In that movement,
the classical references obtain only as part of the order of nature,
not as idols or false gods.

Like Danforth, Richard Steere was inspired more by the power
and beauty of nature than by the doings of any deity other than
the One he saw in all nature. Steere's having written a poem on
the Nativity might lead one to suspect him of crypto-Catholicism,
but Milton also wrote a poem on the Nativity, and Steere's *Antichrist Display'd* is a wholehearted attack on the Catholic Church
and all who serve in her.[18] Like several other poets whose work
we have examined, Steere was sensitive as a Romantic to the beauty
and sublimity of nature. But where the Romantics usually made
the natural world into a god, the Puritans saw immanent in the

natural world the beauty and providence of the God of Scripture. That vision inspired some of their finest poetry.

Steere's *Earth Felicities, Heavens Allowances,* discussed in Chapter 1, is one example. Another is his *Monumental Memorial of Marine Mercy* (pp. 245–252). "An acknowledgment of an High Hand of *Divine Deliverances* on the *Deep* in Time of distress," as its subtitle announces, the poem centers on a naturalistic description of a voyage from America to England in December of 1683. Indeed, Steere insisted on such details as the names of the ship and its captain, and the date on which the ship left Massachusetts Bay behind "and sayling on, / Soon lay'd the Land below the *Horizon*" (lines 14–15). Five weeks of good sailing give the passengers hope that "The Ship might prove an *Ark* of preservation" (line 24), an identification strengthened when near England "a *Land bird* came *a'board*" (line 37). All this time the ship seems quite important and far superior to the wind and sea: it can

> *plough* the Yeilding *Ocean,*
> Whose little *Billows* still her *Bow* out braves,
> Glideing Tryumphant o're the *Curled waves.*
> (lines 25–27)

Cruising along in "a drowsie sleep / Of calme Security" (lines 41–42), the ship is overtaken by a storm that reveals its fragility. The sea rises up to meet

> th' *Impending* Skyes;
> *Flaws* from those lofty *Battlements* are hurld,
> As to a *Chaos* they would shake the world:
> Thus as between a warr of *Sea* and *Heaven,*
> From place to place our little *Ship* is driven;
> And by the Seas tost like a ball in sport,
> From *wave* to *wave* in *Neptunes Tennis Court.*
> (lines 57–63)

Aware now of their former pride and of their danger, those on shipboard try to save themselves from sinking and, for several days, succeed. Steere's description of their plight operates both on the level of factual narration and on that of the spiritual voyage his entire account symbolizes. We see a real, rather than vaguely allegorical, ship in a storm:

> A mighty *Sea* did *Overwhelm* us quite,
> Which falling down with a resistless stroke
> Both our Ships *Waste* (or well built *Gunwalls*) broke
> And carr'd away: now seeming like a *Wreck*
> From the Fore-castle to the *Quarter Deck*
> The *Long boat*, *Windless*, *Captstern*, with the blow
> Besides two weighty *Anchors* from the *Bow*,
> With *Ropes*, and *Ring-bolts* (where ye *Boat* was fast,
> And we constrain'd to cut our *Mizen mast*,)
> All lost at once.
>
> (lines 99–108)

But that ship figures the body of man on his voyage through time. The pride of the passengers in their frangible little boat, the omnipresence of a destroying ocean, the constant threat of potential chaos, all resonate with significances beyond themselves. Given this resonance, it is not surprising that the ship undergoes a death and resurrection. Having shipped so much water that it rides low and the ocean washes over it, the ship seems to have failed utterly: "For we lay *buri'd* in the *Oceans Womb*" (line 152). From that womb, it is reborn when "an Almighty power" causes

> our *buri'd Vessel* to Ascend,
> And by degrees climb up the *Mountain waves*,
> From whence our *eyes* might view our *fluid Graves*.
>
> (lines 154–157)

Using the waves that had threatened to drown it, the ship ascends "by degrees" to the sight of heaven. So the Christian, using the

146

things of this world, could raise his thoughts to its Maker.

Indeed, the God who rescued Steere's ship is quite unlike the God of Wigglesworthian apocalypse. Instead of letting man rest in his security, then melodramatically destroying and irrevocably damning him, this God reminds man of his dependence by showing him His reflected power in nature, then intervening to save him from that power. For Steere, part of the meaning of the event is that it teaches man "How the *Great* God by *Small* meanes doth protect" (line 238). For Steere, as for Bradstreet and Johnson, the world of little, frail, seasick man was alive with cosmic, with divine significance, could man but see it.

It became all the more urgent that man see the meaning of this world when he was faced with someone's departure from it. Death and the concomitant need to make sense of and commemorate life were common; the Puritans wrote many elegies. Faced with the death of a child, Anne Bradstreet had argued herself into acceptance. Faced with the deaths of the aged, Puritan poets attempted to find the patterns and effects, the meaning of their lives. In our time, it has become fashionable to pretend that belief in the afterlife allays the horror of death, that dying is a lucky move in the soteriological game, an occasion to be celebrated with white vestments, singing, and detailed talk of heaven. Less naive, the Puritans centered their elegies about adults on life this side of the grave and only conventionally and briefly mentioned the afterlife. Their elegies, like their sermons, were rarely eschatological. The meaning of a man's life was to be found in the details of that life, not merely in the confidence that he was elect. Though they took comfort in the prospect of an afterlife, they focussed on the significance of this life.

Urian Oakes's elegy on Thomas Shepard II (pp. 209–220), for example, centers on Shepard's accomplishments as minister at Charlestown and on his human virtues:

> Art, Nature, Grace, in him were all combin'd
> To shew the World a matchless *Paragon*:
>
> (p. 213)
>
> . . . .
>
> Learned he was beyond the common Size,
> Befriended much by Nature in his Wit.
>
> (p. 215)

His attempt to describe Shepard's manner affords us a glimpse of how a Puritan minister (indeed any Puritan) was expected to behave:

> Wise He, not wily, was: Grave, not Morose:
> Not stiffe, but steady; Seri'ous, but not Sowre;
> Concern'd for all, as if he had no Foes:
> (Strange if he had!) and would not wast an Hour.
>
> (p. 215)

Oakes's elegy, then, tells us what kind of man Shepard was, how he fulfilled his ministry, and the significance of his life. Oakes likened Shepard to Christ and then to Jacob, as one who interceded for man: "He was . . . our wrestling *Israel* . . .

> The man that stood i' th' gap, to keep the pass,
> To stop the Troops of Judgment[s p]ushing on.
> This man the honour had to hold the hand
> Of an incensed God against our Land.
>
> (p. 212)

The sorts of significance that Oakes made explicit are implicit in the symbolism of Peter Bulkeley's elegy on Thomas Hooker. Thomas Hooker, who died in 1647, was a man, not just an allegorical sign: his life was therefore to be recounted in some particularity. But that life was fraught with meaning, and Bulkeley expressed that meaning through a complex system of biblical symbols:

148

To sinners stout he was a son of dreadful thunder.
When all strong oaks of Bashan us'd to quake . . .
He clave the rocks, they melted into tears.

Sacvan Bercovitch has observed that "a complete analysis of the symbols would entail pages of biblical exegesis." He noted that Christ is the "son of thunder," that the woods of Bashan were enemy ground through which the Israelites passed on their way to the promised land, that Hooker's cleaving the rock alludes, through the "typical" Moses, to Christ's blood, the waters of baptism, and the crossing of the Red Sea, and that the "tears" allude to the tears of Jeremiah, of Christ entering Jerusalem, and of Christ at Gethsemane.[19] The God-wrought linkings of the temporal and eternal order endowed the Puritans and their history with multiple significances similar to those they read in their Bible. Because of these linkings the elegist was justified in seeing the divine significances of Hooker's life.

One reading of such significances that seems misguided to modern taste is the elegy based on anagram. Some Puritan poets read in their subject's name the significance of his life. The poems resulting from this procedure are nearly all terrible, judged by modern standards for poetry. Though they undoubtedly pleased some Puritans, they say nothing to the modern reader. What we may conclude from this evidence is less simple than previous critics have supposed. Hyatt Waggoner cited as evidence of Puritan insensitivity to poetry the allegation that the Puritans took anagrams seriously while their English contemporaries, having evolved far beyond them, did not. As Roy Harvey Pearce has pointed out, however, so sophisticated an Englishman as George Puttenham, author of *The Arte of English Poesie*, could not bring himself to dismiss entirely the prophetic value of anagrams: "Puttenham, in spite of all his protests to the contrary, was of half a mind to take his anagrams seriously." Pearce demonstrated that some Puritans considered the letters of a person's name prophetic,[20] but we have evidence that several Puritans considered the anagram merely a flash of wit, of man's ingenuity. Of his friend John Wilson, the most prolific of Puritan anagrammatists, Nathaniel Ward wrote:

> We poor Agawams
> are so stiff in the hams
> that we cannot make Anagrams,
> But Mr. John Wilson
> the great Epigrammatist
> Can let out an Anagram
> even as he list.
>
> (p. 368)

The jingling rhymes and rhythms, the paraphraseable content, and the choice of central image all contribute to a tone somewhat less than reverent. If being stiff in the hams prevents one's producing anagrams, then writing anagrams is figured either as tumbling or, as the phrase "let out an anagram" suggests, breaking wind, neither of them likely metaphors for prophecy. We know from his other writings that Ward was capable of such humor, and we can see from other Puritan writings that Ward was not alone in taking the prophetic value of anagrams with something less than total seriousness. (For example, someone sent Thomas Dudley an anagrammatic elegy while he was still alive.)

"There is," wrote Cotton Mather in his biographical sketch of Wilson, "a *little sport of wit*, in *anagrammatizing* the *names* of men." Wilson was to be praised because he turned this little game, not to prophecy, but to moral edification: "I believe there never was a man who made so *many*, or so *nimbly*, as our Mr. Wilson; who together with his *quick turns*, upon the names of his friends, would ordinarily *fetch*, and rather than *lose*, would even *force*, devout instructions out of his anagrams."[21] For Ward, then, anagrams were not quite the same as seeing the Lord's order in the universe and uttering it in poetry; making them, like doing acrobatics or breaking wind, was a purely human and fairly unimportant activity. For Mather, anagrams were sports of wit; their meaning lay in Wilson's ingenuity rather than in the Lord's having providentially ordered the letters of a man's name. To be sure, some American Puritans, like some Englishmen, took anagrams seriously. But it is clear that not all Puritan poets placed anagrams on a par with their most serious poetry.

Some sixty years after Ward's *Simple Cobbler*, anagrams were still taken seriously enough that Benjamin Tompson began his elegy on Elizabeth Tompson with an appropriately religious anagram. But when in midpoem he found the anagram restricting, he abandoned it to write "this apostrophe," in which he expressed his sorrow and consolation artfully, but without artificiality:

> A lovely Cluster on a vine I saw,
> So fair it did my admiration draw,
> Climbing the sun side of a house of prayer
> And solacing itself in heavenly air;
> Yet suddenly upon an eastward blast,
> The beauty of his boughs was overcast,
> The fairest grapes were pickt off one by one,
> [The] Dresser looking like one half undone.[22]

These lines express a vision that starts with the sensible world, then moves beyond it. As Sacvan Bercovitch has noted, these lines possess all the figural intricacy that Rosemond Tuve has found in Herbert's poetry; they praise Elizabeth and her family as church members, clinging to Christ, Who is the "ladder-tree, vine-grapes, and Son-church."[23] In discarding the anagram, Tompson chose to write what we may still sincerely believe to be poetry. As his choice of symbols indicates, he still believed that the temporal order was intimately connected with the eternal.

Roger Williams did not. Most of his contemporaries believed in the intimate connection of the temporal and the eternal orders. For them, New England was the New Israel, its people a chosen people, its history, like biblical history, both fact and symbol. In his extended pamphlet debate with Cotton, Williams rejected such connections between the visible and the invisible. As Sacvan Bercovitch has observed, Williams followed Augustinian typology, according to which the types of the Old Testament, having been fulfilled in Christ, no longer referred to any historical state (say Puritan New England in the seventeenth century) but only to "a-temporal states of the soul." Cotton, however, followed Eusebian typology and proclaimed a "literal-spiritual continuity between the two Testaments and the colonial venture in America." Now if the Puritans were a version of the Israelites, and if the objects, persons, and events recorded in the history of the Israelites had symbolic as well as literal significance, then the objects, persons, and events composing New England's history must also have symbolic as well as literal significance. New Englanders could read and make sense of their own lives even as they had read and made sense of the Bible. Both were alive with spiritual, with divine significance. Such was the belief of Cotton and his contemporaries. As we have seen, it invested the secular with something of the sacred and fostered concrete, imagistic poetry; the poet saw the supernatural meaning of natural experience and uttered it.

Williams's theology, his assertion that Cotton had erred in mingling "*Heaven and Earth*, the *Church* and *worldly state* together," his belief that the historical and eternal orders were completely separate,[24] may seem to have had disastrous implications for poetry. If poetry demands some sense of the sacred, some sense that human experience is significant, and if it requires that one record such experience through figuration, then the religious poet who sees no "visible church" that approximates the "invisible church" of God's elect, who sees nothing of Joshua in John Winthrop, nothing of Israel in New England, may ignore the sensible world altogether and write a poetry only of religious abstractions.

But Williams did not. He remained a poetic naturalist, committed to the value of the worldly order. He believed that though sanctification, or good works, could not buy heaven, though sanctification could never provide certain evidence of election, though the civil honest man had no claim on God, yet God had commanded man to obey the law; God had commanded man to be civil and honest; and the uncivil dishonest man was both a threat to human society and an affront to God. He considered it ironic that the Indians, who had not heard that commandment, often obeyed it, and sacrilegious that the English, who had, did not. Williams wrote that the English, who considered themselves a people chosen to fulfill the new covenant of grace, could not even fulfill the old covenant of works, of obedience to God's moral law.

He came to this conclusion during his visit with the Narragansett Indians. Though most Puritans listed the desire to convert Indians among their reasons for coming to New England, Williams was one of the few who did anything about it. As his early career in New England indicates, he believed that a pastoral minister should not preach to the unregenerate. He thought that the work of conversion should be carried out by an apostolic minister who would, like the Apostles, go through the land preaching to the unconverted. Unfortunately for Williams, the Apostles had received their charge to do so directly from Christ. Though any congregation of believers could ordain a pastoral minister, no one could ordain Williams an apostolic minister. Williams decided, therefore, to embark upon his apostolic ministry without ordination, to learn the language of the Indians so that he could prepare them for conversion. Longing "after the natives' souls," as he wrote to John Winthrop, Williams began, while he was living at Plymouth and Salem (1631–1635) to visit the Wampanoags and the Narragansetts "in their filthy smoky holes" in order to learn their language and eventually convert them.[25]

He later decided that the Indians were not yet ready for conversion[26] and therefore wrote up his *Key into the Language of America* so that others could continue the long work of preparation that he had begun. Published in London in 1643, while Williams was there to apply for a charter for Rhode Island, the *Key* contains thirty-two "particular observations" in verse, Williams's only extant poetry. In these poems Williams found much to admire in the Indians, who kept many of God's commandments without knowing them, and much to despise in his fellow Englishmen, who often broke the same commandments while claiming to be God's chosen people:

> 1. *The courteous* Pagan *shall condemne*
>   Uncourteous Englishmen
>   *Who live like Foxes, Beares and Wolves,*
>   *Or Lyon in his Den.*
>
> 2. *Let none sing* blessings *to their soules,*
>   *For that they Courteous are:*
>   *The Wild* Barbarians *with no more*
>   *Then Nature, goe so farre*
>
> 3. *If Natures Sons both* wild *and* tame,
>   *Humane and Courteous be:*
>   *How ill becomes it Sonnes of God*
>   *To want Humanity?*
>   (pp. 38–39)

In the *Key* Williams put a poem at the end of each chapter as a summary of or reflection on the substance of that chapter. This poem closed a chapter in which Williams had praised the Indians for their hospitality, kindness (p. 36), and civility (p. 38), even to strangers.

For Williams, the Indians were minimal men, men in the state of nature; yet with no knowledge of Christian moral imperatives, they behaved better (in Christian terms) than many of Williams's fellow Christians. To appreciate the cutting edge of Williams's charges against the English settlers we must understand that Williams's view of the Indians as natural men, men in the state of nature, was closer to that of Hobbes than to that of Rousseau. In the *Key* itself he mentioned the cannibalism of nearby tribes (pp. 42, 73, 77); he noted their cruelty and treachery in war (p. 79); he considered their painting of their bodies a metaphor for deception (p. 208); and he refused to convert them to Christianity, even when he clearly could have done so, because he felt that they were not yet ready to repent of their allegiance to false gods. Years later, he spoke worse of them, though perhaps in ironic condescension to the ignorance and stereotypical expectations of his audience. On 5 October 1654 he wrote to the Commissioners of the United Colonies to persuade them not to interfere in the quarrel between the Narragansetts and the Indians of Long Island. Williams pointed out that the Narragansetts had allied with the English during the Pequot Wars, that the Narragansetts had not yet shed English blood as had the Long Islanders, and that "many hundred English have experienced them [the Narragansetts] to be inclined to peace and love with the English nation"; he went on to ask the Commissioners (who had intended to protect the Long Island Indians from the Narragansetts) to consider "if, for the sake of a few inconsiderable pagans, and beasts, wallowing in idleness, stealing, lying, whoring, treacherous witchcrafts, blasphemies, and idolatries, all that the gracious hand of the Lord hath so wonderfully planted in the wilderness, should be destroyed."[27]

Though Williams admired the Narragansetts, then, he was clearly no Romantic believer in the unsullied moral superiority of natural man. The point of his poem is that one can be morally superior to the English without being very moral, that *even* the Indians avoid the sinfulness and folly of the English settlers. "The Courteous Pagan" condemned the hypocritical Englishmen by his comments to Williams, to be sure, but more so by his example.

Williams wrote for his fellow English, both in England and America, and he aimed at their moral edification less by offering the Indians as paragons of Christian virtue than by using the disparity between the Indians as they were and the Indians as English prejudice portrayed them to glance ironically at the English assumption of moral superiority. Having noted that the Indians shared their food, Williams concluded with a general observation: "It is a strange *truth* that a man shall generally find more free entertainment and refreshing amongst these *Barbarians*, than amongst thousands that call themselves *Christians*" (p. 46). In his poem, he cast this generosity as an amazing providence:

> 2. *Sometimes* God *gives them* Fish *or* Flesh,
>   *Yet they're* content *without*;
>   *And what comes in, they* part *to* friends
>   *and* strangers *round about.*
>
> 3. *Gods* providence *is rich to his,*
>   *Let none* distrustfull *be*;
>   *In* wildernesse, in great distresse,
>   *These* Ravens *have fed me.*
>
> (p. 46)

Puritans called the Indians ravens both because they were dark and because they were considered, as ravens were considered by the Hebrews, unclean. Ravens' feeding Elijah (1 Kings 17:6) exemplified God's providential intervention in the order of nature since ravens do not ordinarily cater to men. But Williams had just written that such generosity *was* the Indians' custom. His tone, then, was clearly ironic, clearly intended as a caustic comment on the belief that the Indians were at best unclean beasts and at worst agents of Satan.

This criticism becomes explicit in his observation that, though the English may go on whoring, "*The* Pagans *wild confesse the* bonds / *Of* married chastitie" (p. 59); in his statement that the Indians were "born white" (p. 80) and became dark only through long exposure to the sun and their annointing themselves with oil; in his praises of the Indians' intelligence, sense of brotherhood, altruism in aiding Englishmen lost in the forest, courage, sense of justice, care over boundaries (here he mentioned that the English had no right to the Indians' land), toleration of other religions, concern with paying their debts, and all the other virtues that Puritans categorized under good works. The Puritans may dismiss the civil honest man, implied Williams, but in matters of works, in matters of civility and honesty, they could not even bear comparison with Indians.

And the Indians knew it. Illustrating the Narragansett word for "faithfulness," Williams mentioned that Canonicus, Sachem of that people, feared the English had none and cited ten instances to support his fear. Williams reassured him, but later repeated the charge:

> 1. *Oft have I heard these* Indians *say,*
> *These* English *will deceive us.*
> *Of all that's ours, our lands and lives.*
> *In th' end they will bereave us.*
>   (p. 185)

And in several poems he gave the Indian point of view the language it needed to charge the English in their own terms. In the best of such poems, these heathen agents of Satan, these living *topoi* of Puritan histories—"wild men" of a "howling wilderness"—have their say:

> *Adulteries, Murthers, Robberies, Thefts,*
> 1 *Wild* Indians *punish these!*
> *And hold the Scales of Iustice so,*
> *That no man farthing leese.*
>
> *When* Indians *heare the horrid filths,*
> 2 *Of* Irish, English *Men,*
> *The horrid Oaths and Murthers late,*
> *Thus say these* Indians *then.*
>
> *We weare no Cloaths, have many Gods,*
> *And yet our sinnes are lesse:*
> *You are Barbarians, Pagans wild,*
> *Your Land's the Wildernesse.*
>
> (p. 167)

The Indians themselves lacked the knowledge of biblical symbolism necessary for them to make this charge for themselves, to charge "God's people" with having brought a moral, typological, wilderness to a wilderness that had been only physical. Williams's *Key*, then, gave Englishmen the Indian language with which they could charge the Indian with his paganism and call upon him to repent: but its poetry put into the mouths of Indians the typological, symbolic language of the colonists, and charged them with their sins in language they could not help but understand.

Paradigmatic of the Indian reaction to English hypocrisy is the question they addressed to Englishmen who had broken promises to them: "You know God, Will you lie Englishman?" (p. 158). To the Indians, wrote Williams, such hypocrites were not saints, and therefore above other men; they were beasts. In the poem immediately following the Indian reaction to Puritan hypocrisy, Williams placed their reaction to Papist hypocrisy, thereby setting the good citizens of Massachusetts Bay in the worst possible company. When the Indians hear of the disparity between papist doctrine and papist behavior:

> *They aske if such doe goe in Cloaths,*
> *And whether God they know?*
> *And when they hear they're richly clad,*
> *know God, yet practice so.*
>
> *No sure they're Beasts not men (say they,)*
> *Mens shame and soule disgrace.*
> *Or men have mixt with Beasts and so,*
> *brought forth that monstrous Race.*
>
> (p. 172)

Having implied that Puritan hypocrites are no better in Indian eyes than papist, Williams wrote in several poems that in the eyes of God Puritans were no different, collectively, from Indians. Both Indians and English are busy with their own pursuits yet idle till God calls them; both flee storms and pray to God for deliverance, then forget Him in sunshine; both *"shall naked stand. / Before the burning ire"* of God at Judgment (p. 162); both inhabit bodies that must die, leaving their inhabitants to face Judgment together; and neither has any communal guarantee of God's favor, in this world or the next:

> *Boast not proud* English, *of thy birth and blood,*
> *Thy brother* Indian *is by Birth as Good.*
> *Of one blood God made Him, and Thee and All,*
> *As wise, as fair, as strong, as personnall.*
>
> *By nature wrath's his portion, thine no more*
> *Till Grace his soule and thine in Christ restore*
> *Make sure thy second birth, else thou shalt see,*
> *Heaven ope to* Indians *wild, but shut to thee.*
>
> (p. 81)

Indians may be saved, Christians damned. In his prefatory "To the Reader," Williams had hoped both for the salvation of Indians and for their eventual conversion.

The Indians' worship of nature, moreover, was, though ultimately wrong, a step in the right direction. Though he did not believe that the temporal order mirrored the eternal in that any "visible church" contained the "invisible church" of God's elect, Williams did see in the natural world the "irradiations" of God, and did read the natural world as a message from God. He observed that the Indians worshipped the sun, and like Bradstreet sympathized with them: "The *Sun* and *Moon*, and *Stars* and *seasons* of the year do preach a *God* to all the sons of men, that they which know no letters, do yet read an *eternal Power* and *Godhead* in these" (p. 94). Of God in nature,

> 1 *The* Sun *and* Moone *and* Stars *doe preach,*
> *The* Dayes *and* Nights *sound out*:
> Spring, Summer, Fall *and* Winter *eke*
> *Each* Moneth *and* Yeere *about.*
> (p. 95)

Like Bradstreet, he considered the beauty and order of the cosmos *a fortiori* arguments for the immanence of a glorious and provident God: "*When Sun doth rise the Starres doe set,* / *Yet there's no need of light*" (p. 106). Indians can name the constellations far better than the English, yet Williams would tell both

> *Whose hand these Candles hold*:
> *Who gives these* Stars *their Names himself*
> *More bright ten thousand fold.*
> (p. 107)

Like Bradstreet, he saw in the sun God's figure for Himself: "As the same Sun shines on the Wilderness that doth on a Garden! so the same faithful and all sufficient God, can comfort feed and safely guide even through a desolate howling Wilderness" (p. 103). Williams distinguished, moreover, between the natural wilderness which still obeyed God even as it had in Eden and the

typic moral wilderness into which man fell at his first disobedience.
His distinction between fallen man and nature is quite similar to
the one of which Bradstreet wrote in the "Contemplations":

> *Yeeres thousands since, God gave command*
> *(as we in Scripture find)*
> *That* Earth *and* Trees and Plants *should bring*
> *Forth fruits each in his kind.*
>
> *The Wildernesse remembers this,*
> *The Wild and howling land*
> *Answers the toyling labour of,*
> *The wildest* Indians *hand.*
>
> *But man forgets his* Maker, *who,*
> *Fram'd him in Righteousnesse.*
> *A paradise in Paradise, now worse*
> *Then* Indian *wildernesse.*

(p. 126)

Adam's soul, framed in righteousness, was a paradise in Paradise,
an ordered moral park in Eden, until he turned his soul into a
moral wilderness far worse than the natural wilderness of the
Indians, a natural order which still keeps the commands man
broke.

Like Bradstreet and the other naturalists discussed here and in
Chapter 1, Williams wrote poetry alive with the sense of God
in the world. He realized that man would have ultimately to
transcend this world, but that during this life God had given
him the natural world as an apprehensible version of Himself, to
be loved and studied, to be learned from. God's altar did not
need man's polishings. But man needed God's altar, gathered from
the materials of the natural world to make God understandable
in human terms, to love and worship his God as he ought, seeking
his God through metaphor, and practicing his religion through
poetry.

V

Edward Taylor:
Christ's Creation and
the Dissatisfactions of Metaphor

Natural things are not unsuitable to illustrate supernaturals by. For Christ in his parables doth illustrate supernatural things by natural, and if it were not thus, we could arrive at no knowledge of supernatural things, for we are not able to see above naturals.

But Grace excels all Metaphors.

EDWARD TAYLOR

IN A WORK devoted, as this one is, to revising the critical commonplaces about Puritan poetry, a chapter on Edward Taylor may seem superfluous. The attention that I have attempted to bring to other Puritan poets has been focused steadily and intensely on Taylor since Thomas Johnson first began to make his poetry available. Earlier critics have noted Taylor's use of images drawn from the sensible world to figure the invisible things of God, and, after some initial disagreement, later critics have agreed that Taylor was neither a closet idolator nor a crypto-Catholic, but an orthodox New England Puritan, a category that recent scholarship has shown to be much larger and more various than we had earlier believed.[1] What has not yet been done, however, is to read Taylor's poems in the context provided by his fellow Puritan poets, to note, along with the expected similarities, how significantly he differs from them in his treatments of death and metaphor—the two great bridges linking the sensible world the poet inhabits with the divine world he seeks—and, finally, to suggest a crucial

162

distinction in theology and poetics as the explanation for these differences in the poetry.

These similarities and differences are most immediately apparent in Taylor's poems on death, the intersection of this life and the next and, for the saint, of earth and heaven. These poems often begin traditionally enough. "Upon Wedlock and the Death of Children" opens with the same central metaphor used by Bradstreet in her elegy "In Memory of My Dear Grandchild Elizabeth Bradstreet": the child is a flower, beautiful but short-lived. Such flowers "gay and glorious grow: / Unless an Hellish breath do sindge their Plumes."[2] In introducing the metaphor, Taylor attributes the death of flowers to "an Hellish breath." Then heaven takes his daughter Elizabeth:

> But oh! a glorious hand from glory came
> Guarded with Angells, soon did Crop this flowre
> Which almost tore the root up of the same
> At that unlookt for, Dolesome, darksome houre.
>
> (lines 19–22)

Though he had not expected heaven to act like hell, Taylor uses the metaphor and its implications to work himself toward resignation:

> But pausing on't, this sweet perfum'd my thought,
> Christ would in Glory have a Flowre, Choice, Prime,
> And having Choice, chose this my branch forth brought.
> Lord take't. I thanke thee, thou takst ought of mine,
> It is my pledge in glory, part of mee
> Is now in it, Lord, glorifi'de with thee.
>
> (lines 25–30)

The consolation that the child, chosen from all the world, is now with Christ in heaven brings a temporary comfort. For a flower to die so quickly, God had to intervene in the natural order, and Taylor, like Bradstreet, takes comfort in that. Were the poem by

Bradstreet, it might end here, with a willed resignation wrought through metaphor. But Taylor's poem moves on to the death of another flower:

> But praying ore my branch, my branch did sprout
> And bore another manly flower, and gay
> And after that another, sweet brake out,
> The Which the former hand soon got away.
>   (lines 31–34)

At this point the metaphor rips apart. These are not plucked flowers but dying children, and no metaphor can hold the two together:

> But oh! the tortures, Vomit, screechings, groans,
> And six weeks Fever would pierce hearts like stones.
>   (lines 35–36)

The pain of human death and the time-bound human mind cannot be concealed in the pleasant but nonhuman image of flowers, and the actions of a human gardener cannot figure the incomprehensible actions of a loved but nonhuman God. Before such difference, the poet can either rage or be mute, and Taylor, like Bradstreet, chooses acceptance. But unlike Bradstreet, he ends his poem abruptly, reintroducing his metaphor only to subvert it:

> Griefe o're doth flow: and nature fault would finde
> Were not thy Will, my Spell Charm, Joy, and Gem:
> That as I said, I say, take, Lord, they're thine.
> I piecemeale pass to Glory bright in them.
> I joy, may I sweet Flowers for Glory breed,
> Whether thou getst them green, or lets them seed.
>   (lines 37–42)

The poem ends with acceptance, but with an acceptance quite different from his first acceptance, which was based on the flower-child metaphor. Nature would continue to find fault were not Taylor's dominant standard of value the blank, inscrutable will of God. The metaphor is from nature, and as soon as Taylor reverts to it he ends with the ending that nature would desire, that God would not take his flowers in youth, but let them seed. The metaphor, then, does not do its work, does not reconcile the speaker to the death of children. It fails first because the agonies of dying children are nothing like the silent beauty of plucked flowers: it is subverted finally by being used to express, not the acceptance of early death, but the humanly desirable alternative of life and fertility. Taylor's poem ends, then, with an agnostic acceptance of God's will and with just the slightest metaphoric expression of the residuum of regret and discontent that remain in tension with that acceptance.

It is his recognition that the metaphor is not, finally, satisfactory that enables Taylor to tear it apart, then resurrect it in a new form, a form in which it expresses complexly the conflicting emotions with which even the most devout Puritan contemplated the death of those he loved. Other Puritan poets, accepting the metaphoric world, worked their way toward metaphor and ended their poems with it. Taylor often begins with metaphor and is left to work his way beyond it and sometimes back to it. The three central stanzas of this poem begin with the word "But" as Taylor posits his endings, then denies them, changing direction again and again in the hope of finding a resting place. In revising this poem, moreover, Taylor changed the first line of consolation from "this sweet refreshed my thought" to "this sweet perfum'd my thought," a change noted by Donald Junkins, who concluded, "in my judgment, the change is unwarranted."[3] Junkins is quite right in arguing that the revision weakens the metaphor and leaves it more fragile than the original. Though the change would not be warranted if the poem ended with this weak, consoling metaphor, it is I think warranted in a poem that explores the very weakness of that metaphor and the difficulty of consolation.

Since Taylor can rarely rest content with a single metaphor, his poems often seem able to go on indefinitely, forever multiplying comparisons and adding new metaphors, forever finding new facets of a central metaphor. The sense of an ending, albeit a qualified one, that we have in this poem occurs far more rarely in Taylor than in such poets as Bradstreet or Steere, who found their endings in metaphors that seemed final.

This sense of endless struggle to the limits of metaphor pervades Taylor's elegy "Upon the Death of my ever Endeared, and Tender Wife" (pp. 471–476), a poem quite different both from his earlier poems to her and from his more public elegies on the deaths of famous men. When Taylor was courting Elizabeth Fitch, he had sent her an elaborately patterned acrostic declaring his love. The harmony of their love for each other and their love for God he figured through an isosceles triangle, bordered by ornate scroll work and containing a figured heart. The poem itself is composed of exuberant conceits and farfetched comparisons—the poem of a young man in love, and in love with language. Taylor defended this barrage of wit in a letter to Elizabeth, arguing the harmony of conjugal love with Christian and of acrostic and metaphor with logic and theology. The former harmony he figures through the metaphor of two strings in a musical instrument, which produce "a jarring harsh sound" when they are not tuned. "But when equally drawn up, and rightly Struck upon, sound together, make sweet music whose harmony doth enravish the ear; so when the Golden Strings of true affection are Struck up into a right conjugal love, thus sweetly doth this State then Harmonize to the comfort of each other, and to the Glory of God when Sanctified." Lest Elizabeth think such language inappropriate, Taylor argues that metaphor is the best possible expression of his love for her: "Look not (I entreat you) on it as one of Love's hyperboles. If I borrow the beams of Some

Sparkling Metaphor to illustrate my Respects unto thyself by, for you having made my breast the cabinet of your affections (as I yours mine), I know not how to offer a fitter Comparison to Set out my Love by, than to Compare it to a Golden Ball of pure Fire rolling up and down my Breast, from which there flies now and then a Spark like a Glorious Beam from the Body of the Flaming Sun." Acrostic, metaphor, poetry, then, are inevitable and appropriate expressions of love.

Yet they are limited, and Taylor is aware that his experience loses much in its translation into language, that in "striving to Catch these sparks into a Love Letter unto yourself, and to gild it with them as with a Sun Beam, [I] find that by what time they have fallen through my pen upon my Paper, they have lost their shine, and fall only like a little Smoke thereon instead of gilding them." Knowing that his language cannot contain his love, Taylor turns this defect to figurative advantage by urging Elizabeth to allow for the limits of language, to "know that it is the coarsest part thereof 'tis couchant there. For the purest is too fine to clothe in any Linquas huswifery; or to be expressed by words, and though this letter bears but the coarsest part to you, yet the purest is improved for you." Aware of the limits of metaphor, Taylor then buttresses it with logic and theology: "But now, My Dear Love, lest my Letter Should be judged the Layish Language of a lover's pen, I shall endeavor to Show that Conjugal Love ought to exceed all other love."[4] He does so with a list of numbered reasons and with reference to the Bible. It is apparent from his love poems and letter that, despite their limitations, Taylor considered acrostics and metaphors appropriate to the expression of his love. That he also considered them appropriate to the elegy is evident from the anagrams and acrostics on which he builds his elegies on John Allen, Charles Chauncy, and Francis Willoughby.

We might expect, then, that his elegy on the death of his wife

would be similarly built on elaborate conceits and acrostics. And
Taylor implies as much in remembering his earlier poem to her:

> What shall my Preface to our True Love Knot
> Frisk in Acrostick Rhimes? And may I not
> Now at our parting, with Poetick knocks
> Break a salt teare to pieces as it drops?
> (lines 41–44)

But the acrostic never materializes. Like Ward, Mather, and Benjamin Tompson (who abandoned his anagram in the middle of
his elegy on Elizabeth Tompson and went on to write the most
moving part of that poem), Taylor uses anagrams and acrostics
for displays of wit and the drawings of morals, not for vehicles
in serious attempts to understand the intersection of this life and
the next. Metaphor is such a serious vehicle, but in this poem even
metaphor eventually breaks down and is discarded. Even the metaphors left in the poem are singularly conventional and transient,
one giving way to another with little but contiguity to link them.
Taylor is compelled by "bitter Griefe" (line 29) and "Dutie"
(line 49) to write a poem that he knows must be unnecessary to
his wife, now in heaven, and unable to allay his own grief. Her
grace will grace his poem "Although a Poem be no grace to
thee" (line 54). Only if an Angel translates the poem into fit
language will it serve its purpose of bringing joy to his wife and
comfort to Taylor:

> Maybe some Angell may my Poem sing
> To thee in Glory, or relate the thing,
> Which if he do, my mournfull Poem may
> Advance thy Joy, and my Deep Sorrow lay.
> (lines 57–60)

But if the poem can serve no purpose in heaven, it can, here on
earth, help her descendants to remember her. Having asked God's
pardon for his poor verse and grief in the first part of his poem,

and having asked in the second that his wife not blame him for singing at her grave, Taylor recounts her earthly life in the third, in language far more imagistic and metaphoric than the language in the earlier parts of the poem. Yet even here the metaphors fall away as she gets closer to death, and Taylor can find no metaphor to bridge the final contradiction—horrible pain and death sent to a saint, "a Reall, Israelite indeed" (line 132), by a just and merciful God:

> When Pains were Sore, Justice can do no wrong,
> Nor Mercy Cruell be; became her Song.
> (lines 149–150)

No acrostic or metaphor makes sense of this. All tropes have dropped away in a journey past the limits of metaphor to final acceptance that is not esthetic but doctrinal. The God Who is the defining standard of justice and mercy simply could not be unjust and merciless, no matter how much earthly evidence might inform against Him. So Taylor must end his elegy, not with the consoling metaphors in which Bradstreet had found comfort, but with the world-denying verses of Michael Wigglesworth and with the simple statement that Elizabeth, unlike the Puritans cited in Chapter 2 and those studied by David Stannard,[5] had taught herself not to fear death: "The Doomsday Verses much perfum'de her Breath, / Much in her thoughts, and yet she fear'd not Death" (lines 151–152).

This unusual acceptance informs both his meditations on death and his "Valedictory" poems, written after a serious illness in 1720, in which he readies himself for his own death. More than any Puritan poet save Wigglesworth and Pain, Taylor focuses on the attractions of physical death as the gateway to spiritual life. "Nature's amaz'de, Oh monstrous thing Quoth shee, / Not love my life?" (1.33, 13–14). Now all Puritans would have agreed

that the life of nature is insufficient, is not to be loved immoder-
ately, but Taylor is one of the few who writes that grace has
transfigured death and robbed it of its terror:

> To free from Death makst Death a remedy:
> A Curb to Sin, a Spur to Piety.
> Heavens brightsom Light shines out in Death's Dark Cave.
> The Golden Dore of Glory is the Grave.
> (1.34, 21–24)

Since heaven beckons through the door of death, "The Painter
lies who pensills death's Face grim" and death becomes a boon
granted by God, an occasion for exultation:

> Then Death is mine indeed
> A Hift to Grace, a Spur to Duty; Spell
> To Fear; a Frost to nip each naughty Weede.
> A Golden doore to Glory.
> (1.34, 38–41)

In "A Fig for thee Oh! Death," Taylor makes the attractions
more detailed. Even "My Body, my vile harlot" (line 24) will
be transfigured, "raised up anew and made all bright" (line 43),
and body and soul, so often in conflict here on earth, will finally
find harmony in heaven: "The Soule and Body now, as two true
Lovers / Ery night how do they hug and kiss each other" (lines
47–48). Joying in such knowledge, the speaker does not merely
accept death; he hurries it on:

> Why camst thou then so slowly? Mend thy pace.
> Thy Slowness me detains from Christ's bright face.
> (lines 53–54)

The speaker's attraction to death is not Romantic, nor is it a willed
resignation. It is positive and joyous. Where Bradstreet expected
to find in heaven a perfect and endless continuation of "earthly
pleasures," this speaker insists that heaven will differ from earth

in kind as well as in degree. The poetic movement from earth to
heaven insists on difference, not on the similarities emphasized by
Bradstreet.

That Taylor has in mind one central difference becomes clear
in his "Valedictory" poems, his "Valediction to all the world preparatory to Death," which he wrote in three versions from 1720
till about 1724.[6] Here on earth poets "Onely do produce a Lisping
stut, / A piece of Sorry Non-Sense in a Rhyme / That none can
read, Construe, scan or decline" (3, 251–253). This limitation
applies not just to Taylor but to all poets. Taylor's poetry fails
for him, not in comparison with the works of other poets, but
in comparison with the poetry that his subject deserves. So long
as he and other poets write here on earth they can never write a
sacred poem worthy of its divine audience. They must work in

> staining words, & filthy all Sent out
> From rotten Lung & heart full false by thee,
> Yea bawdy tongues that rattle round about
> With Cursed Oaths, & hellish blasphemie.
>
> (3, 68–71)

As long as he remains "in these foggy Vailes I can't devise / What
tune's to sing" (3, 318–319). All earthly instruments are unsatisfactory: "Those used here in our melodious tunes / Seem like
to Smutting Smok in varnisht rooms" (3, 320–321), and Taylor's
best poetry on earth can never be condign either to the God he
praises or to the devotion and love he experiences:

> As for the praise I give thee here Most High,
> I bring it but in bits & Sorry Scraps
> And were it altogether certainly
> 'Twould fall out of my lips in slobbered drops.
>
> (3, 322–325)

For that reason, the poet hungers for death and heaven, the one
state in which, finally, he will be able to sing well the songs he

has sung badly through a lifetime of frustrated effort. Heaven is the place of the best sacred poetry, and the earthbound poet anticipates the contrast between his present frustration and his future joy:

> I hope to take a trip or e're 't be long
> Into a purer air by far than this,
> That is not charriot to a bawdy Song
> Nor ever staind with any thing a miss.
>   To th' Aire that's Charriot of Celestiall joyes
>   Enravishing with Spirituall Melodies.
>   (3, 86–91)

In such an air even he, the poet of so many failures, will finally be able to sing a song free of the limitations that have dogged him here on earth:

> But when I entred am in that bright Glory
> Of thy most Shining Habitation,
> My praise shall be raisd to the highest story.
> Praise can ascend up too; & here upon
>   Refind most bright & raised up most high
>   And to thee Sung by me Eternally.
>   (3, 328–333)

Taylor's last version of the valedictory poem ends, then, in anticipation of a poet's heaven, where the unsatisfactory poems through which he struggled here on earth will give way to perfect poems sung to God by the singular poet forever.

It is important to note that what we see here is not an old man giving up and waiting for the inevitable. Taylor's valediction is filled with joy and anticipation. He is not, like Anne Bradstreet in "As Weary Pilgrim," praying that God will make him ready for death: he is ready. Nor is he merely making a virtue of necessity now that he is old and ill. The sense that earthly poetry must fail and that heavenly poetry is worth dying for informs all his

verse, as we shall see, and is made explicit quite early in his career
in a sermon copied into the church records as part of his "Profession of Faith." In this sermon on the Day of Judgment, Taylor
lists all the heavenly influences that will delight the soul of the
saint, leading up from sensuous and sensual delights through the
delight of the understanding, now able to see clearly the glories
formerly obscured, to what he calls "the Ultimate Influence of
heavenly Glory upon the Soul." The greatest of the glories of
heaven

> is this it sets the Soul a Singing forth the Praises of the
> Lord. God having made the Soul Such a glorious Musical
> Instrument of his praises, & the holy Ghost having so
> gloriously Strung it with the gold wire of grace, & heaven-
> ly Glory having Shored up the Strings to Sound forth the
> Songs of Zion's King, the pouring forth of the Influence
> of glory play upon the Soul Eternal praises unto God.
> & now the Soul beg[inning] to Sing forth its endless
> Hallelujahs unto God.

The ultimate glory of heaven, the central difference between
heaven and earth, the heavenly gift worth dying to attain, is
that there, finally, one can sing. All of Taylor's petitions that
God give him the grace to sing, that God open his pipes, tune up
his wires, make him the bell, the organ, the trumpet to sound
forth glory had come to this at last. The poetic gift would be
given, but only in heaven. There only would his prayers for a fit
poetry be fulfilled, and the poet's soul would finally have the joy
of a divine song: "If it were possible it would fly in pieces under
its glory if this glory got no vent. & there it being filled with
glory for God's glory it falls to singing most heart-ravishingly
out the Glory of God in the highest Strains."[7]

Such joy came at a high price, death for the saint's body and
death to the world and the "earthly comforts" that Bradstreet had

believed would be simply made lasting in heaven. But Taylor is
willing to pay that price. He thanks God for earthly comforts:

> But yet my Lord I give thee Hearty thanks
> Thou'st lent me them to tend me to the banks,
> Of thy all glorious Eternall Throne.
>   (3, 170–172)

Yet when he bids goodby to the world his tone is one of scorn
and independence: Thomas Taylor, Richard Baxter, and Richard
Steere (among others) had proclaimed that God intended us to
use the creatures of this world as a ladder, that we might ascend
by degrees from the creation to the Creator. Yet Taylor denies
that possibility, arguing that he does not need the creatures for
that purpose, and never did. Addressing the sun and moon, he
denies their salvific value:

> Your golden Beams, your Silver Tressell shall
> In no wise be my ladders rounds to soare mee
> To Christ's bright Mansion house, his glorious Hall
> Nor to carry mee up to Gods house of Glorie.
> I never purposed on these Stares t' ascend
> Up to Christs brightest Hall, deckt for his Friend.
>   (3, 26–31)

Most other Puritans certainly did purpose to ascend on those very
stairs, not that they any more than Taylor believed that they could
climb to heaven but that they believed God had put those stairs
there for their striving, for their meditation and religious exercises. Taylor says that he has "a better ladder far than one of
gold / Or one of stars most shining, I'se will climb" (3, 32–33),
but he never says what it is. Perhaps he cannot, since such a ladder
would have to be a divine abstraction: if it cannot be figured by
sun and stars, it surely cannot be figured by a mere ladder and
must therefore be left unstated, as it is in all three versions of his
poem. Taking leave of "the Terraqueous Globe," Taylor seems

to deny not only its significance but also its reality, calling it "Thou realm of Sense & Sensualities / Enveagling our Senses by shadow verities" (3, 100–101). It is hard to find a more thorough and searching treatment of limitations of the sensible world.

I should add quickly that most Puritans would have agreed with any one of the statements noted here: none of Taylor's poetry is heretical. Only in degree and only in aggregate do his treatments differ from theirs, but that difference is significant for his poetry. Like Bradstreet he can begin an elegy with a metaphor taken from the physical world and presumably placed there by God to offer comfort in the face of death. But unlike Bradstreet, he cannot rest content with metaphor; he must strain it, tear it apart, show that it cannot possibly be an adequate mode of understanding death. Like Urian Oakes, he can use a poem to make sense of the life and death of a saint and can use metaphors to figure the saint's virtues for the benefit of his descendants, but unlike Oakes he does not use the metaphors to make sense of the death itself and to argue himself and his audience toward acceptance. Either he moves from failed metaphors to a final acceptance that is doctrinal rather than esthetic, as he does in the elegy on his wife, or he simply multiplies disparate metaphors at great length, then breaks off abruptly, as he does in his elegy on Samuel Hooker. Like Ward, Tompson, and Mather, he puts little credence in the prophetic value of anagrams and acrostics, but unlike them, he sees limits to metaphor as well. Like Steere, Bradstreet, Baxter, Willard, Richardson, and others, he sees the world as a gift of God and filled with divine portent, but unlike them he focuses on its inadequacy as a figure for the communicable glories of its Creator, and in his "Valedictory" poems, he bids it all farewell with an eagerness of which Wigglesworth and Pain might have been proud.

Metaphor is one bridge from earth to heaven, death another.

Bradstreet saw the similarities between earth and heaven, found the metaphoric bridge satisfactory, and continued to fear the other bridge in every poem she wrote. Taylor saw the dissimilarities between earth and heaven, found the metaphoric bridge necessary but ultimately unsatisfactory, and often hungered for the second bridge to unlock his poetry as the first had not.

All this is not to suggest that Taylor was a closet Gnostic, a Neoplatonist, or a victim of "declension," a process that we now have reason to believe never occurred outside the realms of worry and rhetoric.[8] Larzer Ziff's recent comment that "the younger generations wanted nothing more hungrily than they wanted to be given an assurance of their gracious state, together with a few of the family acres so that they could get on with being just like their parents"[9] surely includes Taylor, whose attitude toward metaphor and the religious uses of it has much in common with those of such predecessors as Thomas Taylor, Baxter, Bradstreet, and Williams, and such contemporaries as Steere, Sewall, and Willard. But his actual use of metaphor is subtle, and if we are to understand his poetry and the complex but consistent system of poetics and theology that informs it, we must examine Taylor's theory and use of metaphor in the context his fellow Puritans provide.

For him as for them, the world itself is a metaphor, the gift of a loving God, and is intended to raise our affections to Him and to make us sing. In the sensible world the poet sees "Glory, thou Shine of Shining things made fine . . . the brightest blossom fine things bring / To please our Fancies with and make them sing" (2.101, 1, 5–6). The poet recognizes the divine tenor of this metaphoric world, which gives him both the only possible knowledge he can have of God (all private revelation having ceased with the death of the last Apostle) and the method he can use in singing his gratitude and praise:

But spare me, Lord, if I while thou dost use
  This Metaphor to make thyselfe appeare
In taking Colours, fancy it to Choose
    To blandish mine affections with and Cheare
    Them with thy glory, ever shining best.
    Thus brought to thee so takingly up dresst.
             (2.101, 7–12)

Since God gives His glory to man through metaphoric creatures,
it is appropriate that man answer through metaphoric poetry. Of
course Taylor, like his predecessors, knew that these creatures
would pale if set beside the Glory of God Himself. "Created
Glory dangling on all things," indeed the stars themselves, whose
light is a God-wrought metaphor for grace, "Do blush and are
asham'd of all their grace / Beholding that bright Glory of thy
Face" (2.101, 31, 34–35). But man cannot look upon God directly, and the world-metaphor is God's metaphor, a lover's gift,
not to be scorned:

But, Lord, art thou deckt up in glory thus?
  And dost thou in this Glory come and Wooe
To bring our hearts to thee compelling us
    With such bright arguments of Glories hew?
    Oh! Adamantine Hearts if we withstand
    Such taking Charming pleas in Glories hand.
             (2.101, 49–54)

For Taylor as for Steere, then, the world is God's courting gift,
gilded "ore with sparkling Metaphors" (2.152, 7), through which
God "Courtst mine Eyes in Sparkling Colours bright, / Most bright
indeed, and soul enamoring" (2.12, 7–8). Through "the Shining
Sun . . . Embellisht knots of Love assault my minde" (2.12, 8,
11). Through "Thy Lower House, this World well garnished /
With richest Furniture of Ev'ry kinde" (2.93, 13–14), God
figures "that bright City fair" (2.93, 1), the heaven whose glories
are made humanly apprehensible in the glories of earth. God uses

the law of nature to lead men to grace, and there is no innate contradiction between the two orders: "Everyone is a friend to him that gives gifts. . . . The Law of Nature teacheth us to love them that love us Matt. 5. 46. And Grace doth not debilitate, or disgrace, but regulate, and exalt the Law of Nature, and improve it, to attend matters not Contrary to, but above the Precepts of the Law of Nature" (*C*, p. 31). God's method is based upon a metaphoric similarity between the orders of nature and grace, a similarity He has designed to accommodate the limits of man's cognition.

But unlike Steere, William Wood, and Edward Johnson, Taylor almost never writes about the world on its own terms. He is interested only in the metaphor, not in the world itself but in "The glory of the world slickt up in types / In all Choise things chosen to typify" (2.1, 13–14). Though Donald Junkins has counted 1,749 references to the natural world in Taylor's *Preparatory Meditations*, Karl Keller is surely correct in observing that in Taylor's poetry "Nature is important for analogy only."[10] When Taylor chronicles the creation of the world, for example, we see God creating similes and metaphors:

> Who Lac'de and Fillitted the earth so fine,
> With Rivers like green Ribbons Smaragdine?
> Who made the Sea's its Selvedge, and it locks
> Like a Quilt Ball within a Silver Box?
> Who Spread its Canopy? Or Curtains Spun?
> Who in this Bowling Alley bowld the Sun?
> (*GD*, p. 387)

Perhaps because he focuses on the world only as a metaphor and not as a separate force that one must control in order to discover its metaphoric content, Taylor rarely writes poems hinging on the necessity of weaning one's affections from the immoderate love of this world. In his poetry, this world has no literal value: that it is vain goes without saying, and Taylor writes next to nothing on the literal vanity of the physical world, a theme central to the poetry of Anne Bradstreet, who had to work her way from her celebration of this world on its own terms to an understanding that the world was properly conceived as metaphor.[11] Indeed, on one of the rare occasions when Taylor mentions the world—"And hence the heart is hardened and toyes, / With Love, Delight, and Joy, yea Vanities" (GD, p. 410)—he puts the speech into the mouth of the Devil, and he argues in his *Treatise Concerning the Lord's Supper* that a person "overrun with evil and carnal thoughts" with all his concerns "laid out upon the things of the world" might still be one "of the choicest of God's children" since "this is the condition of God's children here in this life. While we have these bodies of clay to look after, and are betrusted with the concerns of families, towns, and public duties in our hands, they necessitate our thoughts" (pp. 153–154). Though such worldly concerns as organizing Westfield's defenses during King Philip's War and serving as the town physician throughout his life necessitated much of Taylor's thoughts, war and medicine turn up in his poetry only as metaphor. The sensible world has its primary reality as a metaphor. A love letter from God, it could teach man: God "Plac'de man his Pupill here, and ev'ry thing, / With loads of Learning, came to tutor him" (2.41, 5–6); it could figure forth communicable glories of God Himself: "Thou'rt that Sun, that shines out Saving Grace" (2.68, 24); and it could inspire sacred poetry: "Then Glory as a Metaphor, Il 'tende . . . While in my heart thou'rt thron'd my Quill shall greet / Thyselfe with Zions Songs in musick Sweet" (2.100, 7, 42–43). Throughout Taylor's poetry he would sing the glories and failings of earth. But its glories were metaphoric, and when it failed, it would fail as a metaphor.

A second major metaphor was God's other book, "thy Holy

Word, the golden Key" (2.115, 13), which, "Rooted in Rich Relation, Graces Sluce" (2.35, 4), provides Taylor not only with a key to the metaphors immanent in the world but with an explicit precedent for his own metaphoric method. First, the Scripture clarifies the divine tenor only dimly apparent in nature: "Now the will of God is revealed to us: More obscurely, as in the law of nature and of the creation. For there stands imprinted upon the nature of the creature a declaration of the will of God . . . More clearly, as in the law of grace, and holy scriptures" (*TCLS*, pp. 61–62). Second, the Scripture gives man a theological basis for daring to use metaphor himself. Presuming to explain God's metaphoric intentions would be damnable pride if He had not already made His correspondences explicit for us, made them part of our perceived world and given us their explanation in a metaphoric Scripture that explains its own metaphors. Taylor could therefore allude both to Scripture and to creation in justifying man's use of metaphor:

> Natural things are not unsuitable to illustrate supernaturals by. For Christ in his parables doth illustrate supernatural things by natural, and if it were not thus, we could arrive at no knowledge of supernatural things, for we are not able to see above naturals.
> God hath a sweet harmony of reason running the same throughout the whole creation, even through every distinct sort of creatures; hence Christ on this very account makes use of natural things to illustrate supernaturals by, and the Apostle argues invisible things from the visible. So that on this account there is argument enough, if we have but skill to take it and use it aright.
>
> (*TCLS*, pp. 43–44)

Not only God, but Christ, who was God and man, and Paul, a mortal man, could see, recognize, and use metaphors. One had

only to look at the creation and the Bible to find his precedent and
to justify his practice.

But the greatest metaphor, for Taylor, is Christ Himself, the
living link between grace and nature, God and man, the metaphor
who uses metaphors and whose union of earthly and divine is
figured through another metaphor, the Lord's Supper. Like other
metaphors, Christ derives considerable imaginative force by vio-
lating these logical categories. But for Christians His violation is
factual as well as figural. For Taylor, Christ is totally divine:
"Jesus Christ, which words are not to be taken exclusively to exclude the Other persons of the Trinity, for they are also concerned there in, hence the whole undivided."[12] And He is also
fully human, one with us: "For our nature, as we are man Kind,
is the Same with his Humane nature. And so he, and we are united
together (*Genere*) in one and the Same common Nature" (*C*, p.
320). Taylor insists that this metaphor is satisfactory, that neither
term is suppressed. He insists that Christ retains his body in heaven
and keeps his manhood forever, specifically refuting Calvin's argument that Christ has subsumed His humanity into His Deity and
lives in heaven only as God.[13]

This perfect metaphor, neither the world nor heaven but this
union of the two, inspired Taylor's poetry. First, Christ completes the order of nature, and love of Christ enables the poet to
sing as love of the world cannot. Meditating on Canticles 5:13
"His Cheeks are as a Bed of Spices, as sweet Flowers," Taylor's
only criterion for love is beauty. Christ is more beautiful than the
world, but His beauty is enough like that of earth that the two
can be compared. If the creatures were more beautiful, "true
Wisdoms voice would bee, / That greater Love belong'd to these
than thee" (2.120, 11–12). True wisdom seeks only a beauty
that will inspire song, and if that beauty could be found on earth,

> Love to thyselfe might slacke its pin
> And Love to Worldly Gayes might screw up higher
> Its rusty pin, till, that her Carnall String
> Did raise Earths Tunes above the Heavenly Quire.
>   (2.120, 13–16)

As it is, Christ's beauty completes the earthly metaphor suggested by spice beds and sweet flowers. His more beautiful face inspires a better song:

> A Spice bed shining with sweet flowers all fair,
> Enravishing the very Skies so Cleare
> With their pure Spirits breathing thence perfumes
> Orecoming notes that fill my Harpe with tunes.
>   (2.120, 45–48)

In this poem Christ completes the natural metaphor, which in turn provides the poet with a way of praising him. Second, Christ completes the order of grace by instilling grace in man and by keeping it alive there. Not only would man be dead to God without the intermediation of Christ, but without Christ's having taken on a body, man could have no notion of God. Without the mediation of the Christ-metaphor, the image of God would fade: "The Image too of God is grown thrid bare / If this Choice Life be n't with Christ's body fed" (2.80, 39–40). Finally, Christ had left behind a metaphor to feed the image of God in the mind of each man, the Lord's Supper. Christ had spread "Dainties most rich, all spiced o're with Grace" to appeal to the sensuous appetites of men and

> To entertain thy Guests, thou callst, and place
> Allowst, with welcome, (And this is no Fable)
> And with these Guests I am invited to't
> And this rich banquet makes me thus a Poet.
>   (2.110, 19, 21–24)

Bradstreet had been moved to song by the beauty of the natural world and by her observation that other creatures sang to God.

Johnson had been inspired to his poetry by his glimpse of the enormous portent behind the history of the Massachusetts Bay Colony, Wood by the mere abundance of interesting creatures in the New World. Only Taylor found his inspiration in a tertiary metaphor, Christ's own metaphor for His metaphoric self. He knew that it would be idolatry and madness to imagine that Christ's body and blood were physically present in the communion bread, an error into which the Catholics had fallen with their doctrine of transubstantiation: "What feed on Humane Flesh and Blood? Strang mess! / Nature exclaims. What Barbarousness is here?" (2.81, 13–14). Taken literally, John's statement that one should eat the flesh of the Son of man and drink His blood is ghoulish nonsense, but there is another, a primary sense: "This sense of this blesst Phrase is nonsense thus. / Some other Sense makes this a metaphor" (2.81, 19–20). And the metaphoric sense becomes more real and true than the literal.

Since the sensible world, the word of God in Scripture, Christ Himself, and the sacrament that inspired Taylor's poetry all have their primary reality as metaphors, since Taylor's own words are inspired by the Word made flesh, we should expect Taylor to follow his predecessors in writing imagistic, highly metaphoric poetry. And indeed he repeatedly argues the necessity and appropriateness of metaphor and repeatedly begins his poems exactly as we would expect. In his *Christographia* Taylor argues the necessity of metaphor and links it to Christ, meditation, and poetry:

> All Languages admit of Metaphorical forms of Speech,
> and the Spirit of God abounds in this manner of Speech
> in the Scripture and did foreshow that Christ Should
> abound in this Sort of Speech Ps. 78. 2. Matt. 13. 35,
> and this Sort of Speech never was expected to be literally
> true, nor Charged to be a lying form of Speech, but a
> neat Rhetorical, and Wise manner of Speaking. Hence

saith God's Spirit in the Psalmist Ps. 49. 3. 4: I will open
my mouth in Wisdom: the meditation of my heart shall
be of understanding. I will incline mine ear to a Parable
and open my dark Saying upon my harp.

(*C.* p. 273)

Elsewhere in the *Christographia* Taylor uses this metaphorical
form of speaking to discuss the imitation of Christ. To aid man
in his attempt to live the holy life, God has written an *exemplum*:
He "hath presented us with a perfect Pattern of right practice in
our nature in Christ, which is most Exemplary, being a most Exact Copy written by the Deity of the Son of God, with the Pen
of Humanity, on the milk white Sheet of an Holy Life" (*C*, p.
34). The "pen of humanity," guided by God's hand, has written
a metaphor for us to copy. Holy living is associated here with writing in metaphors, though the association is only metaphoric, and
Taylor is urging his congregation to "turn poets of righteousness,"
in John Cotton's words, not specifically to take up the writing of
verses. Yet the association is repeated in a later sermon, also on
Christ as the perfect union of earth and heaven, body and spirit:
"This is the best Example that can be: it is a Copy written by the
pen of perfect Manhood, in the Unerring hand of Godhead, in
Christ and wilt thou not endeavour to Write by this Copy?" (*C.*
p. 102). For Taylor, then, writing in metaphors was part of his
imitation of Christ, part of the practice of his religion here on
earth.

Taylor clearly believed that "these Metaphors we spiritualized / Speak out . . . spirituall Beauty cleare" (2.151, 49–50), a
belief exemplified in nearly every poem he wrote. He recognized
and used the figural value of the world and the flesh; he used
everything from flowers to feces to figure the invisible things of
God and heaven; like Bradstreet, Steere, Hooker, Ward, and Willard, he used erotic imagery to figure salvation. Karl Keller and

William Scheick, among others, have admirably examined this aspect of Taylor's poetry and left no need to rehearse their findings here.[14]

What has not yet been examined in adequate detail is Taylor's almost compulsive insistence that his metaphors failed, that they could not possibly be adequate to his theme. Again, the context provided by other Puritan poets proves helpful. Where Wigglesworth and Pain had avoided metaphor, and where Bradstreet, Steere, Williams, Danforth, and nearly every other Puritan poet had concluded with metaphor as a final and satisfactory way of figuring the harmony between their love of this world and their longing for the next, Taylor begins with metaphor, focuses on metaphor often as the subject of his poem, and considers its powers and limits more explicitly and in more detail than had any other Puritan poet.

Taylor cannot sing without metaphors, but he can never be satisfied with them; he must insist repeatedly that his metaphors will not work:

> My Metaphors are but dull Tacklings tag'd
>   With ragged Non-Sense. Can such draw to thee
> My stund affections all with Cinders clag'd?
>   (2.36, 31-33)

> My tatter'd Fancy; and my Ragged Rymes
>   Teeme leaden Metaphors.
>   (2.82, 1-2)

> Thy Ware to me's so rich, should my Returns
>   Be packt in sparkling Metaphors, out stilld
> From Zion's garden flowers, by fire that burns
>   Aright, of Saphire Battlements up filld
>   And sent in Jasper Vialls it would bee
>   A pack of guilded Non-Sense unto thee.
>   (2.35, 13-18)

My Quaintest Metaphors are ragged Stuff,
Making the Sun seem like a Mullipuff.
(1.22, 5–6)

Though examples could be multiplied, these suffice to suggest that
Taylor often considers his metaphors inadequate to raise his affections to God, to express his gratitude, to capture in language
the glory of the metaphoric world. Nor are such disclaimers simple modesty. Taylor never writes that his poetry is in any way inferior to that of any other earthly poet. Indeed, he insists that the
failings of his poetry are common to all poetry. He tries to write
of a "Grace that shines more bright / Than any Pen and Ink can
write" (*MHC*, p. 488). His skill is not less than that of other
poets, and he occasionally reflects that he might have been able
to write secular poetry had he wished to: "Might but my pen in
natures Inventory / Its progress make, 't might make such things
to jump" (2.56, 37–38), and even his "tatter'd Fancy . . . Ragged
Rymes," and "leaden Metaphors" are good enough for secular
poetry and "yet might serve / To hum a little touching terrene
Shines" (2.82, 1–3). But Taylor's aim is not to celebrate the
beauty of this world but to give adequate song to the miracle of
the Incarnation, to the Word-Made-Flesh whose works "Out vie
both works of nature and of Art" (2.56, 44). This subject "doth
better fare deserve" (2.82, 4) than any earthly poet can serve up
in any metaphor, and Taylor must conclude his *Christographia*,
an earthly attempt to understand and utter the significance of
Christ's life, with a final demurrer: "All our pencils in all their
drafts attain not to anything of the Excellencies of Christ's opera-
tions" (*C.* 468). Though metaphor is a necessary and proper way
of seeing and writing, Taylor can find satisfaction neither in his
own metaphors nor in those of any other poet.

Nor, remarkably, can he be satisfied with God's metaphors,
with either the physical metaphors He has placed in the world or

the verbal metaphors He has set out in the Bible. Though Taylor's "Quaintest Metaphors" make "the Sun seem like a Mullipuff" (1.22, 5–6), the Sun itself is, though fine as a fact of earthly life, unsatisfactory as a metaphor:

> The Suns bright Glory's but a smoky thing
> Though it oft 'chants mans fancy with its flashes.
> All other glories, that from Creatures spring
> Are less than that: but both are sorry Swashes.
> (2.100, 31–34)

Taylor must move from creature to Christ, not by focusing on the similarity his metaphor implies, but by insisting on difference. Earth's glory is always "smoky," and Christ's glory, "purely bright, and spotless cleare" (2.100, 35), can be suggested only by contradicting God's own metaphor. Similarly, Taylor insists that "the Worlds Estate's not able" (1.9, 4) to figure a perfect metaphor like the Lord's Supper, that "dirty Earth" and "Earthy Dunghills" (2.120, 19, 21) cannot figure the beauty of Christ's face. Even though Canticles 5:13, the passage on which he meditates, asserts that Christ's cheeks are like spice beds and sweet flowers, Taylor contends that

> Such things as these indeed are Hells black Smoke
> That pother from its Chimny tunnells vile
> To smut thy perfect beauty.
> (2.120, 31–33)

Given the failings of earthly metaphors, Taylor can suggest Christ's face only by saying that it has the "sweetest Beauty that Face ere did ware" (2.120, 8), a beauty infinitely above nature's metaphors.

God has created the earthly metaphor to direct man's attention to heaven, but "this world doth eye thy brightness most / When most in distance from thyselfe" (2.21, 49–50), and all of nature's metaphors finally fail. This insistence on the inadequacy of metaphor goes well beyond Bradstreet's belief that earthly beauties were literally vain but figurally portentous, that while they could not compete with heaven, they could figure it. Taylor repeatedly insists that all metaphoric predications are equivocal, that, applied to God and heaven, all earthly metaphors become inverted, showing forth the glory of God, not by similarity, but by opposition. Such metaphoric vehicles do not merely fall short of the excellency they are intended to figure: they become totally inverted when applied to the order of grace, turning into their opposites. Heavenly glory is so separate from and superior to earthly glory that it darkens any glory that man can find imaged in nature:

> Thou Glory Darkning Glory, with thy Flame
> Should all Quaint Metaphors teem ev'ry Bud
> Of Sparkling Eloquence upon the same
> It would appeare as dawbing pearls with mud.
> (1.13, 1–4)

Since "Created Nature and Uncreated nature are Contraries and as it were Contradictories" (C. 161), metaphors from nature, though necessary and proper to man's perceptions, necessarily fail to link the orders of nature and grace satisfactorily.

Even metaphors explicitly set forth in the Bible fail to satisfy Taylor. He writes in one poem (2.120), as we have seen, all the ways in which Christ's cheeks are not like spice beds and sweet flowers, and in another he meditates on the metaphor in Canticles 5:14 that figures Christ's hands as gold rings, positing the metaphor, then reflecting:

> But yet methinks the glory of thy hands
> As handling thy mediatoriall Acts
> Metaphorized here too faintly stands.
> (2.122, 25–27)

And the rest of the poem, though composed as it must be of metaphors, is generated by their inadequacies. No metaphor, no received linking of nature and grace, is safe from Taylor, who, as
Karl Keller has observed, "is unique among New England typologists in the obvious delight he takes in playing with the conventions, stretching them wittily . . . and extending them. . . ."[15]
Though natural and biblical metaphors had provided conclusions
for other Puritans, Taylor could not rest content with them.

This dissatisfaction is made explicit in the *Christographia,* in
which Taylor, having justified the use of metaphor, explores its
limits: "There are Some things whose Excellency is flourished
over with Metaphors. We borrow the Excellency of other things
to varnish over their Excellency withall. But Grace excels all
Metaphors. The varnish laid upon it doth but darken, and not
decorate it: its own Colours are too glorious to be made more
glorious, by any Colour of Secular glory" (*C,* p. 253). Secular
glory exists to suggest grace to the limited faculties of men, but
the poet who would sing of grace must go beyond secular glory,
which would merely darken and obscure his subject. If he is to
use this world to sing of grace, he must be aware of the limits of
his metaphoric instruments and must find a way to push them to
their very limits, if not to transcend them altogether. Metaphor
may not be simply applied to glory.

Explicit in his sermons, this dissatisfaction with metaphor is implicit in his artistic choices, in his frequently choosing metaphors
that are particularly farfetched: one critic writes that "his metaphors repeatedly seem calculated to repel rather than to invite sensuous apprehension," another that in choosing such metaphors as
souls' paddling their canoes on a Red Sea of Christ's blood, "Taylor seems almost to defy us to react against such a picture, to reject
it as ludicrous or sacrilegious," and a third that "in creating his
celebrated image of God as prize bowler of the universe, Taylor

is actually underscoring the comic disparity between earthly vehicle and divine tenor."[16] From the pattern of Taylor's revisions, moreover, we know that these choices were deliberate, that he often replaced an apt metaphor with a preposterous one, strove to make his prosody rough and tumbling, revised to make clear the inadequacies of his metaphors.[17] Knowing that this apparent inconsistency is deliberate, however, does not provide us with an immediate solution, and we are still left in a quandary: why should Taylor first insist that the sensible world is sacramental and does show forth the communicable glory of God and then strive in his poetry to desacramentalize the images and metaphors he draws from it? Why should he explicitly justify a metaphoric reading of the Bible and then show that biblical metaphors are inadequate to the knowing and praising of God? It is one thing to aver modestly that one's own metaphors are inadequate to one's high theme and quite another to say that so are the metaphors of all other poets and so are the metaphors of the sensible world and the Bible, and to compound this apparent irreverence by subverting, twisting, and extending all metaphors. Is God also a writer of bad poems, a maker of metaphors that fall apart?

Several explanations of Taylor's unusual use of metaphor have been suggested. One can focus on Taylor's positive uses of metaphor, arguing that "nature represents a proper source from which he could fashion his metaphoric bridge to God," that "the reader should not be deceived by the poet's frequent disclaimers," and that "the apparent unseemly effect of such techniques and Taylor's self-disparagement or humble disavowal of his poetic skill should not lead us to conclude that he considered these qualities severe limitations which he was unable to overcome."[18] But Taylor often insists in his poetry that he will never be free of these limitations until death: "And though not now, I then shall sing thy praise. /

In that thy love did tende me all my dayes" (2.96, 54–55) is but one example. While we should not "be deceived" by Taylor's disclaimers into thinking that he ever abandoned metaphor, neither should we ignore those disclaimers or the poetic techniques that they inform.

Another solution is to suggest that "Taylor strains his metaphors to such a breaking point only in a few instances" and then only "to get us to take the leap of the mystic, so that we may see from the other side."[19] But Taylor never claims to have taken that leap: his poems express a longing for the clear vision that he hopes God will grant him on the other side of death. "Although thy Love play bow-peep with me here" on this earth, "Though I be dark: want Spectacles to prove / Thou lovest mee," after death and resurrection, in the final certainty that he is elect, "I shall at last see Clear" (2.96, 5–53). Although he longs for an assurance of grace that would enable him to sing well here on earth, his repeated petitions for that assurance pervade his poetry right up to the last version of his "Valedictory" poems, written two years before his death, and indicate his belief that God has not yet granted him that long-sought gift.

One can also argue that Taylor was working within the tradition of emblem literature or within a Catholic exegetical tradition,[20] but there is little external evidence of such linkings, and even if such evidence could be found, one would still have to explain why Taylor's poems are so different from those of most emblematists, such as Quarles, and from those of most Catholics, such as Crashaw. If Taylor will not fit within a Catholic tradition, one may say that his poetry is informed by a peculiarly "Protestant poetic,"[21] but this tradition, while it surely includes Taylor, just as surely includes all the other Puritan poets, whose treatments of metaphor are often quite different from his. Finally, one can resurrect the old notion of the poet as secret rebel and say that in his verbal ingenuity Taylor is "paying lavish tribute to his own" powers of creation and dramatizing "the possibility that human inventiveness can actually be superior to Heaven's." [22] But we now have reason to lay this ghost once and for all. Most of the presumably heretical beliefs allegedly implicit in the poetry were made quite explicit in Taylor's public sermons to his congregation. Had they found such beliefs shocking, they could have protested publicly, as other congregations did. We now know that there is nothing inconsistent in a Puritan's writing poetry and that Taylor's supposedly having forbidden in his will the publication of his poetry is nothing more than a family legend, since Taylor never made a will and died intestate, leaving us no evidence that he made any plans whatever for either the publication or suppression of his poetry. [23] To read Taylor's poetry as a celebration of man and a denigration of heaven is to read it quite selectively and to ignore his prose and his Puritanism and his own sensibility, all the things that made him different from other poets.

If we are to improve upon these explanations, we must seek an explanation which includes Taylor and which excludes other poets whose treatments of the world and the flesh, and of the metaphors derived from them, differ from his. One such explanation is suggested by a small but significant difference between Taylor and other Puritan poets in their beliefs concerning the creation of the world. For Bradstreet, Steere, and the others, the world and the flesh were created by God the Father. In this characterization they do not exclude Christ. As orthodox trinitarians they could not exclude Him. But they follow most Christians in assigning the work of Creation to the Father.

But Taylor's theology is more Christocentric than theirs. His poetry is inspired neither by the world itself, as Wood's had been, nor by the immanence of God in the world, as Bradstreet's had been, but by the "rich banquet" (2.110, 24) prepared by Christ.

When he looked upon the sensible world, he saw the handiwork, not of the Father, but of Christ. This belief is made quite explicit in a sermon preached in 1702: "The Father himself executes nothing: but hath committed all the Executing of his Decrees unto the Son, and this wisdom executing of the Decrees appears in 1. The Works of Creation." Christ the Mediator, whose human nature is one with ours, is immanent in "the wisdom of the works of the Creation." It is Christ Who has the wisdom "to make the Heavens and garnish them with all their Glory, accomplish them with those glorious bodies of Light, the Sun, Moon, and Stars." Taylor urges his hearers to "Cast an eye upon the Elementary Bodies from the Stars to the Center of Earth," to reflect with him on an almost Whitmanic catalogue of the creatures—"Scorpions, Worms, Insects, Fishes . . . Herbs, Flowers, Bushes, Shrubs, plants, Seeds, Fruits, trees." All these, says Taylor, were made by Christ, and their "Springings, growing, Durations, Decayings . . . Seasons, etc." have been set in motion by Christ, and under His constant control are "successively on to go by the hand of Providence to the end of the World." Taylor then rejoices in the knowledge that Christ has created man and has invested him with enough of His wisdom to see this wisdom in the Creation: "I say, the Wisdom that hath done all this, and chiefly that hath made Man, and put Wisdom into the inward parts, is Wonderful" (C, pp. 114–115). The creatures, then, are linked in Taylor's soteriology to Christ, to His role as mediator, to the Lord's Supper and the meditations through which one prepared for it, to the earthly struggle of the saint for some assurance of his election. Christ had taken on flesh and time, had become man incarnate as well as God, and Taylor associates His creation far more with the temporal struggle of man on earth than with the eternal stasis of God in heaven. It is clear from another sermon that Taylor distinguished Christ from the rest of the Trinity

193

with specific references to his human nature: "Jesus Christ, which words are not to be taken exclusively to exclude the Other persons of the Trinity . . . But Emphatically. Because Christ Jesus, as he is the Son of man hath it peculiarly conferred on him to transact the whole." [24]

Now this belief that Christ created the world is certainly orthodox enough, and Taylor is merely elaborating a similar suggestion made by Paul in Colossians 1:16. But it is different from the beliefs of other Puritan poets, and it helps to explain the ways in which his poetic use of metaphors drawn from the world and the flesh differs from theirs. Like them, he believes that the creatures had been sent to man to lead him toward God, that they are fit objects for meditation, and that poetry is a proper form for this meditation. But far more than they, he associates the writing of satisfactory metaphoric poetry with the assurance of his own election, an election made possible through Christ's atonement, and prays that Christ will give him the grace to sing aright. Hence he constantly denigrates the metaphoric poetry that he is writing and prays that God will give him the grace to write better. Taylor's doubts about his poetry are inextricably interwoven with his doubts about his election. Where Anne Bradstreet believed that "the spring is a lively emblem of the resurrection" for everyone to see and attributed her inability to sing as the rest of nature sings to the common limitations imposed by the Fall of man, Taylor sees the connection of grace and poetry as far more individual. When "I fain would thee advance / But finde my Pen is workd to the very Stumps," that "My tongue my Speeches tabber Stick can't dance" (2.155, 1–3), he immediately wonders "if I be in the Faith . . . if I bee'nt Reprobate" (2.155, 7–8), since a reprobate poet would not be able to sing. He therefore prays for the assurance of his gracious state that would enable him to sing:

Grant me thy Spectacles that I may see
To glorify aright thy glorious Selfe.
And see this Saving Faith grafted in mee.
(2.155, 13–15)

Taylor is asking here, not for the historical faith that he already
had as Puritan believer, but for the saving faith of the grace ex-
perience itself, for an assurance that his conversion was genuine.
Such grace "makes th'Tongue tipt with it silver" (2.155, 39), but
Taylor can never be sure of his election, can never be sure that
God has given him the grace to sing, and must end, as always, in
the conditional: "If thou wilt give me this my heart shall sing /
On'ts Virginall, thy holy praise, within" (2.155, 47–48).

William Scheick has accurately noted that "the saint's ability
to verbalize rightly depends on this act of grace conveyed by the
Spirit,"[25] a point that can be extended with knowledge of Taylor's
belief in Christ's creation. Christ had created the order of nature
and the metaphoric language that derived from it as part of His
condescension to the limited perceptions of man. To aid fallen
man he had instilled "Thy Mediatoriall glory in the shine" (2.3,
8) of natural and biblical metaphors. And man, "not able to see
above naturals," had a duty to use these metaphors. But they offered him a mediated vision of heaven, and to confuse Christ's
loving mediation with the perfect vision of the saints in heaven
is to imagine that earth can indeed outshine heaven. Christ—the
living, perfect metaphor linking man and God—had come to save
man from his depravity, to confer election upon him. For a poet
to be sure of his metaphors and satisfied with them would be tantamount to his being sure of his own election. The saint could yearn
for election and pray for some assurance of it, but to rest content
with any such assurance while yet on earth was to commit the
damnable sin of pride. So Taylor could and must begin writing

in metaphors as part of his imitation of Christ, another poet whose Godhead wrote with the pen of humanity, but Taylor knew that such an imitation had to be a poor one and that to rest content with any metaphor would be an act of pride, since only saints can sing.

It is clear from Taylor's poetry that he had these theological distinctions constantly in mind. Tempted to despair because he can find no certain assurance of Christ's love, Taylor reassures himself that the metaphoric world is neither a lie nor a cause for satisfaction:

> But listen, Soule, here seest thou not a Cheate.
> Earth is not heaven: Faith not Vision. No.
> To see the Love of Christ on thee Compleate
> Would make heavens Rivers of joy, earth overflow.
> This is the Vale of tears, not mount of joyes.
> Some Crystal drops while here may well suffice.
>
> (2.96, 43–48)

His affections stirred by such "Crystal drops" as he is given, Taylor feels the need and duty to sing: "I fain would something say: / Lest Silence should indict me" (1.21, 7–8). But even in his enthusiasm he can never be any more content with his poetry than with his election:

> To see thy Kingly Glory in to throng.
> I can, yet cannot tell this Glory just,
> In Silence bury't, must not, yet I must.
>
> (1.17, 16–18)

His life on earth, then, is best spent by writing poetry with which he can never be content. He always recognizes that all "sparkling Metaphors" (2.35, 14) are "A pack of guilded Non-Sense unto thee" (2.35, 18), but he also knows that such nonsense is exactly what God expects from him, and "seing Non-Sense very Pleasant is / To Parents, flowing from the Lisping Child" (1.34, 7–8), Taylor can in complete good conscience "Conjue to thee,

hoping thou in this / Will finde some hearty Praise of mine En-
foild" (1.34, 9–10). Knowing that on earth "I cannot sing, my
tongue is tide," he can not only ask God to "Accept this Lisp till I
am glorifide" (1.43, 41–42); he can also take a good deal of joy
in the song he is able to sing while here on earth: "Thy joyes
in mee will make my Pipes to play / For joy thy Praise while
teather'd to my clay" (1.48, 41–42).

There is no contradiction, then, in Taylor's use of metaphor.
The very recognition of its severe limitations frees him to explore
its limits. Nor is there any contradiction between the joy he takes
in his verbal ingenuity and the joy he feels in his hope of election.
They are part of the same coherent view of the world and the
flesh and language and God. In writing his preposterous metaphors, in twisting and wittily extending received metaphors, in
playing hob with typology, he is singing his song on earth with a
self-conscious humility, with a properly ironic sense of his own
limitations coupled with a great and thoroughly human joy that
he is able to sing at all. His puns, conceits, and hyperboles are the
appropriate verbal correlatives for this self-conscious song: they
are language pushed to its limits to suggest, if only by negation,
the transcendent glories that lie beyond those limits.

The relation of Taylor's poetry to the poetry of his fellow
Puritans, then, is more subtle than Karl Keller suggests when he
says that other Puritans "wrote so little verse" and then only as
"an expression of tenets," with the result that "they therefore
became dull apologists and he became a real poet."[26] Wigglesworth and Pain viewed the relation of the world and flesh to
God with an almost Gnostic dualism and therefore had little use
for metaphor. The naturalist Puritan poets, of whom Richard
Steere and Anne Bradstreet are the best examples, viewed that
relation as one of God-wrought metaphor and focused on the
similarity between earth and heaven. They knew that the earth

could not compare with heaven literally and that as a substitute for heaven it was merely a dunghill. But they believed that earth could figure heaven satisfactorily and that their permanent house in heaven differed from their transient house here on earth only in degree, that the latter could figure the former. This metaphoric bridge between earth and heaven they found so satisfactory that they could use it even to comfort themselves in the face of that other bridge, death. Like them, Taylor believed that the world and the flesh were metaphors, but for him those metaphors had been created by Christ and could be used well only by saints. Since he could never be sure of his election here on earth, he could never be satisfied with metaphors, could suggest the transcendent glories of heaven only by pushing earthly metaphors to the limits of language and then saying that heaven lay infinitely beyond them, and could bring himself to an acceptance of his wife's and children's deaths only by a final, abstract, doctrinal insistence that God was merciful and just. Because his earthly instruments were so limited, he looked forward more than most Puritans to the final bridge between earth and heaven, sure that if only he could cross it, he would finally have instruments adequate to the praise of grace. While he remained on earth, then, Taylor's poetry was always in process, never completed. All poems were subject to unending revision, even after being copied out in fair copy. Lines from one poem could be expanded into another poem. And he could bring each flawed poem to a close only by asking God to grant him the grace to write a perfect poem, knowing full well that here on earth he could never be sure that that grace had been granted, never be sure of the metaphors he saw and wrote. Though he longed for both, Taylor wrote, finally, neither the poetry of mystical escape nor that of religious comfort. He wrote the poetry of self-conscious earthly struggle, of frustration and joy, doubt and hope.

His complex poetry and poetics help to illustrate both the variety and unity of Puritan poetry. Reading Taylor in the context provided by his fellow Puritans, we have seen, along with the expected similarities, significant differences in their respective uses of the world and the flesh. But we have also seen that he was a Puritan after all, that like his fellow Puritans he practiced his religion through a metaphoric poetry linking earth and heaven. Like them he saw God's glory immanent in the world and the flesh, and he never presumed to ignore either or to abjure metaphor. Like them he strove in this life to obey the command in Exodus, to build God's altar from the mud and stone of this earth.

APPENDIX
In Critic's Hands:
A Bibliographical Essay

In this array 'mongst vulgars may'st thou roam.
In critic's hands beware thou dost not come,
And take thy way where yet thou art not known.
ANNE BRADSTREET

SINCE no book-length study of Puritan poetry yet exists, most critical comments on its nature have been made in passing in works devoted to other subjects. Even when those other subjects have been individual Puritan poets, such as Anne Bradstreet or Edward Taylor, authors have tended to isolate them from the context provided by their fellow Puritan poets, to view them as exceptions to a general rule. That general rule is usually taken from earlier critical generalizations rather than based on a searching examination of the poetry itself. For this reason, the best way to approach the earlier criticism of Puritan poetry is chronological, since only in that way can we see the development of the critical generalizations now current.[1]

Our earliest editors and critics had little to say for or about Puritan poetry. In 1793, Elihu Hubbard Smith published his collection of *American Poems* which, without explanation, he began with the Connecticut Wits.[2] In 1827, George Bancroft reviewed James G. Percival's *Clio* in the *American Quarterly Review* and used the occasion to write an extended survey of early American poetry. His description of the present state of criticism is nearly as applicable today as it was in 1827: "It is not a great while, since any inquiries into the early efforts of our countrymen in belles-lettres, would have seemed fit to be introduced with an apology. Men thought too little of attempting to discern the scattered proofs of literary taste and genius; a general excuse for presumed deficiencies was found in the character of our ancestors; and no investigations were made" of the sort that he was about to undertake. Despite this promising opening, Bancroft soon begins to ride the progressivist thesis that would later inform his *History of the United States*. Moving steadily toward the conclusion that, of all American poets, "Percival, Bryant, Halleck, and Hillhouse are the best," the essay soon becomes an apology for seventeenth-century poetry and a celebration of the eighteenth-century prelude to the impending genius of his own day. American poetry had begun with its substance "very homely, the rhymes common the construction of the sentences unnatural; and the whole . . . without any claim to spirit or elegance." One poet "must have pleased his own generation"; another had a great contemporary reputation but left poetry "too poor to be quoted." Even Anne Bradstreet's "Contemplations" was described as "that which delighted our fathers, and is now acknowledged to be curious. . . ."[3] Less a retrospective critical estimate than a rallying cry for the poets of his own day, Bancroft's article functioned to assure his readers that American poetry had been getting better and better over the preceding two centuries and that the present time was ideal for writing the poetry that would surpass England's, that would finally be worthy of the most potentially poetic country in the world. This schema required that seventeenth-century poets be poorer than all their successors. The earliest American poetry, then, still occasioned apology. And, in 1829, Samuel Kettell merely continued the antiquarian approach by admitting in the introduction to his three-volume collection, *Specimens of American Poetry*, that although the "earliest attempts in the department of polite literature, must certainly be considered rude and feeble . . . they

. . . possess an interest arising from the curiosity we naturally feel to view the most ancient memorials of literary effort on record among us."[4]

In 1842, Rufus Griswold published *The Poets and Poetry of America*. A popular and influential work, it went through sixteen editions in thirteen years. Griswold claimed to have preserved in it all American poetry that deserved preservation and, unlike Hubbard Smith, wrote a long introduction explaining his exclusion of all poets prior to Freneau. He considered "the quaint and grotesque absurdities of Folger, Mather, and Wigglesworth" the best that Puritan poetry had to offer and assured his readers—after twenty pages packed two columns to a page with pontificatory dismissals—that "the poetry of the colonies was without originality, energy, feeling or correctness of diction."[5]

Yet not all critics of early American poetry have been such fools as Griswold. In 1878, Moses Coit Tyler, in the book with which all studies of American literature must still begin, agreed with the enduring notion that Puritanism precluded art:

> It will hardly be said that any typical Puritan of that century was a poetic personage. In proportion to his devotion to the ideas that won for him the derisive honor of his name, was he at war with nearly every form of the beautiful. He himself believed that there was an inappeasable feud between religion and art; and hence the duty of suppressing art was bound up in his soul with the master-purpose of promoting religion. He cultivated the grim and ugly.[6]

Tyler concluded that an "unconscious Manichaeism," a distrust of things natural, pervaded and helped to ruin Puritan poetry. For Anne Bradstreet it was "the fatal taint in all her poetical life" that she "drew her materials from books rather than from nature," a choice for which her fellow Puritans "gave to her their choicest praise, and called her, for this work, a painful poet; in which compliment every modern reader will cordially join." Puritanism also choked the poetry of Michael Wigglesworth, who possessed "the genius of a true poet" but "had given up to a narrow and a ferocious creed what was meant for mankind."[7]

If Puritan theology had effectually destroyed the substance of such poetry, English poetic precedent went far, Tyler thought, toward destroying its form. The Puritans had been influenced by Metaphysical poetry, "the most execrable form of poetry to which the English language was ever degraded," which had given Nicholas Noyes, among others, his "skill . . . at perfectly emptying his verses of the last atom of beauty, and at so packing them with quips, quibbles, conceits, and the most unexpected contortions of unlovely imagery, as to impart to them a sort of horrible fascination" at which "the reader writhes in pain and disgust." Tylor quite explicitly set forth the source of this second explanation for the failure of Puritan poetry: Anne Bradstreet had been "badly instructed by her literary guides," and later poets had failed by trying to write "the sort of poetry that . . . had been the fashion, both in England and in America—the degenerate euphuism of Donne, of Crashaw, of Quarles, of George Herbert."[8] Though Metaphysical poetry subsequently became quite respectable, Tyler's explanation was convincing at the time. Indeed, Tyler's criticism has come to seem paradigmatic in that he spent most of his time trying to account for the failure of Puritan poetry: he concluded that the Puritan was kept from poetry by his Manichaean theology and his degenerate English models.

Tyler published this estimate of Puritan poetry in 1878. It was little changed in 1927 when Kenneth Murdock published his introduction to *Handkerchiefs from Paul*, a brief collection of poems previously unpublished or long out of print.[9] Though he obviously considered the poems worth publishing, Murdock apparently felt that the occasion demanded apology more than explication. Noting "the literary deficiencies of New England," Murdock offered his edition with the disclaimer that its contents "deserve printing not for any appeal they can make to sophisticated students of *belles lettres*, but for their historical implications, for the sidelights they shed upon Puritan character and taste." In his evaluation of individual poems, moreover, Murdock apparently defined "historical implications" as historical information. In his evaluation of John Wilson's elegy on John Howard, Murdock followed a general complaint about the absence of biographical information on Howard with this summary evaluation: "The poem is disappointing in that it tells us so little that is specific in its eagerness to enlarge on general virtues."[10]

But Murdock's criterion seems misapplied: even good poems, read as history or biography, will read badly. We might just as well discredit *Lycidas* for not containing more specific information about Edward King or *In Quintum Novembris* because it tells us so little of Fawkes. And Murdock, like Tyler and perhaps like all students of literature, was limited by the aesthetic standards of his day, many of which seem almost as provincial to us as those of the Puritans seemed to their earliest critics. He wanted poetry to be "picturesque," and found the subjects of Puritan poetry unpoetic: "Brooks . . . fisheries, woodcutting, ice, and Indians and English 'by the ears' gathering the harvest of corn—these are homely things, and not as amenable, perhaps, to the uses of poetry as Herrick's 'Maypoles, Hockcarts, Wassails, Wakes,' or his visions of 'The Court of Mab and of the Fairy King.' " For Murdock, then, the Puritan poets had little to offer the historian and nothing to offer the lover of poetry. They lacked "the breath of that rare spirit which indefinably marks poetry" and could not measure up to the artistic standards set by such touchstones as "Phineas Fletcher's . . . *The Apollyonists*" or "the terse vigor of Cleveland's *Epitaph on the Earl of Strafford,* with its pregnant 'Here lies blood.' "[11] To a modern reader, "picturesqueness" and the choice of "poetic" subjects seem poor standards by which to judge poetry, and the works of Phineas Fletcher and John Cleveland seem something less than the zenith of poetic achievement.

But we cannot content ourselves with sniffing at Murdock's standards and dismissing his work. He appreciated, though he did not discuss, the power of Puritan poetry; he knew the federal theology well enough to know that it could not be as great a block to poetry as Tyler had contended; and in his attempt to find some way out of such contradictions, he created an enduring, though inaccurate, description of Puritan poetry. Murdock's sensibility was apparently superior to his standards, and he wrote of one poet: "If he falls short of picturesqueness, he does at least give us the flavor of the soil, and a sense of our nearness to those men who, for all their Puritanism and their remoteness in time, knew some aspects of American life and loved them and hated them, much as we do still." And he knew that it was "impossible to say that the mere fact that a man was a Puritan prevented his being a good poet." John Wilson, after all, had written no better as a professed Anglican "than he did when he became an ardent Puritan preacher in Boston." How then to explain the Puritan's failure to meet the standards set for good literature? Murdock's answer was that the Puritan considered poetry trivial. "The Puritan was not hostile to art, but he was relatively indifferent to it." His complete devotion to religion "thrust the arts into the realm of pastimes," and the Puritan's life was so devoted to the search for God that "there were few hours left for pastimes." Because he considered poetry trivial, the Puritan never bothered to distinguish good from bad poetry and "would not have known what to say if asked to compare a page of Milton with one of Sylvester's Du

Bartas."[12] Without mentioning that Milton himself admired Du Bartas, Murdock concluded that such admiration marked the American Puritans as poetic tyros who were kept from writing and appreciating good poetry.

Murdock declined to develop and support with evidence his conviction that Puritan theology did not preclude good poetry; he merely elaborated his belief that the Puritans wrote poor poetry because poetry was for them a pastime. The effect of his introduction, then, was to add one more item to the list of explanations for the poverty of Puritan poetry. He had denied that Puritan theology was inimical to the production of poetry, but he had made no case for this denial, and it was ignored by subsequent critics, who continued to base their dismissals of Puritan poetry on the belief that Puritan theology had stultified it.

The same year that Murdock published his apology for adding to the canon of American poetry, Vernon Louis Parrington chose, without apology, to omit from a book subtitled *An Interpretation of American Literature* any consideration of early American poetry. Instead, he chose "to follow the broad path of our political, economic, and social development, rather than the narrower belletristic."[13] And only a year after the publication of Murdock's book, F. O. Matthiessen wrote that Michael Wigglesworth was a "conscious artist" with "an instinctive sense of what the art of poetry should be" but that he and his fellow Puritans "wholly subordinated them [the arts] to a narrow creed" and that therefore "Michael Wigglesworth . . . stands as a symbol of their [the Puritans'] parched sterility. For when poetry is no more than a servant of theology, only the greatest of poets is likely to give his work the enduring character of the highest art."[14] Again some ill-defined aspect of Puritan theology had prevented the realization of a poet's considerable potential. The subordination of all things to "a narrow creed" had made all things other than

theology secondary, trivial. These critical estimates were based on
a body of poetry considerably smaller than that now available. In
this early canon, the poetry of Michael Wigglesworth loomed so
large as to seem typical. But a major addition to the canon of Puritan poetry was soon to be made available, an addition that should
have caused critics to revise their earlier descriptions.

In 1937, Thomas H. Johnson published in the *New England
Quarterly* some of the poems of Edward Taylor.[15] Though the
story of Johnson's discovery has since become famous, the addition of Taylor's works to the canon of Puritan poetry seems to
have had little immediate effect upon Johnson's contemporaries.
After reading Taylor, Johnson himself did challenge one of the
received formulas for describing Puritan poetry, the assertion by
Murdock and Matthiessen that the Puritans never produced lasting poetry because they considered poetry a trivial pastime. In the
first edition of *The Puritans* (1938), he likened the Puritan attitude toward poetry to those of "Spenser, Sidney, and Milton, the
real precursors of the lesser Puritan bards, . . . ethical poets" who
"conceived poetry as philosophy—the highest philosophy, in fact;
one which taught men virtue by example, not through mere didac-
ticism, but by the embodiment of every knowledge." Johnson
convincingly argued the necessity of distinguishing "between the
artistry they lacked, and the honor in which they held the poet's
high office."[16] For the Puritan, poetry was a medium for the discovery and dissemination of truth; as Johnson's evidence illustrates, the Puritans knew that truths expressed in artful poetry
were more likely to be read than those expressed in prose. Richard
Steere chose to set his beliefs "in the Attire of *Measure* and *Ca-
denc*y, whose even and easy Pace being more Alluring and Capti-
vating . . . than the Elaborate *Volumes* of *Prose* left to us by our
Worthy Ancestors, may probably the sooner . . . Invite thy Perus-

al." And Jonathan Mitchell quoted with approval from George Herbert's "Church Porch": "A Verse may find him who a Sermon flies." The man of God should therefore write poetry: "Great truths to dress in Meter; Becomes a Preacher." And he should practice this craft until he attains some skill. He should give his attention to manner as well as matter for "No Cost too great, no Care too curious is / To set forth Truth, and win mens Souls to bliss." The stakes in Puritan poetry, no less than in Puritan life, were limitlessly high. Poetry had its part to play in salvation history and was anything but trivial. Johnson concluded that no seventeenth-century American Puritan would have agreed with Addison's eighteenth-century "conception of poetry as a mental relaxation, an indulgence of the imagination. . . . Not until the eighteenth century did urbane appreciation of poetry as a social accomplishment supersede an enthusiasm for verse as a means of expressing great truths in exalted moods."[17]

Though Johnson had laid the ghost of triviality, he did not allow his reading of Taylor to alter his acceptance of other formulas concerning Puritan poetry. Like some of his predecessors, he found Puritan theology somehow inimical to poetry. Unlike them, he specified the hindrance: the Puritans had no poetic use for the things of this world. "The Anglican poets juxtaposed the flesh and the spirit. . . . But for the Puritans, and especially for those who came to New England, God, not the world, inspired their 'noble numbers.' "[18] In the 1963 edition of *The Puritans*, Johnson changed his introduction to the section on Taylor to exempt him from the standard generalizations on Puritan poetry. The otherworldly poetry lacked the vitality of Taylor's, for "what gave vitality to such poems by Taylor . . . is the intensity of his love for the world God made," an "intensity [which] involved something of a dilemma for the colonial Puritan who happened to be a poet." Taylor's love for this world, in Johnson's view, was less Puritan than it was Catholic or Anglican. That such poetry, "quite literally redolent of altar incense, overleaped the limits of the doctrines he professed, must account in large part for his injunction that his heirs should never publish his verses."[19] We now have reason to doubt that such an injunction ever existed and reason to believe that Taylor was not nearly so unorthodox and unique as those wishing to exempt him from generalizations about Puritan poetry have long asserted.[20]

Subsequent critics, however, were not immediately sensitive to these difficulties. Ignoring Johnson's assertion that the Puritans had not considered poetry trivial, they worked variations on his statement that the constellation of ideas labelled "Puritanism" could not produce lasting poetry, at least from orthodox Puritans. In 1939, Perry Miller carefully excluded literary concerns from his discussion of the "New England Mind": "There is no occasion in this study for a review of Puritan literature; it is enough to point out that the authors of that literature, who in most cases were divines, did not conceive of themselves as writing in literary genres." True enough. Although many divines considered verse a necessary part of their ministry or meditation, most Puritan writers had no sense of themselves as litterateurs: and Miller is certainly entitled to define the limits of his own book, though over two hundred New England minds did in fact busy themselves with writing poetry. Miller justifies his exclusion by briefly examining explicit statements of Puritan poetics, quite rightly finding them wanting, and stating that, because of their openly utilitarian poetic theory, their poetic practice is not susceptible to literary analysis, is in fact worthy of no analysis. He concludes "that any criticism which endeavors to discuss Puritan writings as part of literary history, which seeks to estimate them from any 'aesthetic' point of view, is approaching the materials in a spirit they were never intended to accommodate, and is in danger of concluding with pronouncements which are wholly irrelevant to the designs and motives of the writers." The designs of the writers, are, for Miller, the most reliable paradigm for studying their writings. Since the Puritans studied Ramus, and since Ramists considered rhetoric merely the decoration of dialectic by addition of arbitrary figures and tropes, the Puritans must have used their metaphors merely to decorate axioms. For Miller's Puritans, then, poetry was still trivial; its metaphors were "creations of fancy,"[21] a faculty esteemed even less by the Puritans than by Coleridge. Miller neither apologized for Puritan poetry nor studied it for its expression of at least part of the New England mind; he dismissed it.

Harold Jantz in 1944 neither apologized for Puritan poetry nor dismissed it. He published a collection of previously unavailable Puritan poetry and wrote a long introduction to explain his reasons for doing so. Consciously taking the tone of a spirited advocate, he insisted that "our patronizing attitude" toward Puritan poetry derived from the retrospective imposition of our own critical standards upon the work of poets who had no intention of meeting such standards. To appreciate Puritan poetry, Jantz argued, we must achieve a certain aesthetic relativism and try to read the poetry as a Puritan would have. For Jantz, however, this tolerant relativism demanded that the modern reader learn to love anagrams. About John Fiske, for example, Jantz discovered that "once the basic understanding of his poetic intent was achieved it suddenly became clear that there was a true master of a remarkable technique"; his poetic intent was "to divine an appropriate anagram from the name of the person to be celebrated, take this anagram as the basic theme and develop his poem contrapuntally about it." Jantz admits that "for a person coming fresh from romantic poetry, this does not seem poetic at all, but dull, monotonous and repetitious"; he encourages, however, a suspension of disbelief based on one's own critical standards and insists that one must achieve such a suspension to appreciate Puritan poetry. Jantz had neatly reversed Miller's use of the intentional fallacy, and his defense implied a tacit admission that Puritan poetry, though it surely pleased the Puritans, had little to offer an unregenerately modern reader.[22]

Later criticism of Puritan poetry worked less to complete or refute these early works than to elaborate on them, or accommodate new evidence to fit them. In 1949, Murdock summarized many of the prevailing attitudes toward Puritan poetry. He wrote that "the principles which Puritan authors chose to follow . . . commonly prevented their achieving artistic successes comparable to those of religious writers of other schools of thought," that chief among these principles was avoidance of appeals to the senses. Murdock considered applicable to the Puritans Lord David Cecil's description of the Christian poet who "will allow himself to express only unexceptionable sentiments, love, reverence, humility. . . . As for using any but the most decorous language, the very idea horrifies him." This horror of the sensuous appeal explained why "it would be useless to hunt for a Puritan poet who could write, as the Catholic Crashaw did, of the wounds on Christ's feet as mouths with full-bloomed lips to be kissed with rapture. The Puritan would say that such imagery would so stir the sensual in man as to blind him to anything spiritual in the poem." Appeals to the senses were dangerous, were apt to distract one's audience from the spiritual to the physical. Ignoring Johnson's distinction between the seventeenth-century American concept of poetry as a compelling utterance of truth and the eighteenth-century concept of poetry as intellectual relaxation or recreation, Murdock quoted Cotton Mather's famous statement of the triviality and dangers of poetry—published in 1726 and expressive of the later Addisonian notion of poetry. In his *Manductio ad Ministerium*

Mather advised young ministers to "make a little *Recreation* of *Poetry* in the midst of your more painful Studies," but not to take poetry seriously: "Let not what should be *Sauce* rather than *Food* for you, Engross all your Application." Murdock stated that Mather's warning "sums up admirably earlier Puritan attitudes toward poetry." For Murdock's Puritans, then, much contemporary Anglican or Catholic poetry "seemed to him [the Puritan] too sensuously evocative, dealing too boldly with material that was 'Passionate' [quoting Mather's *Manductio*] enough to kindle dangerous fires in the human breast." Murdock's Puritan avoided such material in his own poetry. If a poet, such as Edward Taylor, used sensuous and even sensual material in describing spiritual states, he must have been somehow more Catholic than Puritan, and Murdock aided in the long tradition of preserving the critical formulas on Puritanism by exempting Edward Taylor from them. Taylor was unorthodox; he feared his "erotically suggestive imagery would offend his graver colleagues"; indeed Taylor's selection of "imagery richest in color and in sensuous or even erotic effect, and his use . . . of the Song of Solomon more often than any other book in the Bible, suggest that as a poet he unconsciously moved away from the relative asceticism of the Puritan toward the Catholic acceptance of the role of the senses in worship."[23] Murdock's book, though it contained fine readings of individual poems, reinforced the theory that Puritan poetry was deficient in imagery because Puritans distrusted the senses, found them the source of hindrances and distractions. The gap between spirit and matter, grace and nature, God and man was too great to be bridged by metaphor, which would only lead man away from God. Puritan poetry had to concentrate therefore on spiritual matters and utter them in abstract language.

This theory has since become a commonplace of American literary criticism. It was repeated and expanded by Stanley T. Williams in 1951. Williams found Wigglesworth, whose scorn for the world and all things carnal is easily documented, the typical Puritan poet.[24] He imputed to the Puritans a poetic theory that "meant the banishment from verse . . . of human passion, human comradeship and the sensuous love of nature." This theory forced him to make exceptions of both Edward Taylor and Anne Bradstreet, who was able "to disengage practice from theory by using in her poetry the everyday stuff of her life in New England."[25] Though Williams had repeated a description of Puritan poetry that left him with one typical poet and two exceptions, he could rest assured that critical opinion was on his side. Despite increasing contradictory evidence, it would remain so.

In 1953, Charles Feidelson presented much of that evidence and went far toward revising that opinion. He recognized that the Puritans were typologists, that they saw certain persons and events of the Old Testament as types, or prefigurations, of persons or events in the New Testament. Thus Adam, David, and Joshua were all types of Jesus, their antitype. The deliverances from Egypt and Babylon prefigured the deliverance of the Church from the Antichrist. Puritans extended this symbolic mode of thinking to their perception of their own experiences. John Winthrop recorded in his journal that during a sermon before the synod at Cambridge a snake crawling behind the pulpit was killed by one of the elders. Since this, like all events, was "by divine providence, it is out of doubt," wrote Winthrop, that "the Lord discovered somewhat of his mind in it." For Winthrop, the spiritual interpretation of this physical event was clear enough. "The serpent is the devil; the synod, the representative of the churches of Christ in New England. The devil had formerly and lately attempted their disturbance and dissolution; but their faith in the seed of woman overcame him and crushed his head." A similarly symbolic account appears in Sewall's diary. Some hail broke the windows of Sewall's house, and Cotton Mather was on hand to provide the spiritual interpretation. God had sent the hail to break one frail dwelling of man so that man would prepare for the breaking of another dwelling, the body. Feidelson recognized that such language expressed a symbolic view of the world, "Within, not superadded to, such happenings was constitutive language; the devil-serpent and the body-house took shape and were experienced as radical metaphors made by God."[26] But Feidelson was concerned primarily with nineteenth-century American literature and remained convinced that Puritan poetry was merely a tissue of rhymed abstractions.

Though Feidelson recognized that the Puritans perceived "a vital symbolism in everyday experience," he argued that their theology and assumptions about language kept them from realizing this symbolism in their literature. He first generalized that "the symbols themselves were meager, for the mental economy of the Puritans gave little scope for aesthetic realization of the natural world." Then, quoting some of Cotton Mather's most adventitious attempts at wit as typical of Puritan literature, he imputed the bad wit of Mather to "a fundamental limitation in the Puritan views of knowledge and language. A properly symbolic method was denied the Puritan writer by his assumptions on method in general. Aquinas held that things have multiple meaning and that language is at one with the structure of reality. The Puritans made a drastic break with this Catholic tradition." For the Puritans, "the only realistic form of language was logical" and the "truth of Scripture was not aesthetic but propositional." Feidelson then equated the concept of propositional language with the much broader concept of substance or dialectic; he equated the symbolic correspondences perceived by the Puritans with rhetoric or trope; he then cited the Ramist doctrine that dialectic contains all truth and that rhetoric is merely ornament. By substitution, these elegant equations reduced to the surprising conclusion that the Puritans considered the symbolic correspondences they saw in life nothing more than man-made ornament when transferred to poetry. Feidelson concluded that "this ornamentalism effectually destroyed the Puritan sense of artistic coherence."[27]

Though his work was far more sophisticated and valuable than that of his predecessors, Feidelson came to conclusions remarkably similar to theirs. He cited Samuel Mather's warning—that "it is not safe to make anything a type merely upon our own fancies and imaginations; it is *Gods* Prerogative to make *Types*"—and concluded from it that "the Puritan typologist was afraid of the types, or rather of the symbolic thinking necessary to perceive them. . . ." Now being afraid to usurp God's job of *making* types is not quite the same as being afraid to *see* them, "to perceive them," and if the Puritans really were afraid of perceiving types, their literature records matchless and consistent courage in conquering that fear. But the Puritans did not make the conflations that Feidelson made for them. They distinguished clearly between, in Feidelson's terms, "radical metaphors made by God" and mere "ornamentalism" made by man. They objected to the strained conceits of Anglican high style and considered them artificial. But they believed in the system of correspondences immanent in God's world and *seen*, not made, by Puritan poets.

Feidelson started, then, on the road toward a better appreciation of Puritan poetry. But that was not the road he himself wished to travel, and he concluded, as had his predecessors, that the Puritans' negative attitude toward the visible world had wrecked their poetry. They had dealt with "a world of sheer abstractions certified as 'real.'" The man to whom only abstractions are real may write philosophy but he cannot write poetry, so "Calvinistic Protestantism . . . had the effect of invalidating the organic structure of poetry and nullifying the organic world of experience that poetry claims to render."[28] Again, curiously enough, the Puritan had been kept from poetry by his conviction that the concrete visible world was unreal and meaningless, even though he perceived that world as a system of "radical metaphors made by God," metaphors which should have linked the visible world to its Maker and thereby have given it meaning.

A similar refusal to follow out the full poetic implications of the Puritan world view occurred in 1963 with the publication of Ursula Brumm's account of the influence of typology on American thought. Though her explication of Puritan typology increased our understanding of the Puritan mind, she insisted on limiting the applications of this typology. She explained that in the seventeenth century, Puritanism "was an intellectual movement decidedly hostile to images and symbols. Symbols were cause of extreme discomfort and even anger to true Puritans, and this holds not only for the symbols of the Catholic Church, including the cross, but for any symbolic representations of religious doctrine whatever." For the seventeenth-century Puritan, wrote Brumm, all types were fulfilled in Christ and all typology stopped with him.[29] According to Brumm, Cotton Mather was a radical innovator in his *Magnalia Christi Americana*, published in 1702: "He extends the notion of typical prefiguration from the New Testament to secular history." Before that time, no such extension was made. Neither history nor the material world gave man a bridge to understand the mind of God. Brumm's "true" Puritan, then could not have seen or uttered the world as type, could not have "spiritualized" his images by noting that they had spiritual as well as material significance.

That Edward Taylor clearly did so indicates to Brumm only that he was not quite a "true" Puritan: "Taylor's fantasy bursts the confines of Puritan sobriety and . . . Taylor yields to an imagery . . . intended to render God's glory visible." Taylor's spiritualization of all images far surpasses what the Puritans considered theologically permissible." Taylor did not publish, wrote Brumm, because he knew that "he would surely have aroused the ire of his fellow theologians, who would have condemned his rich sensual imagery and his radical spiritualization as the latest form of idolatry."[30] Puritanism was still inimical to poetry, and since Taylor was unquestionably a poet, he must have been something other than a "true" Puritan, an unconscious Catholic perhaps.

Of late, literary historians have taken to following the methods and repeating the conclusions of intellectual historians. In 1960, Leon Howard published a history of American literature and thought, which he prefaced with the commonplace that "the first two centuries of America . . . produced little pure literature in the conventional sense of the word" and that therefore he would discuss the literature of this period by following "the pattern of what is often called intellectual history" instead of "literary interpretation."[31]

Other literary critics have recently advanced criticism of Puritan poetry by attempting to view it, not in contrast to later American verse, but as part of the great sweep of American literature. In such writings, the old argument that Puritan theology somehow prevented the writing of poetry was revivified and made specific. The Puritans had been denied poetry by their belief that man could make nothing, that all things needful had already been made, and by their contempt for the things of this world, snares and distractions which, if attended to, would lead them away from their dutiful contemplation of the next. The first argument was put forward in 1961 by Roy Harvey Pearce, the second in 1968 by Hyatt Waggoner.

"An account of the development of American poetry from the seventeenth century to the recent past," Roy Harvey Pearce's

The Continuity of American Poetry records an attempt to find
the gossamer thread that holds together the apparently discontinu-
ous progress of American poetry. Calling this common element
"a curious antinomianism" or the "Adamic impulse," Pearce placed
Puritans, Augustan wits, men of the American Renaissance, and
moderns in a single enormous procession. Whatever their super-
ficial differences, they were all American poets joined in a common task: "The American poet, in his dedication to the idea of
the dignity of man, has had as his abiding task the reconciliation
of the impulse to freedom with the impulse to community, as the
use of language in poetry may help bring it about."[32] American
poetry, then, is essentially an antinomian claim for the complete
freedom of the individual coupled with the claim that the universal attainment of such freedom will bring about not anarchy but
community. Needless to say, this idea conflicts with the orthodox Puritan beliefs in "family governance" and the communal
covenant.

Though Pearce's definition of the antinomian impulse would
become increasingly broad and flexible later in his book, the opposition between poetry and Puritan doctrine was here quite explicit. "American poetry is the history of an impulse toward antinomianism." As Anne Hutchinson discovered, Puritans would
not tolerate antinomianism. The Puritan poet, therefore, had a
problem. According to Pearce he solved it temporarily "by deciding that as an individual he could make or do nothing, that all
depended upon God. He made poems, surely. But he did his best
to make them in such a way that he could declare—if anyone
thought to ask him—that *he* had not really made them." Though
he did not say so, it follows from Pearce's statement that the
Puritan poet would say that God had made the poem in His two
revelations, Scripture and nature, and that the poet had merely
seen it there and uttered it. But Pearce did not develop this line

of reasoning; instead, he concluded, as had so many before him, that one could not be a Puritan and a poet, that to be a poet, one must be an antinomian: "Antinomianism will out, if only because the making of poems demands that the poet, in spite of all his beliefs to the contrary, be a maker. Saying this, we surely gainsay Taylor and the others."[33] We surely do. In fact, we ignore their own attitudes toward nature and language and impose upon them our notion of poem as artifact, a notion they would have considered idolatrous. Given his definitions, then, Pearce was certainly correct to conclude that orthodox Puritans could not write his kind of poetry. One must, therefore, give up either Puritan poetry or Pearce's definitions.

Hyatt Waggoner gave up Pearce's definitions. In his preface to *American Poets from the Puritans to the Present*, he contrasted his own intent with Pearce's: "I didn't want to produce a 'thesis' book which would rate and classify the poets according to a contemporary ideology foreign to their own outlooks and poetic purposes. (A work which seemed to me to do just this, R. H. Pearce's *The Continuity of American Poetry*, had been published in 1961.)" Waggoner resolved to read Puritan poetry in contexts suggested by the poetry itself rather than imposing on it patterns and values derived from the study of later American poets. At one point he asserted quite convincingly that "to the reader of poetry who wishes to share the values of the poetry he reads, as he must if he is to enter into it and let it enter him . . . theology is not irrelevant to his judgment of the poetry." Then "the realization of Emerson's centrality [to American poetry] came to me."[34] Emerson was central to American poetry, and the Puritans were to be read and judged by comparison with Emerson. Waggoner argued convincingly that the Puritans did not do a very good job of anticipating Emerson.

Waggoner imputed to Puritan theology an attitude which—

were it really held—would indeed make poetry impossible. The Puritans, wrote Waggoner, denied the created world. Their "theology . . . is thoroughly world-denying," and "their very nearly Gnostic dualism of spirit and flesh, good and evil, God and the world" prevented their using metaphor to concretize their experience, prevented their reading nature for images of its Maker.[35] Poetry is incarnational; the Puritans were not, as evidenced in "the otherworldliness of Puritan poetry." Arguing from a few examples of bad Puritan poetry, Waggoner concluded that "the general feature of the first century of New England verse is that it tells us almost nothing of the concrete, existential experience of people, places, or things. For this, the kind of thing that poetry can do best, we generally have to go to prose—and even that is not usually very rewarding." Citing Thomas Tillam's "Upon the first Sight of New England," Waggoner noted quite accurately: "What we get from reading it is not any sight of the new land, or any insight into what the experience of sighting it must have been like, except that it produced a sense of thankfulness; what we get is only religious abstractions."[36] From Puritan poetry, then, Waggoner got no sense of the concrete visible world. He got only "religious abstractions."

But Waggoner did pose the problem precisely in the terms in which it must be examined. Gnostic *contemptus mundi* may produce systematic theology: it cannot produce poetry. And rhymed "religious abstractions," however valid their interest for the historian, are not compelling literature. So far we can agree with Waggoner. We can even agree that many Puritans were poor poets and did in fact write verse that was little more than conventional abstractions. But we need not agree that these poor poets were compelled by their theology to write poor poetry or that good Puritan poetry, of which there is a substantial amount, is adequately described in Waggoner's categories. To disparage seventeenth-century American poetry because the bad poets outnumbered the good ones is no more just than to disparage contemporary American poetry by citing the newspaper poets.

The number of good Puritan poets, as I have attempted to suggest in this study, is far larger than has been realized. Even in admirable recent studies of Bradstreet and Taylor, critics have tended to read them *in vacuo*, to make these fine poets exceptions to a Puritan rule derived from precisely the critical generalizations chronicled here and tested in Chapter 1. Hence Ann Stanford depicts Anne Bradstreet as a rebel against Puritan orthodoxy, as the only "worldly Puritan," and Karl Keller, in a book that remains excellent so long as he centers on Taylor, mistakenly argues that other Puritans wrote little poetry (as Tyler noted, they wrote a remarkable amount) before agreeing with Waggoner and others that they suspected the senses and the world too much to write anything other than religious tenets: "To read the poetry is not to become acquainted with why the Puritans wrote but why they wrote so little verse. In its suspicion of the pleasures of the senses, man's creative efforts, and the world as a whole, it is evidence against the value of its own existence." Again, we are told that because they denied the physical world, Puritans could not write poetry. "Their poetry was an expression of tenets." But Taylor was an exception who so loved the world that he alone could write real, concrete, metaphoric poetry: "They therefore became dull apologists and he became a real poet."[37] This refusal to consider the context provided by other Puritan poets not only limits our readings of Bradstreet and Taylor; it also dismisses a great deal of Puritan poetry that is interesting and important in inself, that is considerably more than "religious abstractions."

In his study of all of American poetry, then, Waggoner has performed a service to criticism in accurately summarizing and restating the generalizations we have studied here. Though Waggoner's book was published in 1968, little has changed of our general view of the world and the flesh in Puritan poetry, as is clear from Michael Zuckerman's statement in June of 1977 that "the people of Plymouth and Massachusetts Bay believed that nature everywhere was corrupt and had to be subdued," and from John Seelye's earlier that year: "Most Puritan poets were preachers, so this limitation and emphasis is not surprising, and the effect was to promote the combination of concentricity and transcendentalism which is endemic to sermon literature, resulting in a poetic walling-out of the New World landscape, metric masonry reinforcing the closed theocratic view."[38] Like many of his predecessors and successors, Waggoner was researching another subject and left Puritan poetry much as he found it. Nevertheless, he has given us the clearest summation of the common view, and his generalizations represent the current state of the argument.

Notes

INTRODUCTION:
Puritanism and Poetry

1. John Cotton, preface to *The Whole Booke of Psalms Faithfully Translated into English Metre*, usually called the *Bay Psalm Book* (Cambridge, Mass.: Stephen Daye, 1640), *passim*. Though the preface was long attributed to Richard Mather, Zoltan Harazti has convincingly argued that John Cotton actually wrote it. See *The Enigma of the Bay Psalm Book* (Chicago: University of Chicago Press, 1956), pp. 19–27. In transcribing these quotations from Cotton, I have expanded his contractions and replaced his spelling with modern spelling but retained his capitalization, punctuation, and italicization. I shall do the same in transcribing all quotations from Puritan prose. Since some Puritan poets were fond of eye-rhymes and visual puns, Puritan poetry will, unless otherwise noted, be quoted exactly as it appears in the source used.

2. Thomas H. Johnson, in *The Puritans*, ed. Perry Miller and Thomas H. Johnson, rev. ed. (New York: Harper and Row, 1963), II:556.

3. John Dryden, *An Essay of Dramatic Poesy*, in *Selected Poetry and Prose of John Dryden*, ed. Earl Miner (New York: Random House, 1969), p. 97.

4. *The Second Part of Absalom and Achitophel*, lines 402–403, in Miner, p. 257.

5. David M. Vieth, ed., *The Complete Poems of John Wilmot, Earl of Rochester* (New Haven: Yale University Press, 1968), p. 22. Vieth notes that by the late seventeenth century, Sternhold and Hopkins had become "a byword for bad poetry."

6. Quoted in Miller and Johnson, II: 556.

7. Cotton Mather, *Magnalia Christi Americana, or The Ecclesiastical History of New England, In Seven Books* (1702), ed. Thomas Robbins (Hartford, Conn.: Silas Andrus, 1855), II: 406.

8. Miller and Johnson, II: 548.

9. For a discussion of this chronological development, see the appendix, "In Critic's Hands."

I The World's Body

1. Allan I. Ludwig, *Graven Images: New England Stone-Carving and Its Symbols, 1650–1815* (Middletown, Conn.: Wesleyan University Press, 1966), *passim*. Quotations are from pp. 44 and 3. See also Dickran and Ann

Tashjian, *Memorials for Children of Change: The Art of Early New England Stonecarving* (Middletown, Conn.: Wesleyan University Press, 1974), esp. pp. 3–9, 232–233. For the wide variety of Puritan reactions to religious imagery in England, see John Phillips, *The Reformation of Images: Destruction of Art in England, 1535–1660* (Berkeley: University of California Press, 1973).

2. Marian Card Donnelly, *The New England Meeting Houses of the Seventeenth Century* (Middletown Conn.: Wesleyan University Press, 1968), p. 107. She quotes Johnson on p. 102.

3. Moses Coit Tyler, *A History of American Literature 1607–1765* (1878; rpt. Ithaca, New York: Cornell University Press, 1949), pp. 227–228.

4. These characterizations have been quoted at greater length in the appendix and are from Tyler, p. 228; Thomas H. Johnson, *The Puritans*, ed. Perry Miller and Thomas H. Johnson (New York: American Book Company, 1938), p. 546; and Hyatt H. Waggoner, *American Poets: From the Puritans to the Present* (Boston: Houghton Mifflin, 1968), pp. 14–15.

5. Anne Bradstreet, "Contemplations," in *The Works of Anne Bradstreet*, ed. Jeannine Hensley (Cambridge, Mass.: Harvard University Press, 1967), pp. 205–206. All further quotations from Bradstreet are from this edition. Page numbers appear in parentheses.

6. Both terms imply a hatred and distrust of the material, sensible world. Gnostics despised the sensible world, many of them contending that it was the creation of a decidedly inferior deity named Ialdabaoth, whom the Jews mistakenly worshipped as Yahweh. They believed that all things visible, including the sun and stars, were creations of this essentially evil spirit and that, among earthly things, only the soul of man had any goodness. Manichaeism was the belief that God ruled only half the universe, the good half. All goodness resided in spirit. The Devil ruled the material universe, and the evil principle was embodied in matter. The American Puritans were, of course, neither Gnostics nor Manichaeans.

7. Wood's *New Englands Prospect* (London, 1634) is cited from *Seventeenth-Century American Poetry*, ed. Harrison T. Meserole (New York: New York University Press, 1968), pp. 399–401. Unless otherwise noted, all citations of minor Puritan poets are from this anthology and will be identified in the text in parentheses.

8. See Meserole, pp. 413–419.

9. The exact nature and extent of Steere's Puritanism remain open to question. In a court brief defending liberty of conscience for all Protestants, he identifies himself with Puritan Dissenters in England but with Baptists in America. Yet there was no Baptist church in New London at the time Steere lived there, and we know that, unlike many other Baptists, he always paid the minister's rate to support the Congregationalist (later Presbyterian) establishment. His editor and biographer, Donald P. Wharton, has said that although Steere'e Puritanism, in the general sense, was quite real, he was throughout his life in America a man without a church. In any event, his

poetry and poetics are very like those of people who we know were Puritans. For that reason, I include in this discussion both his poetry and this caveat, pending the discovery of new information that may enable us to settle the issue. For a clear discussion of nearly all that we now know about Steere, see Donald P. Wharton, "*Novus Homo*: The Life of Richard Steere (1643–1721), to Which Is Added, an Edition of His Complete Poetry and Major Prose" (Diss., Pennsylvania State University 1976). For an account of Steere's part in the Rogerene affair, see Donald P. Wharton, "The Poet as Protester: Richard Steere's 1695 Defense of Liberty of Conscience," *Seventeenth-Century News* 34 (Summer-Fall 1976): 46–50.

10. Edwards's brief essay on the beauty of the world was not published in his lifetime. It is quoted from Perry Miller's edition, *Images or Shadows of Divine Things* (New Haven: Yale University Press, 1948), p. 135.

11. Joseph Crouch, *Puritanism and Art: An Inquiry into a Popular Fallacy* (London: Cassell, 1910), p. 366.

12. Kenneth B. Murdock, *Literature and Theology in Colonial New England* (Cambridge, Mass.: Harvard University Press, 1949), pp. 38, 49.

13. Thomas Taylor, *A Man in Christ, or: A new* CREATURE. To which *is added a Treatise, containing Meditations from the* CREATURES (London: Printed for *I. Bartlet* at the gilt Cup in *Cheapeside*, 1628), pp. 2–3, 5–8, 19, 83.

14. Roger Williams, *The Complete Writings of Roger Williams*, I—*A Key into the Language of America*, ed. James H. Trumbull (New York: Russell and Russell, 1963), p. 46. All further references to the *Key* (1643) are to this edition and will be identified in the text.

15. Ludwig, pp. 155–156.

16. Thomas Hooker, *The Soules Exaltation. A Treatise Containing The Soules Union with Christ, on I Cor. 6. 17. The Soules Benefit from Union with Christ, on I Cor. 1. 30. The Soules Justification, on 2 Cor. 5. 21* (London: Printed by *John Haviland*, for *Andrew Crooke*, and are to be sold at the black Beare in *S. Pauls* Church-yard, 1638). The three treatises are paginated consecutively. *The Soules Union* is quoted from pp. 3, 5–6, *The Soules Benefit* from p. 59.

17. From the fifteenth century on, "ravish" and "rape" (though both had other meanings) were synonymous in that either implied both transport (being taken up and carried away) and sexual knowledge. (*OED*)

18. Samuel Willard, *A Compleat Body of Divinity in Two Hundred and Fifty Expository Lectures on the Assembly's Shorter Catechism* (Boston: B. Green and S. Kneeland, 1726), pp. 876–879. Though Willard's' lectures were not published until 1726, nineteen years after his death, they were given at Old South Church, beginning in January 1688, and are therefore the public statements of an orthodox seventeenth-century Puritan minister.

19. For other uses of sensual imagery to figure spiritual tenors, see Calvin's *Institutes*, IV, xvii, 1–10; Thomas Hooker, *The Soul's Implantation* (London, 1637), pp. 233, 253, and *The Soul's Vocation or Effectual Calling*

(London, 1638), pp. 238–239; and Richard Sibbes, *Works* (Edinburgh, 1862–1864), I: 47, 59, 265, and IV: 181, 198: Karl Keller, "The Rev. Mr. Edward Taylor's Bawdry," *New England Quarterly* 43 (September 1970): 382–407.

20. René Wellek and Austin Warren, *Theory of Literature*, 3rd ed. (New York: Harcourt, Brace and World, 1956), p. 186.

21. Erich Auerbach, "Figura," in *Scenes from the Drama of European Literature* (New York: Meridian Books, 1959), pp. 54, 29, 57.

22. I. A. Richards, *Principles of Literary Criticism* (London, 1924), quoted in Wellek and Warren, p. 187.

23. Wellek and Warren, pp. 188–189.

24. Ursula Brumm, *American Thought and Religious Typology*, trans. John Hoagland (New Brunswick, New Jersey: Rutgers University Press, 1970), pp. 8–9.

25. Wellek and Warren, p. 188.

26. Ludwig, p. 109.

27. *Ibid.*, pp. 67, 85, 121, 216, 261.

28. Perry Miller has recognized the similarity between the Puritan habit of "seeking out the wisdom of God in the creatures" and the Emersonian habit of reading every natural fact for its spiritual significance: "Emerson dedicated Transcendentalism to a new preoccupation with the old symbolism of nature and the correspondence of the thing and the word, the object and the spirit." There were, of course, differences: for Emerson, idea created or ordered correspondent material fact. For the Puritans, the correspondences were created by God as an act of loving condescension to man's limited faculties. But for both Emerson and the Puritans, nature could be read for its spiritual significance. Miller concluded that for the Puritans "Every single fact was a symbol, not only of the law governing things, but of the laws of the spirit. It is truly strange that the generation of Emerson and Alcott should have had to go to Emmanuel Swedenborg for a doctrine of 'correspondence,' since something remarkably like it had been embedded in their own tradition for two hundred years" (*The New England Mind: The Seventeenth Century* [1939; rpt. Cambridge, Mass.: Harvard University Press, 1954], pp. 163, 213).

29. John Milton, *Paradise Lost*, Book III, lines 574–575, in *John Milton: Complete Poems and Major Prose*, ed. Merritt Y. Hughes (New York: The Odyssey Press, 1957), p. 272.

30. "At Joshua's command (Josh. X 12–13) the sun stood still and thus became Copernican in the sense that it did not revolve about the earth. Solstice means literally 'to cause the sun to stand still' " (Meserole's note).

31. Edward Taylor, Meditation 34, Second Series, in *The Poems of Edward Taylor*, ed. Donald E. Stanford (New Haven: Yale University Press, 1960), p. 144. It is clear that other poets often praised the world and that Taylor occasionally renounced it. He was hardly an exception to the Puritan rule, at least in his attitude toward the sensible world.

32. Like most Puritans, Bradstreet used the terms "emblem" and "type" interchangeably, meaning by them what I have defined as symbol. Emblem books entered "England from the Continent during the reign of Elizabeth and remained popular until the end of the seventeenth century" (Ludwig, p. 240). Popular on both sides of the Atlantic throughout the seventeenth century, they were one source for the imagery on New England gravestones. "Borrowing from broadsides was far more popular in New England than copying from the more erudite emblem books, although upon occasion themes were taken from them" (Ludwig, p. 274). Some stonecarvers copied emblems directly from Quarles and Wither, and some poets treated themes also treated by emblem books. At this point, it is tempting to assert that Puritan poets relied on emblem books as visual referents for some of their images, but I have found no convincing evidence that they did so. In his dissertation, Thomas E. Johnston, Jr. mentioned the popularity of emblem books (there were at least nine published in England by 1635) and devoted a chapter to Edward Taylor as "An American Emblematist." But he offered no evidence that Taylor relied directly on the emblem books themselves, rather than on traditional biblical and iconographic imagery. Not a single symbol is illuminated by reference to its counterpart in an emblem book. Not a single image is any clearer or more complex for our having found similarities between it and an image in a contemporary emblem book. (See Johnston, "American Puritan Poetic Voices: Essays on Anne Bradstreet, Edward Taylor, Roger Williams, and Philip Pain" [Diss. Ohio University 1968], pp. 44–64.) Unable to better Johnston's record at finding emblems in Puritan poetry, I have concluded that the emblematic tradition—perhaps because it was not nearly so standardized and universal a tradition in seventeenth-century New England as it was in seventeenth- and eighteenth-century England—did not stand behind and does not illuminate Puritan poetry. Instead of adopting the specific images of the emblem books, the Puritans appear to have imputed to God the emblematist's method of illustrating truths and to have read the sensible world as an emblem for God's truth, the verbal description of which is set down in the Bible.

Particular similarities do of course exist. In an engraving from Francis Quarles's *Hieroglyphics of the Life of Man* (London, 1638), Death carries an arrow and is about to snuff out the candle of a man's life. This scene was repeated with nearly photographic similarity on the stones of Joseph Tapping, Boston 1678, and John Foster, Dorchester 1681 (Ludwig, plates 14 and 15). And Edward Taylor, who explicitly mentioned emblem painters in Meditation 34, First Series (Stanford, p. 55) and in Meditation 112, Second Series (p. 287), devoted a poem to "Death's arrow shot at me" (pp. 286–287). What could be clearer than a tidy and illuminating line of influence? Two things.

First, the emblematists took much of their imagery from the Bible. Man's life is a candle to be snuffed out in Job 18:6 and 21:7 and in Proverbs 24:20. Death has hurled his arrows throughout much of the Bible, notably in

Deuteronomy 32:23 and 32:42. Other imagery was standard in medieval iconography. If a Puritan poet used an image quite similar to one used in an emblem book, then, the chances are just as good that both got it from a common source as that the poet got it from the emblem book. Second, reference to an appropriate emblem never illuminates the poem. It is clear that in Taylor's "Upon a Spider Catching a Fly" (pp. 464–465) the spider figured Satan's catching souls. Taylor made the comparison explicitly. As Rosemary Freeman, in her *English Emblem Books* (London: Chatto and Windus, 1948), has pointed out (without reference to Taylor), an emblem of Quarles's made the same point (p. 121). Bringing the two together is an easy operation, and Taylor may well have seen the emblem. But his poem is completely independent of the emblem, completely clear without it, and the reference tells us nothing of the poem. In the emblem books, themselves, poems often accompanied emblems and were dependent on them. As Norman Grabo has noted, an emblem-book "poem so required the picture that it was often unintelligible without it" (*Edward Taylor* [New Haven: Twayne, 1961], p. 154). This is certainly not true of Puritan poems. Unlike some of his English contemporaries, the Puritan poet did not allude to a rich visual tradition of standard emblems, the study of which would illuminate his poetry. His God may have been an emblematist, but he was not. See also Chapter 5, footnote 20.

For more information on emblems and for an annotated bibliography of emblem books, see Mario Praz, *Studies in Seventeenth-Century Imagery*, 2nd ed. (Rome: Edizioni di Storia e Letteratura, 1964). For a discussion of the ways in which the study of the emblematic tradition illuminates the poetry of one English poet, see Cedric D. Reverand II, "Patterns of Metaphor in the Poetry of Pope" (Diss. Cornell University 1972), especially Chapters 1 and 2.

33. Roger Williams, in a letter to John Winthrop, 24 October 1636, in his *Complete Writings*, VI—*The Letters of Roger Williams*, ed. John Russell Bartlett (New York: Russell and Russell, 1963), p. 11. Perry Miller mentions Williams's use of natural creatures as emblems in *Roger Williams: His Contribution to the American Tradition* (New York: Bobbs-Merrill, 1953), p. 56.

II Ars Poetica

1. John Cotton, *A Practical Commentary . . . upon the First Epistle General of John* (1656), quoted in Norman S. Grabo, "John Cotton's Aesthetics: A Sketch," *Early American Literature* 3 (Spring 1968): 8. Herbert's poem is quoted in the last two pages of Richard Baxter, *The Saints' Everlasting Rest*, 9th ed. (London, 1662); the first edition was published in 1650. Jonathan Mitchell quoted Herbert and stated his own view of poetry in his preface to *The Day of Doom; or a Poetical Description of the Great and Last Judgment*, by Michael Wigglesworth, 6th ed. (1715; rpt. New York: American News Company, 1867), p. 18. John Bulkley's preface to Wolcott's *Poetical Meditations* is quoted from *The Puritans*, ed. Perry Miller and

Thomas H. Johnson, rev. ed. (New York: Harper and Row, 1963), II: 683–684. Cotton Mather's *Manductio ad Ministerium* is quoted from a facsimile of the first edition (Boston, 1726; rpt. New York: Columbia University Press, 1938), ed. Thomas J. Holmes and Kenneth B. Murdock, pp. 40–42. As Thomas H. Johnson has pointed out (*The Puritans*, I: 77–78, and II: 668), the view held by Bulkley and Mather, that poetry is trivial relaxation, is nowhere in evidence in the theory or practice of seventeenth-century American Puritans, though Lawrence A. Sasek finds it expressed earlier in the laws and writings of the English Puritans and demonstrates that in England "the plays, ballads, and romances were looked upon by the puritans as a form of recreation, and placed under the same laws as games or athletic exercises." Even in England, however, not all poetry was considered trivial, and "the puritans could accept the Homeric and Virgilian heroes, but not Robin Hood" (*The Literary Temper of the English Puritans* [Baton Rouge: Louisiana State University Press, 1961], p. 110). Though the American Puritans did not all march in step and wheel precisely at the turn of the century, it is in general true that in America poetry was considered important, often centrally important, in the religious life of seventeenth-century Puritans and came to be considered an entertaining pastime only in the eighteenth century.

2. For a survey of revisionist (usually pluralist) scholarship in Puritan intellectual history, see Michael McGiffert, "American Puritan Studies in the 1960's," *William and Mary Quarterly* 27 (January 1970): 36–67.

3. Alan I. Ludwig, *Graven Images: New England Stone-Carving and Its Symbols, 1650–1815* (Middletown, Conn.: Wesleyan University Press, 1966), pp. 4–5, 18.

4. John Cotton, *A Modest and Clear Answer to Mr. Ball's Discourse of Set Forms of Prayer* (1642), quoted in Norman S. Grabo, "Cotton's Aesthetics," p. 4.

5. Cotton did so in his *Modest and Clear Answer*. For a clear discussion of Cotton's attitude toward the use of objects in meditation, see Norman S. Grabo, "Puritan Devotion and American Literary History," in *Themes and Directions in American Literature: Essays in Honor of Leon Howard*, ed. Ray B. Browne and Donald Pizer (Lafayette, Indiana: Purdue University Studies, 1969), pp. 18–21. See also Larzer Ziff, *The Career of John Cotton: Puritanism and the American Experience* (Princeton: Princeton University Press, 1962), pp. 247–248.

The *Cambridge Platform* is quoted from Williston Walker, *The Creeds and Platforms of Congregationalism* (New York: Charles Scribner's Sons, 1893), p. 195. For the acceptance by the Cambridge Synod of the confession of faith and catechisms of the Westminster Assembly, see also p. 185. For the acceptance by the Reforming Synod of 1679 of the *Cambridge Platform*, see pp. 418, 425.

The Shorter Catechism is quoted from *The Confession of Faith and the Larger and Shorter Catechisms* (London: T. Nelson and Sons, 1860), p. 298.

For a useful discussion of the distinction between the civil and religious uses of images, see Dickran and Ann Tashjian, *Memorials for Children of Change: The Art of Early New England Stonecarving* (Middletown, Conn.: Wesleyan University Press, 1974), p. 6–12.

6. Michael Wigglesworth, *The Diary of Michael Wigglesworth 1653–1657: The Conscience of a Puritan*, ed. Edmund S. Morgan (1951; rpt. New York: Harper and Row, 1965), p. 93.

7. William Bradford, *Of Plymouth Plantation*, ed. Samuel Eliot Morison (New York: Alfred A. Knopf, 1952), pp. 205–206.

8. Ludwig, pp. 202, 66. The Tashjians, p. 187.

9. Samuel Willard, *A Compleat Body of Divinity in Two Hundred and Fifty Expository Lectures on the Assembly's Shorter Catechism* (Boston: B. Green and S. Kneeland, 1726), p. 54. For a detailed reading of this work and for more information on Willard's life and thought, see Ernest Benson Lowrie, *The Shape of the Puritan Mind: The Thought of Samuel Willard* (New Haven: Yale University Press, 1974).

10. For statements that Ramism ruined Puritan poetry, see for example Perry Miller, *The New England Mind: The Seventeenth Century* (1939; rpt. Cambridge, Mass.: Harvard University Press, 1954), pp. 326–327, 359–362; and Charles Feidelson, Jr., *Symbolism and American Literature* (Chicago: University of Chicago Press, 1953), pp. 84–86. Kenneth Murdock guessed without explanation that "even without Ramus, Puritan writing would have been essentially the same" (*Literature and Theology in Colonial New England* [Cambridge, Mass.: Harvard University Press, 1949], p. 217). And Roy Harvey Pearce stated that "Ramist poetics," which he defined as "a poetics of discovery, of examining and stating, of coming upon, of laying open to view—was in effect New England poetics" (*The Continuity of American Poetry* [Princeton: Princeton University Press, 1961], p. 34). But no one examined the matter in any detail.

11. Perry Miller, *The New England Mind: The Seventeenth Century*, p. 337. Though on this page Miller phrases his attribution of the plain style to the influence of Ramus as a question, he changes it to a declaration on p. 345: "It was, obviously, impossible to be a Ramist and still preach like John Donne; to English Puritans it seemed impossible, once they had become Ramists, to preach otherwise than in doctrines, reasons, and uses." Miller also traced clearly the spread of Ramism from France to England and New England (pp. 118–119, 127–128). For other positivistic evidence of the influence of Ramism on Puritan thought, see Walter J. Ong, S. J., *Ramus: Method, and the Decay of Dialogue* (Cambridge, Mass.: Harvard University Press, 1958), p. 12. For Miller's assertion that the Ramist poet would use only decorative imagery, see pp. 326, 360–361.

For this discussion of the Ramist influence on English poetry, see Rosemond Tuve, *Elizabethan and Metaphysical Imagery: Renaissance Poetic and Twentieth-Century Critics* (Chicago: University of Chicago Press, 1947), pp. 331–353. Tuve concluded that "imagery seen in the light of these

[Ramist] conceptions would be indisputably functional. 'Decorative' images would not be a desideratum; they would indeed scarcely be a possibility." She then listed several desiderata implied by her reading of Ramist thought and identified them as "normally the characteristics of Metaphysical imagery" (p. 353).

12. Ong, pp. 273–275.

13. *Ibid.*, pp. 273–279.

14. William K. Wimsatt, Jr. and Cleanth Brooks, *Literary Criticism: A Short History* (New York: Alfred A. Knopf, 1957), p. 225.

15. Miller, *The New England Mind: The Seventeenth Century*, p. 360; Roy Harvey Pearce, p. 33; Ong, pp. 281–282.

16. Miller, *The New England Mind: The Seventeenth Century*, p. 118. Ong, pp. 286, 283. Interestingly enough, American Puritan poets were capable of reading and writing both fine poetry of the sort written by Sidney, Marlowe, and Milton, and poetry as ornamental history of the sort written by Boscovich and Lucini. Bradstreet's "Contemplations" and Taylor's *Preparatory Meditations* exemplify the former sort, Bradstreet's *Four Monarchies* and Taylor's "Metrical History of Christianity" the latter.

17. Ong, p. 282.

18. Miller, Ong, and Pearce all follow this better definition and emphasize this distinction. See Miller, *The New England Mind: The Seventeenth Century*, p. 129; Ong, pp. 182–183; and Pearce, p. 34.

19. Anne Bradstreet, *The Works of Anne Bradstreet*, ed. Jeannine Hensley (Cambridge, Mass.: Harvard University Press, 1967), p. 240.

20. Donald R. Howard, in his introduction to Lothario Dei Segni's *On the Misery of the Human Condition: De miseria humane conditionis*, trans. Margaret Mary Dietz (Indianapolis, Indiana: Bobbs Merrill, 1969), pp. xix–xx. For a brief discussion of the Catharist heresy, see pp. xviii–xx.

21. For my discussions of medieval writings on *contemptus mundi* and Innocent III's contribution to them, I am indebted to Donald R. Howard's introduction and to Rev. James A. Geary, "An Irish Version of Innocent III's *De Contemptu Mundi*" (Diss. The Catholic University of America 1931), in *Catholic University of America Theses* 59 (Washington, D. C., 1931).

Even Lothar's statement of *contemptus mundi* may have been uttered from a point of view somewhat higher than that of mere man. In one of his consecration sermons he "declared that he was less than God, but greater than man, standing as it were in the middle." *National Catholic Encyclopedia* (New York: McGraw-Hill, 1967), VII: 521.

22. For a list of discussions of recurrent themes in such writings, see Howard, pp. xxiv–xxxiii. For treatment of these themes by Puritan poets, see Bradstreet's "The Flesh and the Spirit," "The Vanity of all Worldly Things," and "Upon the Burning of Our House"; Michael Wigglesworth's "A Song of Emptiness"; Roger Williams's "The Indians Prize not English

Gold"; and John Danforth's "A Few Lines to Fill Up a Vacant Page." Lothar is quoted from *On the Misery of the Human Condition*, pp. 6, 24.

23. *Ibid.*, pp. 3, 37–38, 78, 87.

24. For Augustine's assertions that the creatures of a good God necessarily partake, however slightly, of His goodness, see *On Christian Doctrine (De doctrina Christiana)*, trans. D. W. Robertson, Jr. (Indianapolis, Indiana: Bobbs-Merrill, 1958), pp. 21, 27.

25. Alanus ab Insulis, in *Patrologiae Cursus Completus, Patrum Latinorum* ed. J. P. Migne, (Paris, 1844–1864), CCX, col. 579A. All further references to this work will be identified in the text as *PL* followed by the volume and column numbers and a letter to indicate the quotation's position on the page, as *PL* 210, 579A. This selection and the four following came to my attention in a lecture, "Medieval Symbolism and Imagery," given by James Marchand at Cornell University on 24 April 1972. For their aid in translating these passages, I am grateful to Thomas Morrissey and Miceal Vaughan. Of course the final versions of the translations are my own, and I take responsibility for any errors in them.

26. Pseudo-Hrabanus, in *Spicilegium Solesmense complectens sanctorum patrum scriptorumque ecclesiasticorum anecdota hactenus opera selecta e Graecis Orientalibusque et Latinus codicubus*, ed. Jean Baptiste Cardinal Pitra (Paris, 1855; rpt. Graz-Austria: Akademische Druck—U. Verlagsanstalt, 1963) III: 436.

27. Quoted in Perry Miller, *The New England Mind: The Seventeenth Century*, p. 162.

28. Willard, *Compleat Body of Divinity*, pp. 37–45.

29. I have drawn my discussion of Aquinas and Scotus chiefly from Frederick Copleston, S. J., *A History of Philosophy* (London: Burnes Oates and Washbourne, 1950) II: 347–372 and 502–510, and from Allan I. Ludwig, *Graven Images*, pp. 21–32, 440. Willard is quoted from the *Compleat Body*, p. 43; Scotus is quoted and paraphrased from Copleston, pp. 505–506.

30. Samuel Mather (1627–1671), *The Figures or Types of the Old Testament*, 1st ed. (1683), 2nd ed. (London: Nath. Hillier, 1705; rpt. New York: Johnson Reprint Corporation, 1969), p. 55. See also pp. 53, 129. As I have suggested before (Chapter 1, footnote 32), the Puritans usually used the words emblem, type, sign, or similitude to refer to what most modern literary critics have defined as symbol. The Tashjians have noted that the interplay "between allegory and emblem was often so fluid as to render hard distinctions arbitrary" (p. 168). In *The Puritan Origins of the American Self* (New Haven: Yale University Press, 1975), Sacvan Bercovitch has clearly detailed the changing nature of these distinctions in tracing the development of Puritan typology from the orthodox "hermeneutical mode connecting the Old Testament to the New" (p. 35) to a more widely applied "typology of current affairs" that "we would now call symbolic interpretation" (p. 113). The word "symbol" in our modern sense was first

used by Spenser (in 1590) and appeared quite rarely in seventeenth-century writings; its meaning was usually expressed by one of the words listed above, all of which appear far more often (*OED*).

31. For Miller's statement of the originality of Edwards's world view, see the introduction to his edition of Edwards's *Images or Shadows of Divine Things* (New Haven: Yale University Press, 1948), p. 7. Brumm's discussion is somewhat more complete than Miller's. She even hazarded a guess at Edwards's reasons for making this presumed extension of typological method: "From the original correspondence of Old Testament and Christ . . . he transfers it to the enlarged correspondence of the natural and spiritual world. Image 45 gives a biblical text in support of this. But the real reasons for this extension to the cosmos lie in the respect the rising natural sciences were winning for the natural world and its laws" (Ursula Brumm, *American Thought and Religious Typology*, trans. John Hoaglund [New Brunswick, New Jersey: Rutgers University Press, 1970], p. 97). Brumm's quotation in the text is from p. 98. Both Brumm and Miller begin their discussions of typology only with the end of the seventeenth century and so ignore nearly eighty years during which this method informed both theology and literature. This lacuna has begun to be explored, and many of Miller's and Brumm's generalizations have been qualified or corrected by Sacvan Bercovitch in "Typology in Puritan New England: The Williams-Cotton Controversy Reassessed," *American Quarterly* 19 (Summer 1967): 166–191, and by Mason I. Lowance, Jr. in "Images or Shadows of Divine Things: The Typology of Jonathan Edwards," *Early American Literature* 5 (Spring 1970): 141–181.

Jonathan Edwards is quoted from *Images or Shadows of Divine Things*, p. 44. Edward Taylor's Meditation 1, Second Series, is quoted from *The Poems of Edward Taylor*, ed. Donald E. Stanford (New Haven: Yale University Press, 1960), p. 83.

32. Joshua Moody, *Souldiery Spiritualized* (Cambridge, Mass.: 1674) in Miller and Johnson, *The Puritans*, I: 367–368. Although Perry Miller distinguished in his "Introduction" to his edition of Edwards's *Images or Shadows of Divine Things* between the "tedious. . . 'spiritualizing' " (p. 16) of such as Moody and Mather and the natural (as opposed to biblical) typology of Edwards's notebook, it seems clear enough that both sprang from the same habit of mind and the same theological tradition—the habit of reading the natural for its revelation of the supernatural. As I have noted in the preceding footnote, Edwards was not original in his method, which can be found not only in the medieval writers previously quoted, but also in the writings of such earlier Puritans as Alexander Richardson, Anne Bradstreet, Roger Williams, and Samuel Danforth II.

33. See Norman S. Grabo, "The Veiled Vision: The Role of Aesthetics in Early American Intellectual History," *William and Mary Quarterly* 3rd series, 19 (October 1962): 493–510; "The Art of Puritan Devotion," *Seventeenth-Century News* 26 (Spring 1968): 7–9; "John Cotton's Aes-

thetics: A Sketch," *Early American Literature* 3 (Spring 1968): 4–10; and "Puritan Devotion and American Literary History," in *Themes and Directions in American Literature*, pp. 6–23. Grabo is quoted from "The Art of Puritan Devotion," p. 9.

34. For a discussion of the meditative tradition and its influence on English poetry, see Louis L. Martz, *The Poetry of Meditation*, rev. ed. (New Haven: Yale University Press, 1962). Martz asserted that structured meditation became a concern of the Puritans only after 1650, after Baxter had made palatable to them methods of meditation that were essentially Catholic. That Baxter was not nearly so original as he claimed to be has been demonstrated by Norman Grabo in "Puritan Devotion and American Literary History," *Themes and Directions*, p. 12. Grabo discussed the importation into England of Catholic handbooks on meditation in *Edward Taylor* (New Haven: Twayne, 1961), p. 60.

For a discussion of Puritan meditation after Baxter, See U. Milo Kaufmann, *The Pilgrim's Progress and Traditions in Puritan Meditation* (New Haven: Yale University Press, 1966). St. Francis de Sales is quoted in Louis L. Martz, *The Poetry of Meditation*, p. 15.

35. Thomas Taylor (1576–1633), *A Man in Christ, or: A new* CREATURE. *To which is added a Treatise, containing Meditations from the* CREATURES (London: Printed for *I. Bartlet* at the gilt Cup in *Cheapeside,* 1628), pp. 2, 5–8, 23, 104.

36. Thomas Hooker, *The Soules Preparation for Christ. or A Treatise of Contrition* (London: Printed for Robert Dauulman, at the sign of the Brazen-serpent in *Pauls* Churchyard, 1632), pp. 84–86.

37. Indeed, the Puritan dependence upon language and upon literary metaphors (e.g., the creatures are letters in a book written by God) was so great that they could not comprehend a religion based upon "visions and magic" rather than upon words. See Frank Shuffelton, "Indian Devils and Pilgrim Fathers: Squanto, Hobomok, and the English Conception of Indian Religion," *New England Quarterly* 49 (March 1976): 109–116.

38. Drawing the customary distinction between the legitimate act of *seeing* the symbols that God had put in one's way and the idolatrous act of *making* them, Cotton continued: "but he must not take upon him to determine them to be used as signs for such an end and purpose." Written early in his career, these statements were later published as *Some Treasure Fetched out of Rubbish* (London, 1660), p. 29, and are quoted from Grabo, "Puritan Devotion," pp. 19–20. Cotton more than Hooker feared the possibility of idolatry lurking in the religious use of images, but even he acknowledged the value of meditation from the creatures and believed that if one kept clear the distinction between seeing signs and making them, one would be safe.

39. For the failure of such previous critics as Miller and Martz to examine early Puritan writings on meditation and for Norman Grabo's preliminary examinations, see Grabo, "Puritan Devotion," pp. 6–23.

40. This work was in the library of another famous crypto-Catholic, the

sensuous Edward Taylor. See "Taylor's Library" in *The Poetical Works of Edward Taylor* ed. Thomas H. Johnson (New York: Rocklands Editions, 1939), p. 207.

41. Martz, *The Poetry of Meditation*, p. 154, and Louis B. Wright, *The Cultural Life of the American Colonies 1607–1763* (New York: Harper and Brothers, 1957), p. 140.

42. Richard Baxter, *The Saints' Everlasting Rest*, 9th ed. rev. (London: F. Tyton and J. Underhill, 1662), pp. 694, 749–751. Where before he had recognized the dangers of idolatry, Baxter now noted the dangers of dealing only in religious abstractions: "Go to then: When thou settest thyself to meditate on the Joys above, think on them boldly as Scripture hath expressed them: Bring down thy conceivings to the reach of sense. . . . Both Love and Joy are promoted by familiar acquaintance: When we go to think of God and Glory in proper conceivings without these spectacles, we are lost and have nothing to fix our thoughts upon" (p. 751).

43. Willard, *Compleat Body*, p. 233; David E. Stannard, "Death and Dying in Puritan New England," *American Historical Review*, 78 (December 1973): 1315. See also David E. Stannard, *The Puritan Way of Death: A Study in Religion, Culture, and Social Change* (New York: Oxford University Press, 1977), esp. Section II, and David E. Stannard, ed., *Death in America* (Philadelphia: University of Pennsylvania Press, 1975). Puritans also believed in a resurrection of the body, to a heaven where at least some of the delights were figuratively physical. See Anne Bradstreet's "As Weary Pilgrim Now at Rest" (*Works*, pp. 294–295); and Willard, *Compleat Body*, p. 524.

III Anne Bradstreet and the Practice of Weaned Affections

1. John Rogers is quoted from *Seventeenth-Century American Poetry*, ed. Harrison T. Meserole (New York: New York University Press, 1968), p. 422.

Cotton Mather, *Magnalia Christi Americana, or the Ecclesiastical History of New England* (Hartford, Conn.: Silas Andrus and Son, 1855), II: 135.

Evert A. Duyckinck and George L. Duyckinck, *Cyclopedia of American Literature* (1855; rpt. Philadelphia: William Rutler, 1875), I: 52–53.

2. Moses Coit Tyler, *A History of American Literature 1607–1765* (1878; rpt. Ithaca, New York: Cornell University Press, 1949), pp. 277, 242. In 1908, Charles William Pearson published an essay entitled "Early American Poetry," in which he quoted Tyler's few positive comments on Bradstreet, then sidestepped the problem of Puritanism and poetry by stating that "Anne Bradstreet represents the more beautiful, gentle, and tender side of Puritanism. Michael Wigglesworth, her contemporary, represents its darker, more forbidding and terrible aspects" (*Literary and Biographical*

Essays: A Volume of Papers by the Way [Boston: Sherman French, 1908], p. 21). But neither unobjectionable generalizations nor exhaustive demonstrations that Puritan poets were good churchgoers will adequately explain the influence of Puritanism upon the poetry of its adherents.

3. Stanley T. Williams, *The Beginnings of American Poetry 1620–1855* (Uppsala, Sweden: Almqvist and Wiksells, 1951), p. 28.

Ann Stanford, "Anne Bradstreet: Dogmatist and Rebel," *New England Quarterly* 39 (September 1966): 374, 388–389. In this article and in her book, *Anne Bradstreet: The Worldly Puritan* (New York: Burt Franklin, 1974), Stanford made much of Bradstreet's statement in the autobiographical sketch addressed to her children that when she came to New England "I found a new world and new manners, at which my heart rose." Though Stanford imputes to "Puritan dogma" a great number of things (e.g., supremacy of men) at which Anne's heart presumably rose, it seems likely that Bradstreet was referring to the test and confession of saving faith then demanded of all prospective church members. Having been a respected member of a covenanted community in England, she might well have baulked at being treated as an outsider, the sincerity of whose religious professions was to be tested before she could join the New England church. That her "heart rose" at the requirements for church membership rather than at the "dogmas" mentioned by Stanford (most of which were, after all, the same in Old England as in New) she indicated by her next sentence: "But after I was convinced it was the way of God, I submitted to it and joined the church at Boston" (*The Works of Anne Bradstreet*, ed. Jeannine Hensley [Cambridge, Mass.: Harvard University Press, 1967], p. 241).

4. Samuel Eliot Morison, "Mistress Anne Bradstreet," in *Builders of the Bay Colony*, 2nd ed. (Boston: Houghton Mifflin, 1958) pp. 333, 335.

Robert D. Richardson, "The Puritan Poetry of Anne Bradstreet," *Texas Studies in Language and Literature* 9 (Autumn 1967): 317, 331.

William J. Irvin, "Allegory and Typology 'Imbrace and Greet': Anne Bradstreet's 'Contemplations,'" *Early American Literature* 10 (Spring 1975): 44.

5. For a detailed discussion of Bradstreet's evolving critical reputation, see Jeannine Hensley, "Anne Bradstreet's Wreath of Thyme," in her edition of *The Works of Anne Bradstreet*, pp. xxi–xxxv. For an annotated checklist of Bradstreet criticism, see Ann Stanford, "Anne Bradstreet: An Annotated Checklist," *Bulletin of Bibliography* 27 (April–June 1970): 34–37.

6. See Augustine, *On Christian Doctrine*, trans. D. W. Robertson (New York: The Liberal Arts Press, 1958), pp. 27 (1.31.34 and 1.32.35), 68–69 (2.32.50).

7. Perry Miller, *The New England Mind: The Seventeenth Century* (1939; rpt. Cambridge, Mass.: Harvard University Press, 1954), pp. 15, 42. Thomas Hooker, *The Soules Justification, on 2 Cor. 5. 21*, in *The Soules Exaltation. A Treatise* (London: Printed by *John Haviland*, for *Andrew Crooke*, and are to be sold at the black Beare in *S. Pauls* Church-yard, 1638),

p. 310. Edward Reyner, *The Rule of the New Creature*, appended to Hooker, *The Danger of Desertion* (London, 1641), p. 29, is quoted from *The Puritans*, ed. Perry Miller and Thomas H. Johnson, rev. ed. (New York: Harper and Row, 1963), I: 289.

8. Cotton on "Christian Calling" is quoted from Miller and Johnson, I: 319; Miller's remark on Sewall's *Phaenomena* from *ibid.*, I: 290; and the *Phaenomena* itself from *ibid.*, I: 377. Augustine is quoted from his *Confessions*, book seven, chapter nine, trans. Vernon J. Bourke (New York: Fathers of the Church, Inc., 1953), p. 180.

9. *The Works of Anne Bradstreet*, p. 279. All references to the works of Bradstreet are to this edition and will be identified in the text.

10. Allen Tate, "Tension in Poetry" (1938), reprinted in *Essays of Four Decades* (Chicago: Swallow Press, 1968), p. 64.

11. Allen Tate, "The Angelic Imagination: Poe as God," in *Essays of Four Decades*, pp. 401–423. Tate has contrasted Poe's "angelic imagination" with the "symbolic imagination" of Dante, examined in "The Symbolic Imagination," *Essays of Four Decades*, pp. 424–446.

12. Juvenal, "Satire X: The Vanity of Human Wishes," in *Juvenal and Persius*, trans. G. G. Ramsey, rev. ed., *The Loeb Classical Library* (Cambridge, Mass.: Harvard University Press, and London: Heinemann, 1965), pp. 219–221.

13. Solomon is as good a name as any for the unknown author of Ecclesiastes.

14. Edmund S. Morgan, *The Puritan Family: Religion and Domestic Relations in Seventeenth-Century New England*, rev. ed. (New York: Harper and Row, 1966), pp. 47, 61. Wadsworth's *Well-Ordered Family* (Boston, 1712), p. 36, is quoted from Morgan, p. 48. Husbands were similarly warned of the divine command to love their wives, were forbidden by law to strike them, to insult them, or to neglect to provide for them. See Morgan, pp. 29–64.

15. Ann Stanford, "Anne Bradstreet: Dogmatist and Rebel," p. 380.

16. Hyatt H. Waggoner, *American Poets: From the Puritans to the Present* (Boston: Houghton Mifflin, 1968), pp. 15, 19.

17. Roy Harvey Pearce, *The Continuity of American Poetry* (Princeton: Princeton University Press, 1961), p. 24.

18. Cleanth Brooks and Robert Penn Warren, *Understanding Poetry*, 3rd ed. (New York: Holt, Rinehart and Winston, 1960), pp. 238–244. Lowell is quoted from pp. 239–240. Elizabeth Drew, *Poetry: A Modern Guide to Its Understanding and Enjoyment* (New York: Dell, 1959), p. 123 is quoted from p. 243.

19. Rosemary M. Laughlin, "Anne Bradstreet: Poet in Search of Form," *American Literature* 42 (March 1970): 4–5.

20. See Ann Stanford, "Anne Bradstreet: Dogmatist and Rebel," p. 386. Stanford has written that in the second stanza Bradstreet states "how she really feels instead of how she *should* feel. The reply is closer to Herrick

and the Cavaliers than to most Puritan poetry." Having interpreted the first six lines of the second stanza as a near-criticism of God, Stanford asks: "How can she end the stanza? How can she retreat from this approach to criticism of God who orders all things? . . . She concludes by backing down from her near-criticism of the deity" (p. 386). As we have seen, however, the closing triplet is not a lame reversal but the appropriate conclusion of a coherent argument.

21. "The Autobiography of Thomas Shepard," ed. Allyn Bailey Forbes, in *Publications of the Colonial Society of Massachusetts* 27 (1927–1930): 345–400. Shepard is quoted from pp. 391–392, 374, 395.

22. For the reading that Bradstreet's poem is Romantic, see Richard Crowder, "Anne Bradstreet and Keats," *Notes and Queries* (September 1956): 386–388; Josephine K. Piercy, *Anne Bradstreet* (New Haven: Twayne, 1965), pp. 100–101; and Alvin H. Rosenfeld, "Anne Bradstreet's 'Contemplations': Patterns of Form and Meaning," *New England Quarterly* 43 (March 1970): 79–96. Rosenfeld varied this approach by arguing that her Puritanism squelched her Romantic rebellion: "Her poem is forced to reverse itself from its insurgent, Wordsworthian Romanticism, then, because Romanticism and Paganism obviously were too closely allied" (p. 91).

23. Elizabeth Wade White, *Anne Bradstreet: "The Tenth Muse"* (New York: Oxford University Press, 1971), p. 335.

IV   Gnostics and Naturalists

1. Hyatt H. Waggoner, *American Poets: From the Puritans to the Present* (Boston: Houghton Mifflin, 1968), pp. 14, 15.

2. Moses Coit Tyler, *A History of American Literature 1607–1765* (1878; rpt. Ithaca, New York: Cornell University Press, 1949), p. 228.
Charles Feidelson, Jr., *Symbolism and American Literature* (Chicago: University of Chicago Press, 1953), p. 96.

3. Edmund S. Morgan, ed., *The Diary of Michael Wigglesworth 1653–1657: The Conscience of a Puritan* (New York: Harper and Row, 1965), p. v.

4. *Ibid.*, pp. 96, 50.

5. For Wigglesworth's reaction to his wife's death and Crowder's charitable and I think correct interpretation of it, see Richard Crowder, *No Featherbed to Heaven: A Biography of Michael Wigglesworth 1631–1705* (East Lansing: Michigan State University Press, 1962), p. 99.

6. "In Solitude Good Company," quoted *ibid.*

7. Cotton Mather, "A Character of the Reverend Author, Mr. Michael Wigglesworth, in a Funeral Sermon Preached at Malden, June 24, 1705," printed in the sixth edition of *The Day of Doom* (1715; rpt. New York: American News Company, 1867), p. 117. Subsequent references to this edition will be identified in the text in parentheses.

8. René Wellek and Austin Warren, *Theory of Literature*, 3rd ed. (New York: Harcourt Brace and World, 1956), p. 186.

9. Anne Bradstreet, *The Works of Anne Bradstreet*, ed. Jeannine Hensley (Cambridge, Mass.: Harvard University Press, 1967), p. 243. The drawing for Wigglesworth's pillar appears in his *Diary*, p. 93.

10. Samuel Willard, *A Compleat Body of Divinity* (Boston: B. Green and S. Kneeland, 1726), p. 233. Bradstreet is quoted from her *Works*, pp. 250, 295.

11. Crowder, pp. 149–153. Wigglesworth's poem is quoted in Crowder, pp. 150–151. O. M. Brack, Jr., "Michael Wigglesworth and the Attribution of 'I Walk'd and Did a Little Mole-Hill View,' " *Seventeenth-Century News* 28 (Fall 1970): 41–44. Brack argues intelligently that the London edition has no authority, but the evidence is inconclusive, and it seemed uncharitable as well as unscholarly to deprive Wigglesworth of what might be his most naturalistic poem.

12. Larzer Ziff, "Literary Consequences of Puritanism," *ELH* 30 (September 1963): 302.

13. Leon Howard, in the introduction to his edition of Philip Pain's *Daily Meditations* (1668; rpt. San Marino, California: Huntington Library, 1936), p. 6. All quotations from Pain are from this edition and will be identified in the text.

14. Tyler, p. 229.

15. Nathaniel Ward, *The Simple Cobbler of Aggawam in America* (London, 1647). This poem is quoted from Harrison T. Meserole, ed., *Seventeenth-Century American Poetry* (New York: New York University Press, 1968), p. 367. All further references to this anthology will be identified in the text.

16. Though the traditional genres constitute a loose form of classification, they are I think useful in illustrating the variety of Puritan poetry.

17. Waggoner, p. 15.

18. For a discussion of the nature and extent of Steere's Puritanism, and for the sources of more information about him, see Chapter 1, footnote 9.

19. See Sacvan Bercovitch, "Typology in Puritan New England: The Williams-Cotton Controversy Reassessed," *American Quarterly* 19 (Summer 1967): 170–71. Bulkeley's elegy is quoted from p. 170.

20. Waggoner, p. 13. Roy Harvey Pearce, *The Continuity of American Poetry* (Princeton: Princeton University Press, 1961), p. 31.

21. Cotton Mather, *Magnalia Christi Americana* (1702; rpt. Hartford: Silas Andrus and Son, 1855), I: 318.

22. Benjamin Tompson, "The Amiable Virgin Memorized—Elizabeth Tompson," in *Handkerchiefs from Paul*, ed. Kenneth B. Murdock (Cambridge, Mass.: Harvard University Press, 1927), p. 10. Murdock retained original spelling, including contractions, u's for v's and the like. I have given the lines in modern spelling, while retaining Tompson's punctuation and capitalization.

23. Bercovitch, p. 170.

24. For a discussion of Williams's separation of the temporal from the eternal order, see Bercovitch, pp. 166-191. Bercovitch is quoted from pp. 175-176; Williams's *The Bloody Tenent Yet More Bloody* (1652), pp. 181, 403, from p. 175. See also Edmund S. Morgan, *Roger Williams: The Church and the State* (New York: Harcourt Brace and World, 1967), esp. pp. 10, 15, 27, 53, 79-85.

25. For a detailed discussion of Williams's desire to become an apostolic minister, see Morgan, *Roger Williams*, pp. 40-45. Williams's letter to Winthrop (February, 1632) is quoted from *The Complete Writings of Roger Williams*, VI—*The Letters of Roger Williams*, ed. John Russell Bartlett (1874; rpt. New York: Russell and Russell, 1963), p. 2. For a brief discussion of Williams's visits to the Indians and of his *Key*, see Henry Chupak, *Roger Williams* (New Haven: Twayne, 1969), pp. 63-70.

26. Though he began his association with the Indians with the expressed intent of converting them to Christianity, Williams soon decided not to convert them prematurely, but to prepare them for conversion eventually. In his *Key*, he explained his decision: "I was persuaded, and am, that God's way is first to turn a soul from its Idols, both of heart, worship, and conversation, before it is capable of worship, to the true and living God." Since the Indians did not know enough of the Christian God to do anything other than install Him in their own mythology, Williams considered their conversion at this time an "Antichristian conversion" and wrote that it would lead them to hell. Such false outward conversion was "the bane of millions of souls in England, and all other Nations professing to be Christian Nations who are brought by public authority to Baptism and fellowship with God in Ordinances of worship before the saving work of Repentance, and a true turning to God" (Williams, *The Complete Writings of Roger Williams*, I—*A Key into the Language of America*, ed. James H. Trumbull [1643; rpt. New York: Russell and Russell, 1963], p. 160-161). All further references to the *Key* are to this edition and will be identified in the text.

27. *The Letters of Roger Williams*, pp. 274-276.

V Edward Taylor: Christ's Creation and the Dissatisfactions of Metaphor

1. For a detailed study of Taylor criticism, see Constance J. Gevfert, *Edward Taylor: An Annotated Bibliography, 1668-1970* (Kent, Ohio: Kent State University Press, 1971). Two recent book-length studies of Taylor are William J. Scheick, *The Will and the Word: The Poetry of Edward Taylor* (Athens, Georgia: University of Georgia Press, 1974), which contains a selected bibliography, and Karl Keller, *The Example of Edward Taylor* (Amherst, Mass.: The University of Massachusetts Press, 1975). For demonstrations that New England orthodoxy was more various than we had earlier believed, see Robert G. Pope, *The Half-Way Covenant: Church Membership in Puritan New England* (Princeton: Princeton University Press,

1969), and Emory Elliott, *Power and the Pulpit in Puritan New England* (Princeton: Princeton University Press, 1975). For a survey of such pluralist scholarship in Puritan intellectual history, see Michael McGiffert, "American Puritan Studies in the 1960's," *William and Mary Quarterly* 27 (January 1970). 36–67.

2. Donald E. Stanford, ed., *The Poems of Edward Taylor* (New Haven: Yale University Press, 1960), p. 468. Unless otherwise noted, all references to Taylor's poetry are to this edition and will be identified in the text either by page number or, when Taylor has numbered his meditations, by their series, number, and line number. Quotations from Taylor's long poems will be identified in the text, using the following abbreviations: *GD, God's Determinations Touching His Elect; MHC, Metrical History of Christianity*, both in the Stanford edition. Unless otherwise noted, references to Taylor's prose works will also be identified in the text, using the following abbreviations: *C, Edward Taylor's Christographia*, ed. Norman S. Grabo (New Haven: Yale University Press, 1962), and *TCLS, Edward Taylor's Treatise Concerning the Lord's Supper*, ed. Norman S. Grabo (East Lansing: Michigan State University Press, 1966).

3. Donald A. Junkins, "Edward Taylor's Revisions," *American Literature* 37 (May 1965): 139.

4. William B. Goodman, "Edward Taylor Writes His Love," *New England Quarterly* 27 (December 1954): 512–513. Taylor's acrostic to Elizabeth Fitch is pictured in Karl Keller, *The Example of Edward Taylor*, p. 168.

5. See David E. Stannard, ed., *Death in America* (Philadelphia: University of Pennsylvania Press, 1975), esp. Stannard's own essay, "Death and the Puritan Child."

6. Taylor's "Valedictory" poems are quoted from Thomas M. Davis, "Edward Taylor's 'Valedictory' Poems," *Early American Literature* 7 (Spring 1972): 38–63 and are identified in the text by version and line number. I shall cite primarily from the third and final version.

7. Thomas M. Davis and Virginia L. Davis, "Edward Taylor on the Day of Judgment," *American Literature* 43 (January 1972): 540.

8. Emory Elliott's *Power and the Pulpit in Puritan New England* considerably strengthens the theory that there never was any decline in fact, only in the rhetoric of the jeremiads.

9. Larzer Ziff, "Founding Fathers and Sons," *Times Literary Supplement*, 16 July 1976, p. 870.

10. Donald A. Junkins, "An Analytical Study of Edward Taylor's Preparatory Meditations," (Diss., Boston University 1963), pp. 257–408; Keller, p. 57.

11. Peter Nicolaisen overstates this point in arguing that Taylor devalued the physical world so much that he took nearly all his images from the Bible. He does not examine Taylor's dissatisfaction with metaphors based

even on biblical sources. See *Die Bildlichkeit in der Dichtung Edward Taylors* (Neumünster: Karl Wachholtz, 1966), esp. pp. 32–57.

12. Thomas and Virginia Davis, "Edward Taylor on the Day of Judgment," p. 527.

13. See Scheick, pp. 43–44.

14. See Scheick, pp. 43–44, 134–144, and Keller, pp. 206–220.

15. Karl Keller, " 'The World Slickt Up in Types': Edward Taylor as a Version of Emerson," in *Typology and Early American Literature*, ed. Sacvan Bercovitch (Amherst: The University of Massachusetts Press, 1972), p. 175.

16. These observations are made by Alan B. Howard in "The World as Emblem: Language and Vision in the Poetry of Edward Taylor," *American Literature* 44 (November 1972): 361; by Kathleen Blake in "Edward Taylor's Protestant Poetic: Nontransubstantiating Metaphor," *American Literature* 43 (March 1971): 19; and by John Gatta, Jr. in "The Comic Design of *Gods Determinations touching his Elect,*" *Early American Literature* 10 (Fall 1975): 127.

17. See Donald Junkins, "Edward Taylor's Revisions," pp. 135–152, esp. 139; Peter Thorpe, "Edward Taylor as Poet," *New England Quarterly* 39 (September 1966): 356–372; and Charles W. Mignon, "Diction in Edward Taylor's 'Preparatory Meditations,' " *American Speech* 41 (December 1966): 243–255.

18. Scheick, pp. 140, 134, 129.

19. Kathleen Blake, p. 21. The paradoxical matter of Taylor's mysticism has been discussed by Donald E. Stanford and Norman S. Grabo. In Grabo's *Edward Taylor* (New York: Twayne, 1961), he cautiously relates Taylor's symbolic poetry to the experience of "the mystic, transcending the world of sense to achieve union with God" (p. 87). Stanford may be right in arguing in his review that "the great bulk of Taylor's poetry is not mystical, and Mr. Grabo exaggerates this aspect of the poet's writing" in *American Literature* 34 (November 1962): 412. But the distinction is not merely quantitative, and a more accurate characterization is that Taylor was an enthusiast: he longed for complete union with God, for the mystical leap that Grabo and Blake describe. But he knew that such a union was impossible this side of the grave, and his poems record the longing, not the union.

20. For the suggestion that Taylor was operating in an emblematic tradition, see Alan B. Howard, pp. 359–384. For speculations on the possibility that Taylor may have written some of his Meditations as "blind emblems," emblems unaccompanied by a picture, and the possibility that he may have been influenced, before coming to America, by the characterization and structure of tapestries, see Carmine Andrew Prioli, "Emblems, Blind Emblems, and the Visual Imagery of Edward Taylor" (Diss., State University of New York at Stony Brook 1975). For yet another attempt (no doubt part of a Jesuitical conspiracy) to find something Catholic about

Taylor, see Judson B. Allen, "Edward Taylor's Catholic Wasp: Exegetical Convention in 'Upon a Spider Catching a Fly,'" *English Language Notes* 7 (June 1970): 257–260.

21. Blake, pp. 1–24.

22. Clark Griffith, "Edward Taylor and the Momentum of Metaphor," *ELH* 33 (December 1966): 457–458.

23. Francis Murphy, "Edward Taylor's Attitude toward Publication: A Question Concerning Authority," *American Literature* 34 (November 1962): 393–394.

24. Thomas and Virginia Davis, "Edward Taylor on the Day of Judgment," pp. 527–528.

25. Scheick, p. 101.

26. Keller, *Example*, p. 102.

Appendix: In Critic's Hands: A Bibliographical Essay

1. These generalizations are examined in Chapter 1.

2. Elihu Hubbard Smith, *American Poems* (1793), ed. William K. Bottorf (Gainesville, Florida: Scholar's Facsimiles and Reprints, 1966).

3. Percival's was the third book of poems published under G. & C. Carvill's series title, *Clio*. Though its heading identifies it as a book review, the central subject of the essay is better expressed by the running title and the title given in the *Review*'s account book, "Early American Poetry." See *American Quarterly Review* 2 (December 1827): 492, 493, 501, 508. The essay was unsigned, but Ralph M. Aderman has used the *Review*'s account book to identify Bancroft as its author. See "Contributors to the *American Quarterly Review*, 1827–1833," *Studies in Bibliography* 14 (1961): 167.

4. Samuel Kettell, ed., *Specimens of American Poetry with Critical and Biographical Notices* (Boston: S. G. Goodrich, 1829), I: iii.

5. Rufus Wilmot Griswold, ed., *The Poets and Poetry of America*, 11th ed. (Philadelphia: A Hart, 1852), pp. xvii–xxviii.

6. Moses Coit Tyler, *A History of American Literature 1607–1765* (1878; rpt. Ithaca, New York: Cornell University Press, 1949), pp. 227–228.

7. *Ibid.*, pp. 228, 248, 277.

8. *Ibid.*, pp. 248, 292–295.

9. Kenneth B. Murdock, ed., *Handkerchiefs from Paul* (Cambridge, Mass.: Harvard University Press, 1927). Most of the poems were taken from the manuscript journal of Joseph Tompson of Billerica, the brother of Benjamin Tompson, the poet. The title is a phrase used by John Wilson the younger to describe his father's verses.

10. *Ibid.*, pp. lxvii, lxii, xxxii.

11. *Ibid.*, pp. lx, lxii–lxiii.

12. *Ibid.*, pp. lxv–lxix.

13. Vernon Louis Parrington, *Main Currents in American Thought:*

An Interpretation of American Literature from the Beginnings to 1920 (New York: Harcourt Brace, 1927), p. iii.

14. F. O. Matthiessen, "Michael Wigglesworth, A Puritan Artist," *New England Quarterly* 1 (October 1928): 493, 504.

15. Thomas H. Johnson, "Edward Taylor: A Puritan 'Sacred Poet,'" *New England Quarterly* 10 (June 1937): 290–322. He republished these poems in 1938 in the anthology that he edited with Perry Miller, *The Puritans* (New York: American Book Company, 1938). In 1939, he made more Taylor poems available in *The Poetical Works of Edward Taylor* (New York: Rockland Editions, 1939).

16. Johnson, *The Puritans* (1938), pp. 546–547.

17. *Ibid.*, pp. 667–668. See also Chapter 2, footnote 1.

18. *Ibid.*, p. 546.

19. Thomas Johnson, in *The Puritans*, rev. ed. (New York: Harper and Row, 1963): II, 652.

20. For evidence that Taylor died intestate and that therefore the allegation that he forbade publication is no more than family legend, see Francis Murphy, "Edward Taylor's Attitude toward Publication: A Question Concerning Authority," *American Literature* 34 (November 1962): 393–394. For a list of readers who have argued that Taylor was somehow crypto-Catholic—an approach which enables one to preserve Taylor without reconsidering the formulaic dismissals of other Puritan poetry—see Karl Keller, "The Reverend Mr. Edward Taylor's Bawdry," *New England Quarterly* 43 (September 1970): 382–407.

21. Perry Miller, *The New England Mind: The Seventeenth Century* (Cambridge, Mass.: Harvard University Press, 1939), pp. 359–361. For a brief and specific description of Miller's Ramist writer in the act of composition—first writing out his substance, then going back to interlineate his rhetoric—see pp. 326–328.

22. Harold S. Jantz, *The First Century of New England Verse* (New York: Russell and Russell, 1962), pp. 6–7, 31. See "The First Century of New England Verse," *Proceedings of the American Antiquarian Society* 53 (1943): 219–258; reprinted Worcester, Mass., 1944.

23. Kenneth B. Murdock, *Literature and Theology in Colonial New England* (Cambridge, Mass.: Harvard University Press, 1949), pp. vii–viii, 16, 38, 138–139, 167–170. Mather is quoted from Murdock, p. 138. We may recall here that when the translators of the 1651 edition of the *Bay Psalm Book* added metrical translations of other parts of the Bible to the earlier collection of psalms, their favorite source was the Song of Solomon. Taylor's preference for this book, then, is no more Catholic than theirs.

24. Stanley T. Williams, *The Beginnings of American Poetry (1620–1855)* (Uppsala, Sweden: Almqvist and Wiksells, 1951). For Williams's belief in the typicality of Wigglesworth, see especially pp. 15–16, 29, 31.

25. *Ibid.*, pp. 17, 28, 32–33.

26. Charles Feidelson, Jr., *Symbolism and American Literature* (Chicago: University of Chicago Press, 1953), pp. 88, 77—78. Winthrop and Sewall are quoted by Feidelson.

27. *Ibid.*, pp. 96, 78, 84—86. For evidence that Feidelson has misinterpreted Aquinas on the efficacy of language, see *Summa Theologica*, Section 1, Question XIII, Article 1: ". . . we know God from creatures as their cause. . . . In this way therefore He can be named by us from creatures, yet not so that the name which signifies Him expresses the divine essence in itself in the way that the name *man* expresses the essence of man in himself. . . ." See also Article 2 in which Aquinas declares that man's limited apperception limits the correspondence between words and reality. "For as we can apprehend simple subsistents only by way of composite things, so we can understand simple eternity only by way of temporal things, because our intellect has a natural proportion to composite and temporal things. But demonstrative pronouns are applied to God as pointing to what is understood, not to what is sensed" (Tr. Anton C. Pegis in *Introduction to St. Thomas Aquinas* [New York: Random House, 1948], pp. 98—99). For Aquinas, then, we use language because it is all we have and because it is our nature to use language, not because it is, in Feidelson's terms, "at one with the structure of reality."

28. Feidelson, pp. 55, 90, 87. For a repetition of this same generalization—that the Puritans distrusted the sensible world and the use of images drawn from it—see Robert Spiller et al., *Literary History of the United States*, 4th ed. (New York: Macmillan, 1974), pp. 56, 62.

29. Ursula Brumm, *American Thought and Religious Typology*, tr. John Hoaglund (New Brunswick, New Jersey: Rutgers University Press, 1970), p. 15. For the distinctions between Augustinian typology, which Brumm imputed to all seventeenth-century Puritans, and Eusebian typology, which many in fact practiced, see Robert W. Hanning, *The Vision of History in Early Britain: From Gildas to Geoffrey of Monmouth* (New York: Columbia University Press, 1966), pp. 22—38, and Sacvan Bercovitch, "Typology in Puritan New England: The Williams-Cotton Controversy Reassessed," *American Quarterly* 19 (Summer 1967): 166—191.

30. Brumm, pp. 63—64, 82—84.

31. Leon Howard, *Literature and the American Tradition* (New York: Doubleday, 1960), p. 9. As far as I know, there is no conventional sense of the term "pure literature." Wallace Stevens's work is often called pure, presumably because it contains so little mention of the outside world. But this term might also refer to Robert Penn Warren's notion of "pure and impure poetry," to Edith Sitwell's arguments for "abstract poetry," or to the poetics of Walter Pater, referents that have little in common.

32. Roy Harvey Pearce, *The Continuity of American Poetry* (Princeton: Princeton University Press, 1961), pp. 3—6.

33. *Ibid.*, pp. 40—41, 54.

34. Hyatt Waggoner, *American Poets: From the Puritans to the Present* (Boston: Houghton Mifflin, 1968), pp. xi, 12.

35. *Ibid.*, p. 11.

36. *Ibid.*, pp. 10, 14–15.

37. Ann Stanford, *Anne Bradstreet: The Worldly Puritan* (New York: Burt Franklin, 1974); Karl Keller, *The Example of Edward Taylor* (Amherst: The University of Massachusetts Press, 1975), p. 102.

38. Michael Zuckerman, "Pilgrims in the Wilderness: Community, Modernity, and the Maypole at Merrymount," *New England Quarterly* 50 (June 1977): 262; John Seelye, *Prophetic Waters: The River in Early American Life and Literature* (New York: Oxford University Press, 1977), p. 313.

Index

Addison, Joseph, 209
Alain de Lille, 60
Alighieri, Dante. *See* Dante
Allen, John, 167
Anagrams, 149–51, 167–68, 175
Andrewes, Lancelot, 50
Aquinas, Thomas, 66–67, 68, 120, 215
Aristotle, 50
Auerbach, Erich, 28–29
Augustine, 60, 85, 86, 87, 152

Bancroft, George, 201–202
Barlow, Joel, 142
Bartas, Sieur Guillaume Salluste du. *See* Du Bartas, Sieur Guillaume Salluste
Baxter, Richard, 41, 59, 71, 75–79, 174, 175, 176
Bay Psalm Book, 1–4
Bercovitch, Sacvan, 149, 151, 152
Bernard of Clairvaux, 62
Blake, William, 30, 80
Boscovich, Ruggiero, 54
Brack, O. M., Jr., 135
Bradford, William, 48
Bradstreet, Anne, 24, 35–36, 36–37, 55–56, 71, 82–127, 132, 138, 173–76, 188, 194, 203–204, 222; mentioned, 20, 129, 131, 132, 139, 147, 160, 161, 163, 164, 166, 169, 170, 171, 179, 184, 185, 192, 197, 201, 214
—*Works*:
"As Spring the Winter Doth Succeed," 94–95
"As Weary Pilgrim, Now at Rest," 94, 134, 172

"Contemplations," 9, 36, 84, 93, 117–26, 161, 202
"The Flesh and the Spirit," 100
"For Deliverance from a Fever," 102–103
"For the Restoration of My Dear Husband from a Burning Ague," 103
"In Memory of My Dear Grandchild Anne Bradstreet," 114–15
"In Memory of My Dear Grandchild Elizabeth Bradstreet," 110–13, 163
"A Letter to Her Husband, Absent upon Public Employment," 93, 106–108
"Meditations Divine and Moral," 88, 90–92, 116–17
"My Daughter Hannah Wiggin Her Recovery from a Dangerous Fever," 103
"My Son's Return out of England," 103
"On My Dear Grandchild Simon Bradstreet," 115–16
"To My Dear and Loving Husband," 104–106
"Upon the Burning of Our House," 100–101
"Upon Some Distemper of Body," 102
"The Vanity of All Worldly Things," 24, 36, 96–99
Bradstreet, Samuel, 11–12, 20
Bradstreet, Simon, 106–107
Brahe, Tycho, 34
Brooks, Cleanth, 53, 109–110
Browne, Sir Thomas, 117

249

Brumm, Ursula, 30, 69, 217–18
Bryant, William Cullen, 202
Bulkeley, Peter, 148–49
Bulkley, John, 41
Bunny, Edmund, 72
Burns, Robert, 30

Calvin, John, 96
Cambridge Platform, 47, 137
Canonicus, 157
Cathari, 57, 59, 60, 80–81
Cecil, Lord David, 212
Celestine III, Pope, 59
Charles II (king of England), 75
Chaucer, Geoffrey, 58
Chauncy, Charles (1592–1672), 167
Chauncy, Charles (1705–1787), 137
Classicism, 10–11, 142–44
Cleveland, John, 206
Coleridge, Samuel Taylor, 9, 125, 211
Contemptus mundi, 14, 37, 44, 56–60, 221
Copernicus, Nicolaus, 34
Copleston, Frederick, S.J., 67, 68
Cotton, John, 1–3, 40–41, 45, 46, 74–75, 86–87, 152
Crashaw, Richard, 191, 204, 212
Cromwell, Oliver, 49
Crouch, Joseph, 21
Crowder, Richard, 130, 134–36

Danforth, Samuel I, 10–11, 20, 143–44, 185
Danforth, Samuel II, 32–34, 63
Dante, 30, 131
De Lille, Alain. *See* Alain de Lille
De Sales, Francis, 72
Donne, John, 50, 105, 204
Donnelly, Marian Card, 8
Doolittle, Hilda, 89
Drake, Francis (elegist), 35
Drew, Elizabeth, 109
Dryden, John, 3, 53

Du Bartas, Sieur Guillaume Salluste, 206–207
Dudley, Thomas, 83, 150
Dunster, Henry, 3–4
Duyckinck, Evert and George, 83
Dwight, Timothy, 142

Edwards, Jonathan, 21, 69–70
Eliot, John, 25
Emerson, Ralph Waldo, 9, 13, 33, 220
Emmanuel College, Cambridge, 106
Eusebius Pamphili, Bishop of Caesarea, 152

Fawkes, Guy, 205
Feidelson, Charles, 128–29, 214–17
Fiske, John, 211
Fitch, Elizabeth, 166–69
Fletcher, Phineas, 205–206
Folger, Peter, 203
Francis of Assisi, 60
Freneau, Philip, 203
Frost, Robert, 116, 140

Gnostics, 9, 10, 16, 17, 56, 59, 60, 80, 85, 134, 136, 137, 139, 176, 197, 221
Gosson, Stephen, 53, 58
Grabo, Norman, 71
Graham, Billy, 131
Griswold, Rufus, 203

H. D. *See* Doolittle, Hilda
Halleck, Fitz-Greene, 202
Harvard College, 41
Herbert, George, 20, 41, 132, 137, 151, 204, 209
Herrick, Robert, 205
Hillhouse, James Abraham, 202
Hobbes, Thomas, 155
Homer, 42, 142
Hooker, Samuel, 175
Hooker, Thomas, 26–27, 74, 86, 148–49, 184

Hopkins, John, 2–3
Howard, Donald R., 57
Howard, John, 205
Howard, Leon, 137, 218
Hutchinson, Anne, 219

Idolatry, 7, 45–49
Innocent III, Pope (Lothar of Segni), 57–60
Irvin, William J., 84

James II (king of England), 75
Jantz, Harold, 211–12
Johnson, Edward, 8, 25, 138, 140–42, 147, 178, 183
Johnson, Samuel, 96–97
Johnson, Thomas H., 7, 162, 208–210, 212
Jonson, Ben, 109, 110
Junkins, Donald, 165, 178
Juvenal, 96–97

Keats, John, 124–25
Keller, Karl, 178, 184, 189, 197, 222
Kettell, Samuel, 202
King, Edward, 205
Kopit, Arthur, 113

Laud, Archbishop William, 141
Laughlin, Rosemary, 111
Lothar of Segni. See Innocent III, Pope
Lowell, James Russell, 109–110, 112
Loyola, Ignatius, 59, 72
Lucini, Paolo, 55
Ludwig, Allan I., 7, 8, 26, 43–44, 48, 66
Lynde, Benjamin, 12, 20
Lyon, Richard, 3–4

Mallarmé, Stéphane, 96
Manichaeans, 8, 56, 59, 60, 80, 128, 203, 204
Marlowe, Christopher, 54

Mather, Cotton, 3, 37, 42–43, 82–83, 132, 150, 168, 175, 203, 212–13, 215, 217
Mather, Samuel (1626–1671), 47, 69, 216
Matthiessen, F. O., 207, 208
Meditation, 59, 71–81; from the creatures, 22–23, 45, 59, 72–74
Melanchthon (Philip Schwartzerd), 52
Miller, Perry, 43, 50, 52, 54, 69, 85, 87, 113, 210–11, 212
Milton John, 15, 33–34, 54, 109–110, 131, 142–43, 206–207, 208
Mitchell, Jonathan, 35, 41, 43, 209
Moody, Joshua, 70
Morgan, Edmund, 104, 129
Morison, Samuel Eliot, 84
Murdock, Kenneth, 7, 21–22, 204–206, 208, 212–13

Newton, Sir Isaac, 55
Noyes, Nicholas, 204

Oakes, Urian, 147–48, 175
Ong, Walter Joseph, S.J., 50–52, 54
Ovid, 42

Pain, Philip, 71, 128, 137–39, 169, 175, 185, 197
Parrington, Vernon Louis, 207
Paul (apostle), 86, 96, 194
Peale, Norman Vincent, 131
Pearce, Roy Harvey, 54, 109–110, 114, 149–50, 218–20
Percival, James G., 201–202
Persons, Robert, 72
Poe, Edgar Allan, 95
Pseudo-Dionysius, 66
Pseudo-Hrabanus, 61
Ptolemy (astronomer), 34
Puttenham, George, 149–50

Quarles, Francis, 191, 204

Ramus, Peter, 44, 50–56, 211, 215
Rawson, Grindall, 35
Richard of St. Victor, 60
Richards, I. A., 29
Richardson, Alexander, 63, 96, 175
Richardson, Robert, 84
Rimbaud, Arthur, 96
Rochester, John Wilmot, Earl of, 3
Rogers, John, 82
Rousseau, Jean Jacques, 155

Saffin, John, Jr., 35
Sales, Francis de. *See* De Sales,
    Francis
Saybrook Platform, 47
Scheick, William, 185, 195
Scotus, John Duns, 61, 68
Seelye, John, 223
Segal, Erich, 132
Sewall, Samuel, 20, 35, 86–87, 176,
    214–15
Shakespeare, William, 105
Shepard, Thomas I, 113–14, 129–30
Shepard, Thomas II, 147–48
Shorter Catechism, 47, 75
Sidney, Sir Philip, 53, 54, 105, 208
Smith, Elihu Hubbard, 201, 203
Spenser, Edmund, 143, 208
Spinoza, Baruch, 68
Stanford, Ann, 83, 105–106, 222
Stannard, David, 81, 169
Steere, Richard, 12–21, 27, 63, 65,
    144–47, 208; mentioned, 98, 138,
    166, 174, 175, 176, 177, 178, 184,
    185, 192, 197
—*Works*:
    Antichrist Display'd, 20, 144
    *Earth Felicities, Heavens Allow-
        ances*, 12–20, 32, 145
    *A Monumental Memorial of Ma-
        rine Mercy*, 145–47
    On a Sea-Storm nigh the Coast, 20
Sternhold, Thomas, 2–3

Stevens, Wallace, 96
Sylvester, Joshua, 206

Talon, Omer, 50, 52, 54
Tashjian, Dickran and Ann, 7, 48
Tate, Allen, 93, 95, 108
Taylor, Edward, 36, 38, 70, 71,
    162–99, 208, 209–210, 213, 217–
    18, 222; mentioned, 84, 201,
    214, 220
—*Works*:
    Christographia, 178, 181, 183–84,
        186, 188, 189, 193
    "A Fig for thee Oh! Death," 170–
        71
    Gods Determinations, 178–79
    Metrical History of Christianity,
        186
    Preparatory Meditations
    —First Series:
        1.9, 187
        1.13, 188
        1.17, 196
        1.21, 196
        1.22, 186–87
        1.34, 170, 196–97
        1.43, 197
        1.48, 197
    —Second Series:
        2.1, 178
        2.3, 195
        2.12, 177
        2.21, 187
        2.35, 180, 185, 196
        2.36, 185
        2.41, 179
        2.56, 186
        2.68, 179
        2.80, 182
        2.81, 183
        2.82, 185–86
        2.93, 177
        2.96, 191, 196

2.100, 179, 187
2.101, 176–77
2.110, 182, 192
2.115, 180
2.120, 181–82, 187–88
2.122, 188–89
2.151, 184
2.152, 177
2.155, 194–95
Treatise Concerning the Lord's Supper, 179–80
"Upon the Death of my ever Endeared, and Tender Wife," 166–69
"Upon Wedlock and the Death of Children," 163–65
"Valediction to all the world preparatory to Death," 169, 171–76, 191
Taylor, Thomas, 22–23, 59, 72–74, 76, 174, 176
Thomas Aquinas. *See* Aquinas, Thomas
Tillam, Thomas, 221
Tompson, Benjamin, 151, 168, 175
Tompson, Elizabeth, 151, 168
Tuve, Rosemond, 50, 52, 151
Tyler, Moses Coit, 8, 9, 83, 128, 139, 203–204, 205, 222
Typology, 152, 214–15, 217

Vanity, 95–101, 133–34, 136, 179
Virgil, 42

Wadsworth, Benjamin, 104
Waggoner, Hyatt Howe, 9, 109, 110, 128, 140, 149, 218, 220–21, 222–23
Ward, Nathaniel, 140, 150, 151, 168, 175, 184
Warren, Austin, 28, 30, 109–110, 132

Weaned affections, 85–88, 100, 113, 126, 130, 178
Wellek, René, 28, 30, 132
Westminster Assembly, 46–47, 75
White, Elizabeth Wade, 126
Whitman, Walt, 89, 108, 193
Wigglesworth, Michael, 48, 83, 96, 128–36, 143, 169, 185, 204, 207–208, 214; mentioned, 147, 175, 197, 203
—*Works*:
The Day of Doom, 41, 131–32, 134
"Death Expected and Welcomed," 134
"A Farewell to the World," 134
"I Walk'd and Did a Little Mole-Hill View," 134–36
"Vanity of Vanities: A Song of Emptiness," 133
Willard, Samuel, 27, 49, 63–66, 68, 69, 77, 79, 81, 133–34, 139, 175, 176, 184
Williams, Roger, 25–26, 37, 152–61, 176, 185
Williams, Stanley, 83, 213–14
Williams, William Carlos, 140
Willoughby, Francis, 167
Wilson, John, 37, 150–51, 205, 206
Wimsatt, William K., Jr., 53
Winthrop, John, 35, 37, 140, 153–54, 214
Wolcott, Roger, 41–42
Wood, William, 9–10, 12, 20, 138, 178, 183, 192
Wordsworth, William, 23, 125

Yeats, William Butler, 80

Ziff, Larzer, 136, 176
Zuckerman, Michael, 223